REFLECTIONS ON THE FUTURE OF NON VIOLENCE

REFLECTIONS ON THE FUTURE OF NON VIOLENCE

Edited By
S. R. Sharma
Director Education

COSMO PUBLICATIONS
2001 INDIA

REFLECTIONS ON THE FUTURE OF NON VIOLENCE

First COSMO Print 2001

ISBN 81-7755-148-5

Published by
MRS. RANI KAPOOR
for COSMO PUBLICATIONS Div. of
GENESIS PUBLISHING PVT. LTD.
24-B, Ansari Road, Darya Ganj,
New Delhi-110 002, INDIA

Composed at
Cosmo Publications

Printed at
Mehra Offset Press

CONTENTS

1. New Frames of Reference for a Peaceful International Order

Elise Boulding 1

2. Alternatives to the Use of Arms

Beverley Woodward 17

3. The New World Order and a Culture of Nonviolence

Philip Grant 31

4. Nonviolence and the Case of the Extremely Ruthless Opponent

Ralph Sammy 59

5. Recalling the Christian Church to its Pacifist Faith

Lance Robinson 97

6. Nonviolent Strategies for Conflict Resolution in the Post-Cold War Environment: A View from Japan

Takeshi Ishida 127

7. Nonviolent Third-Party Intervention: Towards a New Realism

Andrew Rigby 135

8. Reflections on the Future of Nonviolence

Jan Oberg 163

9. Practical Nonviolent Responses to New Forms of Violence

A.T.Ariyaratne 177

10. Teaching History in the Framework of a Problem-Based Peace Education

Antonino Drago 189

11. Civil Disobedience

Henry David Thoreau 207

12. The "Politics of Love" In the Cause of Peace

Liane Norman 229

13. The End of the Cold War: Implications of Neutrality and Non-allignement

Ramon Lopez-Reyes 255

Chapter-1

NEW FRAMES OF REFERENCE FOR A PEACEFUL INTERNATIONAL ORDER

ELISE BOULDING

Chapter-1

In the following article, Elise Boulding is concerned with giving a model of a new emerging international order based on an androgynous social order with a commitment to peace and nonviolence. The social order as Boulding says, "is essentially androgynous, having the characteristics of both the female and the male." So there has to be a partnership based on the maleness and the femaleness and it is only through this kind of partnership that it will be possible to bring an end to nuclear weapons. Boulding explains in this article how this inclusive international order can be achieved.

The Search for an Inculsive International Order

Love of one's own people, language, culture and societal arrangements has always been a deep source of social energy and creativity for every society. When mixed with the elixir of love of domination and conquest it has taken pathological forms and turned into strident nationalism and ruthless imperialism, aided by age-old patriarchal structures which turn male social energies into the public sphere and female social energies into the private sphere. The resulting political order has been organized around the carefully sustained possibility of war with potentially adversary neighbor nations.

Yet the concept of a more inclusive order joining together a plurality of national societies committed to the maintenance of peace is very old. Not surprisingly, it has tended to be associated with an imperial order. Ashoka's reign of peace in ancient India, The Pax Romana, The Holy Roman Empire and the community of Islam are all examples. The fruitless efforts of the Holy Roman Empire to recover for a Pax Catholica some of its earlier Middle East territories in the face of the expansion of two competing "communities of peace", Byzantium and Islam, left the church of

Rome weak and vulnerable to a long series of religious wars within its own European territories. The subsequent rise of the secular empire in the West proclaiming is own peace has been a temporary success due to a unique concordance of scientific and technological advances and inventions in social organization. However, the claims to a Western-based international order are now evaporating before a host of problems beyond the capabilities of Western culture alone to solve.

But not for lack of trying. The League of Nations was initiated by Western powers to rationalize a more inculsive international order; its successor, the United Nations, was formed with the same goal. After several decades of applying the physical, economic and social technologies of both socialist and nonsocialist West to the development of nonwestern societies it became clear that the quality of life was worsening for many of the countries newly included in that international order, primarily from the South.

In the meantime first, second and third generation social scientists in the countries of Africa, Asia and Latin America, trained in Europe and then increasingly trained in their own universities, were reflecting on the experiences of their people and developing their own critique of European development. As early as the fifties they were pointing out that the development experience of the South would have to fit the geocultural conditions of each region, each society. At UNESCO's first North-South conference on economic and social development held in 1954 the warning voices spoke clearly, but it was not until the late seventies that they were heard. The UN itself has been the forum for these voices, and has provided the birthing room for an emergent order far different from the culture of its founding members.

The New International Intergovernmental Orders

The countries of the South learned a lot from their frustrating experiments with both socialist and nonsocialist models of modernization. The positive outcome of their frustration was an event which signaled the emergence of a new, more genuinely inclusive international order. This event was the coming together of the Group of 77 (now 118) which resulted in the acceptance of the UN General Assembly of a Program of Action on the establishment of a New International Economic Order in 1974. It is not the economic order itself which interests us here, but rather the act of conceptualizing any part of the international order in a different way. The first signals of this new thinking came inevitably in the economic sector because of the concentration of efforts on economic development, narrowly conceived, by specialists of the North. The more comprehensive emergent order has several closely interrelated parts: the international environmental order, the international information order, the international culture order, and the international security order. It is in the elements of and interrelationships among these orders that we will find the ingredients for an appropriately complex understanding of the world task of peacemaking, one that preserves the diversity and creativity of humankind. The fact that each of these orders is highly controversial and bitterly contested by both governmental and nongovernmental groups, particularly in the North, only shows how partial and incomplete our capacity to grasp the world public interest has been to date. Each grouping of nations knows only its own national and regional public interest. It is clearly the task of the humanistic and the social sciences to clarify concepts, explore theories and verify relationships within the international order, in order to build and test collaborative mechanisms which will evoke the capacity to perceive national public interest in the context of world public interest. If world public interest does not develop, peace will continue to elude us.

One serious obstacle to this collaboration is that scientists are citizens of nation states, and nation states have conflicting interests with regard to the international order. One tangible evidence of the new international order will be when social scientists have been able to develop a variant of the Hippocratic Oath which will declare that they will practise their science in such a way as to do no harm to any nation state, and to be of service to all. It will be difficult to apply such an oath in practise, but its formulation will be a great step forward for science, building logically values set forth in the 1945 U.N. Declaration of Human Rights and more recent culture-specific declarations such as the 1981 Universal Islamic Declaration of Human Rights.[1]

Can the conceptual language of a new international order provide the point of departure for considerations of the development of stable peace in the international system? I believe so, for two reasons. First, each of the dimensions—economic, environmental, information, culture, security—involves a more equitable sharing of resources and responsibilities for human welfare than obtains under the "old order", and thus provide for the releasing of new energies into society. Second, the new international order concepts are both interdisciplinary and interparadigmatic, taking account of major schools of thought and development paradigms, including but not confined to free market and central planning paradigms. By drawing on the full diversity of social thinking, across East-West and North-South barriers, they bring a fuller array of problem-solving approaches to the global problematique. The basic documents of each of the international orders exemplify this. The new international economic order documents, the Brandt Reports of 1979 and 1983,[2] were produced by a Commission which included eleven scholars from the South and six from the North. The new international information order document, the 1980 MacBride Report,[3] was produced by nine scholars from the South, six from Western Europe and one from Eastern Europe. The new international cultural order document is being slowly developed out of a series of reports from regional commissions made up of scholars from each region.[4] The new international security order document, the Palme report,[5], was produced by a 17 person group of scholars and statesman, seven from the South, eight from Western Europe and two from Eastern Europe.

Not a single one of these generative documents could have been produced in any one economic or cultural region of the world. Each reflects the diversity of cultural preferences and economic aspirations of many peoples.

The New Information and Culture Orders, and Peace

Because knowledge is so widely valued in the modern world, insufficient attention has been paid to the distinction between socially productive and socially exploitative information processes. Information technology can be used for economic and political exploitation. Human transmitters can also clarify or distort social images of reality by the pictures they construct of world events as they practise their reportorial craft. They can trigger war hysteria or feature peaceable overtures by an adversary. What would a Hippocratic Oath for information technologies and journalists look like? How convey information without doing harm? The idea of a new international information order is so revolutionary, so contrary to the conventional western ways of thinking about the "free" flow of information (to those who can pay for it), that it will take decades to come to an understanding of how information should be gathered and disseminated on our planet for the benefit of all.

The UN itself is the great undergirder of the world information order. The data it collects year in and year out, by country and in many categories of economic and social behavior, resource development and environmental degradation, give to those who pay attention to it an unparalleled picture of the wants, needs and activities of member states. Closely related to the information order is the cultural order. The national cultural policy studies supported by UNESCO provide valuable contextual material for peacemaking programs, by tapping deeper layers of cultural aspirations. Each formerly colonized country, for example, has as a major item of cultural policy some degree of reconstruction of indigenous culture destroyed by colonialism. Similarly, many countries are giving priority to recovering the knowledge structures found in their oral traditions. These knowledge structures are critical for determining a development policy uniquely productive for each society.

International diplomacy should be the first to benefit from indigenous knowledge stock because traditional practices of mediation, negotiation and conflict resolution are an important part of the oral tradition of every society. The proverbs, the poetry and the strategy of pacemaking are found in a variety of UNESCO publications about third world cultures, but they tend to be treated as curiosities rather than as serious resources by scholars and governmental officials steeped in the political wisdom of the West. As part of the International Cultural Order, they will regain their proper role in world diplomacy.

The New International Securty Order And Peace

Nowhere is the process of selective reinforcement of one aspect of our social order at the expense of other aspects as pronounced as in the area of national security. The most technologically advanced nations have become mesmerized by their own advanced military capabilities, and have forgotten that international differences are political differences that have to be solved by political means. A new theology prevails, the theology of nuclear deterrence, which postulated that the capacity to threaten extinction of another country makes the threatener nation safe. Based on faith, not reason, the doctrine of nuclear deterrence has outlasted every attack that reason has so far been able to mount.

The significance of the Palme Commission report is that it makes visible in a new way the dependence of individual national securities on the security of the spaceship earth itself, and demonstrates that the insecurity of any nation is the insecurity of all. There can be no "policeman" countries, neither among the superpowers nor among the smaller powers. There does not have to be any magical trust, since nations, whether allies or enemies, have never trusted one another anyway. There does need to be a highly developed craft of peacemaking, based on a recognition of each nation's national interest. By negotiation on the basis of the national of all affected nations, some modicum of positive outcome becomes possible under even the bleakest of negotiating conditions.[6]

Arriving at the conditions for international conflict resolution depends, however, on the recognition of the multidimensionality of the international order we have been discussing. Deriving from the intellectual, moral and aesthetic contributions of every tradition, this order will be evolving over centuries to come. A completely new educational system, that teaches children about their planet, must evolve with it. Monoculturalism will be a thing of the past.

The Androgynous Nature of the International Order

Ordinarily in analyses of contemporary social institutions, phenomena are described with their male face. As an addendum, a writer may add a special section to describe "the role of women" in the subject under discussion. As well describe a one-handed, one-legged human being and add a postscript on the "role of the other hand and leg". The social order, like the individual human being, is essentially androgynous, having the characteristics of both the female and the male. Androgeneity is the new frame of reference needed for the emerging social order. Society gives birth to new ideas and institutions, nurtures its members, settles conflicts, enforces priorities, searches out new resources and methods for maintenance and growth. It does this through the interrelated institutions of the family, the economy, the state, the church and institutions for cultural transmission. Historically, at different times and places, both men and women have carried out the work of each of these sectors. Yet the rules of the social order generally assign certain roles to men only, others to women only. The survival-oriented flexibility of ancient specializations has frozen into a rigid, creativity-lessening division of labor for men and women in recent centuries. In its present form it make men tenders of military machines and women tenders of men and children. Is the women's hidden culture of creative problem-solving only to emerge in crisis to rescue societies from total collapse? This has happened before in history, and could happen again.[7]

The message in the UN Women's Decade theme of "Equality. Development and Peace" is that women are needed side by side with men to make the social order work in all its aspects. Social behaviors become twisted and bent out of shape when women and men cease to be jointly available for the whole range of political, economic and social tasks of a society. This is so because that social order requires both nurturance and repair, and exploration and construction, in every part of its functioning, from household to workplace to civic forum. The fullest human potential for creative problem-solving can only be realized in a social order based on a free-flowing, flexible partnership drawing on the maleness and femaleness which lives within every man and woman. Only such a partnership can topple the "gods of metal", the nuclear weapons, in which nations now place their faith.

The Peoplem's International Order: The New Peace Movement

Acting partly on signals about the new international order, partly on new understanding of how men and women can work together, and partly out of older, more traditional international attitudes, the new peace movement has gone beyond the old elites that helped provide leadership for the pre-World War I and pre-World War II peace movements into a different kind of grassroots antinuclear movement. The basic premise of the new localist movement in all its diversity is that public interest groups have both the possibility and the responsibility to reshape the social order according to new perceptions of social need, through the political process. The European movement has its own diversity, including a diversity of types of relationships of various sectors of the peace movement to governments. The frame of reference of the new peace movement is a perceived need for social change in the national and international order to ensure survival, accompanied by a willingness on the part of a variety of civic groups to contribute their skills to the change process. In the U.S., as one example, three new sets of civic actors have become available as change agents: (1) Local community groups originally organized around a concern for the environment, human rights, and other issues; they are now supporting, on their own initiative, the antinuclear movement in general and the nuclear freeze in particular. They do not belong to any national organization. (2) Professional groups from the communities of the natural sciences (mostly physics), the social sciences, medicine, law, business education and social work who have all organized themselves into continuing associations using their professional expertise to educate the public and governments on the dangers of nuclear war, the possibility of alternative nonmilitary strategies. (3) All the major religious denominations and 50 of the smaller ones who are now collaborating art their own initiative in a massive nation-wide effort to educate their parishioners on the danger of nuclear war and to lobby Congress and the President for nuclear disarmament. While each of these groups works in their own way, all have agreed on a specific, politically feasible first step, the nuclear freeze, as a precondition for further disarmament and the development of effective non-military international conflict resolution procedures. Older peace organizations do of course work with these new actors.

The New Skills

Much space would be needed to detail how each civic, professional and religious group is bringing to bear its knowledge and expertise on the problem of ending recurring arms races and eliminating the specific threat of nuclear war. In the professional community, the most effective international voices are probably those of the International Union of Physicians for Social Responsibility and the International Council of Scientific Unions. They are calling attention to scientific data suggesting that no nation can bomb another country without also "bombing" itself, independently of possible retaliatory action, since the earth's atmosphere is one unitary envelope. An international educators group[8] is courageously preparing materials for school children on nuclear war and its alternatives, in spite of considerable negative pressure by governments which fear that the next generation if educated in this way will lose its "will to fight".

One of the most interesting "new skill" developments is the international focus at the present time on negotiation and mediation skills. The interest in 1983 is much more sophisticated than the comparable interest aroused by the Hague Peace Conferences which stimulated the pre-World War I peace movement at the beginning of this century. This is in part owing to the work of the international Peace Research Association,[9] which has brought scholars together from all continents since its founding in 1965. By helping to formulate the nature of conflict and peace processes at th einternational level it has paved the way for new reseach paradigms. One example of thenew developments in mediation occurred this past spring, withthcfirst-ever gathering of all the associations and centers in the U.S. concerned witht he process of peacemaking, negotiation and conflict resolution at the University of Georgia. The purpose of the conferece was to bring together practitioners at every level from the local community to the international sphere, toexplore how the development and practice of peacemaking skills might be strengthened through collaboration. Manyof th epeople at that conference were in their private capacities also supporters of the peace movement, and ssaw the relevance of their skillsto problems in international negotiation. A new international association, a new NGO, will certainly develop as the networks established at that meeting link with approapriate transnational contacts.

Thenew and currently forming nongovernmental networks described here will remain, along with older international peace organizations, as a permanent part of th einternational scene, independent voices and independent actors for peace.

The same nomentum which led to th enew mediation sassociation has also led to pegislation now before the U.S Comgress to establish a U.S. National Peace Academy. This Academy would teach the skills of conflict resolution and negotiation, a missing part of the curriculum in the current training of government negotiators, foreign service officers and State Department decisionmakers.This curriculum lack of course obtains in every nation, and Peace Academies are needede in every nation.

What the peace movement is slowly learnign is that it takes skill and effort to make and maintain peace, not just emotional commitment. Sustained action for social change is a new part of the movement's self-defined social role.The rank and file are as convinced of th eneed for change as the professionals, and as aware of their need for skills. This may have a profound effect on the kind of education demanded by the public for its children in coming decades.

Coordinating the Frames of Reference and Resources Available for Peace in the 1980's

I have suggested three essentially new frames of references and new sets of intellectual resources which are available for peacemaking at this difficult moment in history. Each of these frames and accompanying resources can help nations and alliance blocs break out of their traditional military defense modes. First, there are the new international orders. An unprecedented North-South collaboration is taking place among scholars trained in the disciplines of economics, the environment, informatics, culture and security. Drawing on both traditional and new knowledge and methods of seeking knowledge, the collaborating scholars are forging new understandings of the interrelated culturally patterned elements and processes involved in achieving peaceful development for all countries. The UN documents on the New International Order provide a new conceptual frame for this type of thinking.

Second, the world view and accompanying skills stemming from the experiences gained in the previously segregated women's sector are now in the UN Women's Decades increasingly being made available to the social order as a whole. Only as the skills of the women's sector become everyone's skills can the ideas of the new, more inclusive international order be implemented. This means an end to all practices of gender segregated policy-formation. Because of resistance by member states, and of the UN itself—a creation of member states—this desegregation will be hard to achieve. It will be no harder, however, than the other steps that relate to the development of a more peaceful international order.

Finally, the contemporary peace movement brings to the social order a unique constellation of social perceptions of civic participation in a new global interdependence. The movement puts into the hands of each national societies as well as into the ever-stronger translational networks of concerned world citizens, new paradigms, of peace processes and new competencies more adequate to the complexities of the merging international order than the traditional competencies of the elites of the North. New mediation practices will blend with the traditional mediation practices of the countries of the South, including the less understood mediation practices of Islam.

Each of these three new resource groups—the North-South collaborators who are spelling out the dimensions of the new international order, the women who have been the hidden partners in the work of peacemaking, and the new activist professionals, all suffer from incomplete social imagery about the kind of world they are trying to build. The diversity and clarity of that imagery needs to be fostered through interaction between these three groups. A "vision pool" is needed, for without continuing vision social efforts will slow down. Only the rich fullness of all the ways that humans in different traditions can picture a good life for their children's children can sustain the necessary hard work that lies ahead. Perhaps it is the task of philosophers to stimulate and explore the vision pool. How else will people know what they are working for, any why?

References

1. The Universal Islamic Declaration of Human Rights, prepared by eminent Muslim scholars, and jurists, was issued by the Islamic Council of Europe, Salem Azzam, Secretary General, on September 19, 1981 in Paris.
2. Willy Brandt, Commission chair, *North-South: a Program for Survival,* 1980 and *Common Crises North-South:Cooperation for World Recovery,* 1983. London: Pan Books.
3. Sean MacBridge, Commission chair, Many Voices One World, Paris: UNESCO, 1980.
4. For an account of the cultural policy regional meetings, see Herbert Shore,
Cultural Policy: UNESCO's First Cultural Development

Decade. Washington, D.C.:U.S. National Commission for UNESCO, 1981. Also note the National Cultural Policies Studies, published by UNSECO, Paris, between 1975 and the present.

5. Olof Palme, Commission chair, *Common Security: A Blueprint for Survival,* New York: Simon and Shuster, 1982.
6. John Burton has developed these concepts in both theory and practice. See his *Dear Survivors*. Boulder: Wastview Press, 1982.
7. For example, see Elise Boulding's *Underside of History: A View of Women through Time,* Boulder: Westview Press, 1976.
8. The international liaison person for the END affinity group for peace educators and teachers is Dr. Nigel Young of the University of Bradford School of Peace Studies. A collaborating group in the U.S. is Educators for Social Responsibility, with a nuclear war curriculum project based at Harvard University.
9. The International Peace Research Association has for the past 4 years been located at the Faculty of Law, Tokyo University, with Yoshikagu Sakamoto as Secretary General. The quarterly IPRA Newsletter with news of peace research activities and conferences has been published from the Tokyo headquarters. Its 1983 Congress is being held at Gyor, Hungary, with a special focus on the study of peace movements.
10. Conferences has been published from the Tokyo headquarter.s Its 1983 Congress is being held at Gyor, Hungary, with a special focus on th estudy of peace movements.

Chapter-2

ALTERNATIVES TO THE USE OF ARMS

BEVERLY WOODWARD

Chapter-2

After reading the different articles in this book related to non-violence, the question naturally arises, "Is possible to apply nonviolence to the political system?" In the following essay, Beverly Woodward answers this question in a positive way by explaining the process of transformation to a nonviolent political order and proposes certain techniques that should be used to make this transformation in the political order possible.

Two kinds of changes would be essential for the institution of an alternative security policy in which violence no longer served as the ultima ratio: on the one hand, the substitution of unarmed for armed modes of action; on the other, general policy changes with respect to both domestic and foreign affairs. The latter sorts of changes would be aimed primarily at creating an environment in which conflict would be less acute and basic rights more readily recognized than in our present world order. Examples are: environmental measures designed to protect dwindling resources and to impede pollution across international boundaries; treaties and other legislation to implement the right to food; and measures to stabilize international commodity markets.

It is the former kind of changes, however, that will be the focus of attention here: the replacement of armed modes of action by unarmed modes. The three key elements in such a transformative effort are: nonviolent struggle, nonviolent defense, and nonviolent peacemaking (i.e., various kinds of unarmed intervention in violent or potentially violent conflict situations).[1]

The adoption of any or all of these forms of action by any body politic is an aspect of the process I call "the institutionalization of nonviolence." While the use of nonviolent strategies in a direct action campaign by a particular interest group may leave the global violence system essentially intact,[2] a decision to substitute unarmed forces and nonviolent behaviors for the activities traditionally carried out by armies, police forces, armed liberation units, or similar bodies *ipso facto* modifies that system as long as the decision is in effect. To be sure, no single shift of this kind will bring about the transformation of traditional nation-state politics, in which the use of violence is the ultima ratio, to global community politics. But each such change can contribute to the process of transformation and a series of major institutional changes of this kind might generate the momentum that a thoroughgoing transformation of the nation-state system would require.

The term "nonviolent" as used here, then, does not refer simply to *any* behavior where arms are not employed, but to those particular unarmed behaviors that may take the place of armed behaviors—and in fact have done so on some occasions. In what follows I shall consider each of three nonviolent substitutionary elements separately, certain of their similarities and differences, and the kind of activities that may be required to gain their adoption.

The means of *nonviolent struggle* are quite familiar. They include the means employed in such well-known campaigns as those of Gandhi in India an Martin Luther King, Jr., in the United States. Gene Sharp in his path breaking book *The Politics of Nonviolent Action* subdivides nonviolent struggle into five sorts of methods: (1) the methods of protest and persuasion; (2) the methods of social noncooperation; (3) the methods of economic noncooperation; (4) the methods of political noncooperation; (5) the methods of nonviolent intervention. (By "intervention" Sharp does not mean "mediation" or related activities, as I do in speaking of unarmed intervention above, but a particular type of direct action, to be illustrated in the next paragraph.

Examples of actions which belong to these different categories are: (1) a vigil or a march; (2) ostracism of persons or withdrawal from social institutions; (3) strikes or boycotts; (4) civil disobedience against laws considered "illegitimate" or refusal to recognize the authority of a public official; (5) a nonviolent land seizure or a "reverse strike," i.e., an insistence on working in order to fill a community need even though the work is unpaid and is opposed by property owners, public authorities, etc.

The possible objectives of nonviolent struggle are exceedingly varied and need not be what would be called "progressive." Indeed nonviolent struggle has been used to achieve ends that many consider quite objectionable, e.g., the overthrow of a democratically elected government in Chile. Nevertheless, it can be argued that the use of nonviolent means, to the extent that the means are *in fact* nonviolent, is preferable to the use of violence. The point would be especially forceful if there were a way of replacing *all* violent struggle with nonviolent struggle. The "wrong" side, as defined by one's particular political perspective, would doubtless win part of the time in such a world, but at least the dire threats that the war system now poses to humankind would be eliminated.

The use of arms has traditionally been the last resort of groups seeking radical change in domestic affairs, e.g., the overthrow of a government. In this century in particular violence has been the ultimate resort of movements that have perceived themselves as liberation movements. A commitment to nonviolent struggle involves a renunciation of this option whether on grounds of principle or simply because such a choice seems wisest. Gandhi followed this course with significant success in India. It is also the course followed, although with less consistency, by several post-World War II liberation struggles in Africa. More recently it has been the course chosen by the people of Poland, with remarkable results (a shift of power from Communist to non-Communist political forces).

While nonviolent struggle may be used to bring into being new political institutions and to secure the recognition of rights not yet recognized, *nonviolent defense* is used to protect and defend institutions already in existence and rights already honored. Generally, nonviolent defense is thought of as a form of defense against invasion and occupation. But the methods of nonviolent defense can also be used to protect a country against an internal coup or against other kinds of threats to the constitutional order (Nonviolent defense can also be used by social entities other than nations).

Nonviolent defense has not yet been adopted as the long-term defense policy of any nation. It has, however, been used an *ad hoc* basis by a number of countries faced by a difficult circumstance in which the use of arms could not be expected to be effective (It is important to note that there are a large number of potential circumstances of this sort for which national governments are ill-prepared due to their habits of believing in the efficacy of violence in all extreme situations). Examples cited by Sharp include the nonviolent resistance by the civilian populations of Denmark and Norway to Nazi occupation in World War II, the German resistance in 1923 to the French/Belgian occupation of the Ruhr (*the Ruhrkampf*), the resistance to the Kapp putsch of 1920 (a right wing putsch against the Weimar Republic), and the widespread Czech resistance to the invasion of Czechoslovakia in 1968 by the Warsaw Pact. While the latter effort did not prevent the installation of a new government obedient to Moscow, a number of commentators have insisted that it cannot be chalked up simply as a failure. For one thing, the resistance continued longer than would have been possible for an armed resistance. In addition, the resistance (in part because it was nonviolent and not immediately defeated) highlighted the issues at stake clearly and thus laid the groundwork for the end of monolithic communism in Europe.

Although no national government has yet adopted a nonviolent defense policy in recent years a number of governments in Western Europe have sponsored official studies of the potentialities of this mode of defense. These include Sweden, Norway, and the Netherlands. Advocates of nonviolent defense argue that advance preparation generally can be expected to enhance the effectiveness of this form of defense. If strategizing, training, etc., have taken place in advance of an attack or threatened attack, a better coordination of efforts can be achieved.

The tactics of nonviolent defense are closely linked to those of nonviolent struggle. In particular, noncooperation is a key element in both types of nonviolent action. Sharp writes that nonviolent defense (which he calls "civilian-based defense") works "not simply by efforts to alter the will of the attacker, but by the capacity to make effective domination and control impossible by both massive and selective noncooperation and defiance by the population and its institutions. The aim is to make the populace unrulable by the attackers and to deny them their objectives..."[3] Emphasizing the coercive potentialities of nonviolent action, Sharp adds: "It is possible to exert extreme pressure and even coerce by nonviolent means. Rather than converting the opponent, civilian struggle has more often been fought by disrupting, paralyzing, or coercing by denying the opponent the cooperation he needed..."[4] In certain cases, of course, "winning over" the opponent or at least some segment of his armed forces will be an important element in a defense campaign against an invasion or an illegitimate seizure of governmental power.

Research on nonviolent defense cannot by itself create the popular climate necessary if nonviolent defense is to be adopted. but research can help illuminate the advantages and difficulties of this approach, how surrounding circumstances may affect the efficacy of nonviolent strategies, the role of particular tactics in particular situations, the elements of a foreign policy appropriate to a nonviolent defense policy, etc.

In the case of the superpowers, armed forces exist not only for the purpose of defense of territory, but for the purpose of interventionsometimes represented as a kind of defense. These powers may intervene to protect their "sphere of interest," their "way of life," (including its material accoutrements), or simply what is called "international stability." Most of the time such interventions appear morally questionable or simply plainly imperialistic. Nevertheless, intervention *per se* cannot necessarily be rejected on these grounds. The Charter of the United Nations speaks of disputes which "endanger the maintenance of international peace and security" and it is apparent in our present highly interdependent world that violent conflict in any country or region may pose threats that reach beyond the parties immediately involved. This state of affairs may legitimate unarmed intervention or *nonviolent peacemaking* efforts.[5]

Most great power intervention is partisan. Ideally intervention should not serve a particular interest, but should aim at finding a just solution to the conflictor at a minimum a solution that is no less just than the status quo ante. Traditionally, it has been held that a mediator in a conflict should be neutral. The ideal of neutrality, however, may be misleading. It should not imply that all parties in a conflict are to be regarded as equally in the right whatever the facts of the case may be (although some conflicts *do* involve clashes of more or less equally compelling claims.) Nor can it mean that the mediator is some kind of god or inhuman robot without feelings and prejudices that may affect his or her actions. Neutrality should indicate an equal willingness to consider all claims and the intention to be as fair as possible within the limits of one's human capacities. When these conditions are met, we may speak of third party intervention. When the mediator hopes to facilitate a fair solution to the conflict, but nevertheless has stronger ties to one side, we may speak of 2½ partly intervention.

Mediation, negotiation, and arbitration are obvious instances of interventionary techniques that may be employed when violence threatens or has already erupted. Another interventionary techniques is the interposition of unarmed (or armed) "peacemaking" forces between the parties in conflict. I have placed the term "peacekeeping" in quotation marks, beaus such forces generally are employed after violence has broken out; strictly speaking, at this point there is no peace to keep. The aim of the peacekeeping forces is to secure and to maintain a cease-fire. Unless there is a parallel effort to solve at least some of the issues in dispute, interposition is unlikely to be more than temporarily effective. Interposition can be a useful *element* in a peacemaking effort, but by itself is unlikely to establish the conditions for a lasting peace. While the United Nations interpositionary forces have nearly always carried some kind of arms (but been restrained by a rather strict protocol concerning when they could be used), such forces do not necessarily have to be armed. (In fact, in some operations certain components of the

UN forces have been unarmed and have been more effective as a result.)[6]

The use of police forces, whether armed or unarmed, is sometimes considered an interventionary technique. In fact, police carry out a wide variety of duties, only some of which could be considered non-partisan intervention. Police forces have been used quite often for interposition, probably less frequently to mediate disputes (the proportions of the activities engaged in vary a great deal, of course, from one police unit to another). Generally the key function of police units is to monitor observance of the law and to apprehend lawbreakers, i.e., to carry out enforcement action. In these cases the conflict might be said to be between the lawbreaker and the community. In their enforcement role, the police cannot be said to be non-partisan, for they clearly stand on the side of the community. This fact among others may lead to a certain self-righteousness and overzealousness in the performance of enforcement duties and a consequent disregard for the rights of suspected lawbreakers. Because even a nonviolent police force may have considerable coercive capacity at its disposal, careful attention must be given to preventing the kind of abuse that any police activity risks, if such a police force is to remain true to a nonviolent ethos.

The emphasis on conciliation appears to differentiate nonviolent peacemaking from both nonviolent struggle and nonviolent defense. In both nonviolent struggle and nonviolent defense the emphasis is clearly on advocacy, on trying to secure the recognition of particular claims, not on building bridges. Nevertheless, the dichotomy is not absolute.

The various forms of nonviolent action generally involve elements of both advocacy and conciliation. Securing the recognition of a claim may require some conciliatory gestures. Similarly, successful intervention may depend on the ability to be an advocate for *both* sides in a two party conflict. As noted above, when an interventionary force intervenes to enforce community norms, then it acts on behalf of the whole community whose norms it enforces, and in a sense is its advocate.

Initiative in nonviolent peacemaking need not be and in general have not been limited to actions undertaken by governmental or inter-governmental bodies. In the years immediately ahead, in fact, we may anticipate that the most significant peacemaking efforts will be undertaken by nongovernmental groups (NGO's). NGO's may be active both in the training of skilled intervenors (mediators, negotiators, unarmed interpositionary forces, nonviolent enforcement units) and in the establishment of new "extragovernmental" channels of communication through which intervention in conflict can occur.

In the late 1950's there was an effort to create an unarmed World Peace Brigade. A.J. Muste, Jayaprakash Narayan, and Michael Scott played a leading role in the experiment. After some sections in Asia and Africa, the Brigade foundered due to financial and logistical problems. In 1981 Peace Brigades International was established, another international nongovernmental effort to provide unarmed teams to intervene in and to monitor situations of violent conflict. Thus far, PBI has been principally active in Guatemala and EI Salvador. PBI has also sent exploratory teams to Israel, South Africa, Northern Ireland, and Sri Lanka and has carried out an exploratory project on the nonviolent defense of Nicaragua.[7] Some years ago Robert Johansen proposed the creation of an international "nonviolent police force" with NGO status.[8] As envisaged by Johansen, such a force would employ both the techniques of direct action and of mediation to bring about the acceptance of global norms. It would operate on the basis of a moral authority which would take the place of the more conventional public authority based on a monopoly of the right to use violence.

Although the terms "substitute" and "technique" have been used a number of times in this exposition, the adoption of nonviolent approaches involves changes that go considerably beyond the substitution of one set of techniques for another. To be sure, different theorists have different viewpoints in this regard. My own is that the adoption of a nonviolent stance involves a far-reaching shift in philosophical and political outlook.

Although the focus in this essay is on a shift in techniques, this kind of shift involves a fundamental reorientation in the way in which political is conducted. To deny that, it seems to me, is to deny the way in which the use and threat of violence permeates all of political life, even such seemingly pacific activities as elections, legislative actions, etc. In brief, the renunciation of violence will require or entail a great many other changes. It is important not to lose sight of this point, even while focusing on the transarmament aspect of the shift to a nonviolent politics.[9]

The adoption of nonviolence only involved a substitution of one set of techniques for another, we might have seen more progress in this regard than we have this far. As just indicated, however, the shift from a willingness to employ violence to a renunciation of this option involves a profound cultural change. In this area there has been insufficient research and reflection. Moreover the "answers" regarding how to facilitate a change to a nonviolent politics necessarily will vary for different contexts. The variations in the history, geography, "national character," and customs and beliefs of different people will lead to various conclusions regarding the way or ways in which any given people might come to be a participant in nonviolent global community politics.

In any case, the transition process from violent to nonviolent politics requires a heavy reliance on the ends as means. That is, we should not expect violent means to bring a nonviolent world order. Even the catastrophe of a nuclear war cannot be counted upon to bring about this result. It might only generate a rather violent anarchic chaos.

Space does not permit a detailed consideration of how we might get from a violent to a nonviolent world order. But one example may illustrate the kind of steps that such a transition process would include. The example concerns the effort to achieve disarmament. (From what has already been said, it should be clear that disarmament is only one component in the process of transformation to a nonviolent political order. "Disarmament" as a concept provides a wedge for discussion, but it is not a policy that is likely to be implemented without other changes.).

To achieve, or to make progress toward disarmament it is obvious that concerted *nonviolent struggle* at the popular level will be required. Further, the groups that make up such a popular movement may need to use measures of *nonviolent defense* to protect themselves against convinced militarists who feel threatened by the changes that are advocated or actually undertaken. As disarmament progresses, the establishment of *nonviolent defense forces* for the disarming body politic as a whole (or bodies politic if the disarmament is multilateral) will come to seem both necessary and desirable. (Some would argue in fact that progress in disarmament cannot occur unless a capacity for *nonviolent defense* and *nonviolent peacemaking* is developing more or less simultaneously.). Finally, the monitoring of multilateral disarmament may require the creation of a *transnational nonviolent interventionary enforcement unit.* This unit would act as an agent of the global community and would alert it to any failure to carry out the measures that had been agreed upon. Where its reports did not in themselves bring a remedy, the unit might take other more coercive steps to enforce the global community will.

This example indicates how nonviolent struggle, nonviolent defense, and nonviolent intervention may be used to help bring about their own institutionalization. If experience is any guide, a positive demonstration of their efficacy is more likely to assist their adoption than a demonstration of the bankruptcy of violence—a demonstration that has already occurred repeatedly (or so some of us believe).

References

1. For clarification regarding my use of the term "peacemaking," see note 5. See also the second paragraph on page 284.
2. Except in a situation of civil war, most domestic political activity is nonviolent. To speak of nonviolent action in this context, therefore, may be somewhat misleading, since it may appear to involve a more radical choice than in fact is the

case. When we speak of nonviolent action in the domestic context we usually mean action that is "extraparliamentary," i.e., outside the normal legislative framework, and "militant" by virtue of a willingness to break the law. To the extent that the expectation of violence in domestic politics is low, the renunciation of violence by a group will not clearly set a new example for the conduct of political life and therefore is not likely to affect greatly what I call the "violence system."

3. Gene Sharp, *Making the Abolition of War a Realistic Goal,* (N.Y.: Institute for World Order, 1981.) This essay can be ordered from the World Policy Institute, 777 United Nations Plaza, N.Y., NY 10017. The essay won first place in the Wallach essay contest for published articles on the theme "the abolition of war."
4. *Ibid.*
5. I am using the term "peacemaking" here to include activities that are sometimes labeled "peacekeeping" and "peacebuilding." Although the conceptual distinction which separates these three activities is sometimes useful, we need also a comprehensive term which refers to any interventionary activity which is guided by the twin goals of reducing violence and protecting the rights of the various parties to the conflict. The term "peacemaking" seems to me best suited to express this concept. Ideally the activity of peacemaking, in the larger sense, will encompass all the kinds of actions needed to secure a lasting peace.
6. In April 1989 the Foreign Ministers of five Central American countries asked the United Nations to establish an international peace force of unarmed observers to patrol the region against violations of an accord banning aid to insurgent armies. (*New York Times,* April 1, 1989.).
7. For further information regarding PBI, write: Peace Brigades International, Traprock Peace Center, Keets Road Deerfield, MA 01342.
8. Robert C. Johansen and Saul H. Mendlovitz, "The Role of Enforcement of Law in the Establishment of a New International Order: A Proposal for a Transnational Police Force," *Alternatives* VI (1980), pp. 307-37. For Johansen's

suggestion, see the appendix, pp. 335-37.

9. Among nonviolent defense theorists, the term "transarmament" is generally used to indicate the process by which lethal arms are replaced by the strategies and tactics of an organised nonviolent civilian-based defense. I am using the term more broadly here to indicate the process of adopting nonviolent struggle, nonviolent defense, and nonviolent peacemaking to replace the use of violence within and by the body politic.

Chapter-3

The New World Order and a Culture of Nonviolence

Philip Grant

Chapter-3

THE CURRENT MOMENT in history contains the conjunction of two unprecedented events: the end of the Cold War and the conclusion of the five-century-old struggle for global domination by the great powers. This struggle was the main cause of the proliferation of "the warfare stale" paradigm throughout Europe and then the world. Since the warfare stale is the chief engine driving the culture of violence, its demise as a model for political development could have enormous implications for the emergence of a nonviolent culture in the twenty-first century. The organizing principle of a new world order would be derived from the new types of human personality and consciousness appearing from within the new culture of nonviolence. Its expression on the global level would be accompanied by a rebirth of political philosophy that stresses the theory and practice of dynamic, multiple allegiance between individuals, communities, national groupings, and regions.

The Old World Order

The effects of the titanic five-century-old struggle for world supremacy among the great powers are just now being understood. Without doubt, it significantly influenced most of the developments that have since come to define modernity: the demise of feudalism; the triumph of nationalism; the division of the globe into independent states; the emergence of mass industrialism; the uncontrolled development of science and technology; the rise of ideology; and the establishment of state and corporate bureaucracies. This unrelenting great-power war of "all against all" was also responsible for the subjugation of the globe by the European nation-states and, in turn, their own self-destruction and replacement by the US and the former USSR as the leading powers of the middle and late twentieth century.[1]

These two Super Powers, however, merely assumed the roles that had been created, played, and replayed by earlier great power actors since the beginning of the age of global discovery. In fact, the ideological conflict that raged between the USSR and the US eerily reenacted the religious dimension of the global struggle between the Counter-Reformation forces of the Habsburgs and those of the loosely-allied Protestant nations during the sixteenth and seventeenth centuries. As in those days, our own time has witnessed, on each side of the Iron Curtain, mass inquisitions, charges of heresy, ritualistic trials, and well-publicized punishments. Anyone fundamentally questioning the logic of one's own system was regarded as ideologically suspect, ostracized, harassed, and often murdered by inquisitorial state security services. Given the enormous immorality displayed by each party to this conflict, writers as eminent as Graham Greene have held that there was not a penny's worth of difference between them, while others have claimed that despite failings the seeds of freedom were somehow preserved by NATO and its allies.[2]

Predictably, in this war for world domination the battle was unhesitatingly transferred by the Super Powers to the far reaches of the globe. In each emerging polity, the two giant combatants used every influence imaginable to serve their own ends. Leaders were corrupted, often assassinated. Independent nations were invaded and sometimes destroyed. The results of free elections were overturned and free institutions eradicated. The Super Powers weighed and responded to the domestic social and economic policies of each new nation, chiefly in terms of how they might influence the outcome of the Cold War.[3]

While the full scale of the violence unleashed by this super-struggle has yet to be fully calculated, not many will disagree with the estimate that the local and regional conflicts which took place under its aegis caused as many violent deaths as occurred in any forty-year period in recorded history. Even more tragically, the moral, social, economic and environmental systems of the entire planet were altered beyond recognition. There is now more world poverty, disease, genocide, torture, ecological collapse, and outright despair than ever before.

Astonishingly, the end of this gigantic battle, this almost

mythic crusade against evil that has ruined so much of the planet, has been greeted by the intellectual and political leadership of the victorious side in a manner reminiscent of a punch-drunk prize fighter who cannot understand that he was won his fight. Having knocked out the opponent, he still flails away in the ring, his brain so damaged from the match that even as his enemy lay prostrate at his feet, he cannot grasp what it all means. Even when assured that there are no more opponents to challenge, like some musclebound Don Quixote, he can only make sense of his life through training to fight again.

In the US, Western Europe, and Japan, compelling reasons now exist for a complete reassessment of the challenged international situation and its implications for all aspects of foreign and domestic policy. In most areas of social and economic life, the values, plans, and allocations of resources that were conditioned by the overwhelming strain of the Cold War await revision, reform, and in some cases, revolution. But since no acknowledgement seems forthcoming of the terrible cost that almost fifty years of bitter struggle has visited upon victors, few can visualize the healing benefits that might be possible in the light of its demise. The most glaring example of this is the almost routine budgeting by the great powers of trillions of dollars for "deterrent" nuclear forces, although no one knows exactly what or who they are deterring in the changed international setting.

The Looking Glass World

Much of the current failure in moral and political thought lies in the denial of the vital role played by *nemesis,* or imitation, in international affairs. For too long the democracies of the North have refused to recognize how much they have been shaped in the image of their enemy. Today, however, research by scholars like Paul Kennedy is revealing just how much the modern "world system" was from the onset a self-exciting one in which power was assessed in terms of how faithfully a nation could imitate the post powerful.[4] This was nowhere more apparent than in the US where the original idea of a society free of militaristic values and other legacies of feudalism gradually gave way as the country became, along with the USSR, the ultimate bearer of the ethos of global militarism.

America's unique experience of the Second World War paved the way for its response to the challenge of post-war Soviet-led communism. For most Americans, the Second World War is remembered with nostalgia. Except for Pearl Harbour, in the Second World War, the country was never touched by the destruction suffered by the other combatants and its casualties were relatively slight for a nation of its size. More importantly, the war marked the final recovery from a depression that had deeply scarred the lives of the vast majority of its citizens. Under the need for war production, a coalition of labour, business, and government spent its way to high prosperity and full employment, repudiating the conventional economics of the age. Forever after, Americans would look back with gratitude at the military-industrial complex, especially in those parts of the country where defence industries employed the majority of industrial workers. Intellectual and cultural life was pressed into service on behalf of the great struggle against the Axis. Universities, research centers, popular entertainment and the mass media all became instruments for winning the war. No part of the US was immune from the eager embrace of a military struggle that brought such wealth where before there had been such poverty.

Once American intellectuals became acquainted with the full benefits of a government-stimulated economy, plans were laid for the post-war utopia that might emerge. Urban renewal, environmental protection, racial, sexual, and economic equality, universal health care, revolutions in education, and many other progressive ideas were thought to follow the full employment that a government-managed economy would bring. These plans were not implausible given the incredible economic strength of the US after the war. Yet the fundamental contradiction between welfare and warfare was never fully faced. It was lost amidst abundance and praise for the collectivist, administrative state that had made it possible.[5]

Underlying this hope for full social democracy was also a rejection of more radical reforms. The realities and the myths about the Soviet state that emerged during Allied wartime cooperation, coupled with the immensed prosperity of the US, marked the end of populist and anarchist versions of the "American dream" in favour of status quo "interest group democracy" and "brokerage politics." The unique historical and economic position of the US was interpreted to mean that if only the rest of the world would adopt the newly discovered American version of a "semi-managed" society, all would share in the great banquet of life.

This abandonment of serious thinking about fundamental change in the US was then extended to the newly liberated nations of Europe and Asia. Indeed, from all of the victorious Allied powers that comprised the newly formed UN Security Council, there was violent opposition to any of the radical, social visions that had once flourished within the resistance movements in previously Axis-controlled societies.[6] Ironically, many of the radical democratic and anarchistic plans of the antifascist liberation groups that the US now opposed had drawn ideas and inspiration from utopian ideals of the Enlightenment and social experiments in North America. Equally ironical was the fact that the Saint-Simonian tradition of planned, state-coordinated progress that had been eagerly adopted by the USSR and the fascist powers in the 1920s and the 1930s was now resurrected in a new form by an America which was previously the chief opponent of such ides. A managed, post-war America became the image of the future for much of the world which chose not to imitate the even more managed USSR.

But Western antagonism to fundamental social change was based on something more than the fear of Stalinism and full American bellies. The war also brought the death of confidence in optimism, rationalism, and "the assumption that there were certain moral limits civilized nations would not dare exceed, even in war."[7] With the revelations about the full savagery of the Second World War, including the holocausts of the death camps, the fire bombings, and Hiroshima and Nagasaki, American elites became extremely disenchanted with the hidden potentials of human nature. In international affairs the so-called realistic,

Hobbesian, or Machiavellian social theory became the vogue among "hard-headed" intellectuals—one of them even proclaiming that this offered a way to renounce ideology altogether.[8] In turn, political philosophy was confused with ideology and was proclaimed dead.

Such cynicism accounted for much of the transference of the Second World War mentality by the Western powers to the struggle with the Soviet Union. By the time of Potsdam, Stalin had begun to be identified with Hitler and socialism with totalitarianism. With the increasing use of Fascist intelligence reports and agents by the US, and assistance to former Nazi-supported "liberation" movements inside and outside the Soviet bloc, the image of the "other side" became more and more static.[9] Since no change could be expected, total, absolute, unyielding opposition was insisted upon. Under the producing of anticommunist Eastern European social scientists and former Marxist intellectuals now turned anticommunist, the distinction was forged between unalterable "totalitarian" societies and "authoritarian" regimes more potentially sensitive to democratic currents. Wherever possible, the authoritarian states were supported, or even installed, by Western intelligence services, to oppose the former, making American rhetoric about freedom and democracy a laughing-stock throughout the world. Intellectual life in the US became conservative and complacent. Practical post-war plans for social democracy were dropped.

Not only did the status quo in America go unchallenged, it was celebrated as the "last, best hope on earth." American historians and social scientists self-righteously proclaimed the US as being commensurate with the future. The wide gap between the ideas Americans held about their society and its actual condition stretched ever larger until the Civil Rights Movement, the Vietnam War, the Counter-culture, and Watergate. Within the West grew the almost unchallenged conviction that a small elite would have to run the defence establishment in a way that shielded it from public scrutiny, accountability, and meaningful debate. As the economic and social requirements for defence accelerated, this secrecy removed the most important decisions from any involvement with the democratic process. An American political culture that despised ideas and a consumer culture fuelled by adolescent desires became celebrated as the epitome of modernity for much of the world.

Enormous economic and social rewards were given to any intellectuals who went along with the deception. The amazing myth was propagated that democracies do not make war, or at lest do not fight with one another, as Western intelligence services unleashed coup after coup to overturn election results thought favorable to the Soviets.[10] Most American intellectuals dismissed any thinking other than mainstream as doctrinaire, prompting one commentator to remark: "Ironically at the very moment they welcomed the 'end of ideology,' they had become the ideologues of the American Way."[11]

In the 1970s, much of the propaganda praising American society was subjected to fierce criticism. One best-selling writer began his analysis of American society with the words."...we no longer understand the system under which we live, hence the system has become obsolete and we have become powerless; in turn, the system has been permitted to assume unchallenged power to dominate our lives, and now rumbles along, unguided and therefore indifferent to human ends."[12] In the 1980s, Americans turned to an ex-movie actor, Ronald Reagan, to "lead" them out of this "malaise"—a term coined by his predecessor—which prompted Eric Hobsbawm to remark that for the first time in history the values arising from the commercial requirements of the cinema were decanted into high policy.[13] The resulting realization in the 1990s, after the Gulf War, that Madison Avenue, Hollywood, and Wall Street really did not have the answers, has intensified political unrest. Revelations about the machinations of the security services in domestic politics, the phenomenal rise of Ross Perot, and riots in Los Angeles have merely sealed an unprecedented American disillusionment with their own system.

Mimesis and the Apotheosis of Violence

The process by which the US was corrupted had really begun

in the fourteenth century with the emergence of the Renaissance "warfare state," a term usually used to described Tudor England, Valois France, or Habsburg Spain. But if we examine carefully the roots of this form of political organization, it seems to have appeared as early as the thirteenth century among the city-states of Northern Italy. These polities, although small in territory, were the most complete expressions to date of societies organized for war. Their principles of organization differed from those of the feudal states surrounding them, in that they integrated rather than separated the different orders of society by reviving the classical concept of "citizen" and linking it to the duty of bearing arms in defence of the city. The role of "warrior" was thus extended to all of the people rather than restricted to a special military caste.

This revival of such "republican" values—giving people a sense of common ownership of the city and its way of life—enabled the Italian city-state to resist aggression from Pope and Emperor alike J.G.A. Pocock even credits this kind of political organization as marking a new era in medieval thinking, one in which men's identities and status became shaped by their participation in the temporal destiny of their city rather than by their place in the feudal hierarchy or a future, other-worldly paradise.[14]

This change in consciousness is distinctively modern and the connection between it and militarism has until recently been neglected by students of the Renaissance who have preferred to stress other, more pacific developments. From the perspective of our century, however (the most violent of any), it now seems rather incredible not to have noticed that the social and economic advances that are said to have laid the basis for the march into modernity—especially the Florentine meshing of banking, trade and production, and the marriage between science, invention and art—were also pressed into the service of a persistent and ruinous military competition with the other city-states of Italy. If nothing else, the writings of Machiavelli served notice that the Renaissance political system of competing city-states had developed the logic of power politics to a hitherto unsurpassed degree. The continuity between the political system he was analyzing and our own was marked by the amazing popularity of Machiavelli's ideas in this century, especially after 1945, among Western political scientists.

Once the Italian city-states exemplified by Florence organized themselves in a modern manner, warfare began to prove so deadly and efficiently financed that other states in Europe began to arrange their political and economic systems in a similar fashion. In a systematic way, trade, finance, and war became locked into a vicious circle or iron triangle with each term of the equation becoming dependent on the other two Hence the practice of treating international trade as an integral part of a state's "national interest" was placed on a par with territorial boundaries as a legitimate cause of war.[15]

All of this was accompanied by the growing importance of *mimesis* in international affairs. The city-states of Northern Italy were continually comparing and contrasting themselves to each other, almost frantically reacting to any change in power or wealth that could be discerned among their rivals. Unlike the system of city-states that had existed in ancient Greece, in which agrarian economies were most common, the Italian system was primarily dependent upon trade and commercial activities. This and the mass suggestibility fostered by medieval Catholicism made them much more externally oriented and reactive than their Greek counterparts. With the fall of Constantinople, Florence became the envy of all of Europe, regarded as the leading state of Christendom: the richest, most beautiful, and especially the most powerful. All states felt compelled to imitate her success and only her internal divisions led her, half a century later, to be eclipsed by the Spanish and French. Forever after, international relations in Europe would be increasingly influenced by *nemesis* until it would reign supreme through the adoption of the nineteenth-century belief that political supremacy would fall to those nations highest on the ladder of social evolution.[16]

Each succeeding century witnessed more and more expensive wars, requiring more efficient economies to bear the cost. In an even more ominous development (again foreshadowed in

Florence during the reign of Savonarola), the Habsburgs transformed the Renaissance state into the "Counter Reformation state," combining a crusading, ideological purity with a unified and organized polity.[17] Although liberal history claims that this moral totalitarian model was subsequently imitated by the French, Russians, Austrians, and Prussians—and rejected by the Dutch, the English and later the Americans—the reversal of roles in the late eighteenth century, when England joined Russia, Prussia, and Austria to become the bastion of resistance to social renewal, testifies to how the principle of *nemesis* in international affairs impelled every European polity to succumb to the image of its rivals. Subsequent American imperialism, militarism, and McCarthyism can best be understood in this way.

With the onset of industrialism, social theory largely ignored the subsequent strengthening of the warfare state. This was especially evident in the distinction drawn between the logic of the industrial economy, based on the principle of peace through economic interdependence, and that of the feudal Ancient Regime, grounded on martial values and zero-sum conflicts. It later came as something of a shock when the twentieth century finally realized that within the womb of the promising "new society" was also gestating a hideous, demonic twin, later to be named the military industrial complex.

Characteristically, it was Gandhi who first saw through the facade of the great-power system better than any other social thinker of this century. In his *Hind Swaraj,* published in 1909, he pointed out in scathing tones how the industrial system provided the state with the ideas, machinery, and workforce to pursue its raison d'être, the waging of war, and diffusion of violence.[18] Later writers have pointed out that the violent nineteenth century "top down" industrialization of Europe was actually a response to the equally violent and socially disruptive "bottom-up" industrialization of England in order to challenge her assumption of world hegemony.[19] The stop-down process was then imitated by Japan, whose Meiji reformers modernized her in the image of the most successful imperialists: Britain, and Bismarck's German Empire.[20]

The industrial warfare state then became the chief carrier of violence in the twentieth century. Its influence permeated and affected every aspect of society through the new instruments of socialization: mass production, mass education, and mass media. The Prussian military uniforms worn by Japanese students today are merely an atavistic remainder of the connection that existed in every great power of the twentieth century between the state, education, militarism, and murder. The conduct of war by the industrialised powers was regarded as a duty by men, copied by children, idolized b women, celebrated by the media, and worshipped in the churches, most usually in the image of an angry and vengeful god slaughtering his enemies. Adulation to the strong, contempt for the weak, and, above all, and exaltation of selfishness set into motion the systems of structural violence that still permanent all contemporary societies. Today, in almost every nation,the young are enthralled by the image of a "Terminator," an indestructible assassin, the highest creation of a future robot-run state engaged in a determined effort to exterminate the human race.

The full consequences of this massive, global organization of violence culminated in the "seventy-five-year" world war beginning in 1914 and ending in 1989. It is unthinkable, therefore, that the conclusion of this conflict, and perhaps the Renaissance state system that produced it, will not have dramatic, long-term effects on all aspects of life in the twenty-first century. Given the depth and breadth of the warfare state's influence, however, we can only speculate about the rate and direction of the change.

Withering away of Violence?

In the sequel to the movie *Terminator*, humanity has developed its own counter-assassin who successfully defends it against the evil designs of the robots. In the real world it is also possible that with the end of the military struggle for global mastery, humanity has developed an effective antidote to the reign of violence inaugurated centuries ago by its robot creation, the Renaissance warfare state. There is now no imperative in the international system to support it. In fact, the two most economically successful states, Japan and Germany, were rebuilt after 1945 with peace constitutions that prevented them from fully redeveloping the military industrial state machines that had been destroyed by the Allied powers. These societies are not free from structural violence, nor are they free from state police systems and militarist values; but it is significant that during the Gulf War the populations of these nations refused to allow their governments to contribute troops to the war, despite enormous pressure from the US and other belligerents. This is a sure sign that the considerable weakening of the Renaissance state link between militarism and citizenship has permeated deep within the political cultures of these former warfare societies. It also reveals the potential for similar changes in other nations, now that the old international system stimulating state aggression has been radically altered.

Today, in fact, in many parts of the world, the identify of the citizen is no longer defined by the state's position in an international hierarchy of military strength. Instead, what is of growing importance to the idea of citizenship is the social and economic fabric of a society and the moral values that give shape and meaning to daily life. Ironically, this new movement in history was made possible by the concentration of militaristic energies within the US and former USSR. The assumption of military responsibility for the entire planet by these huge Super Powers for almost half a century allowed regions of the world like Germany and Japan to develop a new understanding of duty and obligation to the state that entailed a reconsideration of "authority" and "freedom" as well. The loss of the state's power to demand that citizens lay down their lives in defence of whatever the leadership declared was in the national interest has made the individual's connection to the traditional framework of the state much weaker than ever before. In Germany and other parts of Northern Europe, this has enhanced individual freedom, while in Japan social organizations like the corporation seem to have been the chief beneficiaries.

This withdrawal of allegiance from the state also occurred among the young in the US during the 1960s. The collectivist social conformity that accompanied the emergence of the national security state gave rise to a large youth movement that questioned all of the myths justifying mass society and the military-industrial complex. The subsequent dehumanization left within the educational system and other mass institutions in America fostered a generation of rebels who were determined to build new lives outside of the system. In all of these cases, the meaning and relevance of "authority" and "power" were redefined, while that of "freedom" was enhanced. This revolt spread to Europe and merged with the pacifist temperament there, where the common enemy of the young was a corrupt leadership that had abandoned the real concerns of the people for their own interests in perpetuating the warfare state system.

This realignment of the relationship between state, society, and citizen now seems to have spread universally. No longer limited to the young, the questioning of the status quo has led to the most stupendous changes in the former Soviet Empire and is daily influencing events in Asia, the EC, and the US. The great nonviolent revolutions that ended the Cold War were only possible because of an intuitive recognition by the citizens of the Soviet Empire that authority relies on the willingness of the people to accept it. Freedom, in other words, is the necessary precondition for authority to be exercised, and if it is denied, the regime becomes dependent upon power and force, which eventually demoralizes the entire population and destroys the citizens' sense of obligation to the state.

For the past quarter century, this idea had been forcefully carried throughout the world by American popular culture. Itself heavily influenced by the great youth rebellion of the 1960s and the early 1970s, popular culture in the US became a potent transmitter of counter-culture values which themselves had not been fully realized within the American system. As entertainment markets became global in scope, this discontent with US society became an important force in stimulating resistance to the status quo everywhere. Surprisingly to many Americans, a pop culture laced with images at once self-deprecating and self-indulgent, decadent and transcendental, helped accomplish overseas what was frustrated at home.[21]

In one of history's more surreal marriages, the military might of the American system, combined with a popular culture subversive of it, helped liberate a large portion of the planet from the Soviet system. The great military build-up under Reagan in the 1980s convinced the leaders of the Soviet Empire that the continuation of the warfare state would bring bankruptcy before world supremacy, while the great message of the American popular culture was that some combination of freedom and material prosperity would bring happiness. Ironically, this so-called victory of capitalism over communism has produced startling repercussions within that bastion of capitalism, the United States.

Today Americans, no longer fixated on the Soviet nightmare, are looking with alarm at their own self-produced horror show of class warfare, drug abuse, urban lawlessness, educational collapse, family disintegration, and financial and economic decline—all made more pressing by a colossal failure of leadership. Now, instead of seeing other cultures as catastrophic examples of what would happen were they to question their own system, Americans are often stimulated to emulate what they see overseas. Stereotypes of other cultures might persist as popular frustration mounts. But few American can now travel abroad or read about foreign societies, especially Europe and Japan, without feeling that there are more creative ways of living together than have been realized at home, especially in those nations not primarily organized for war.

Furthermore, as American's social, moral, and economic weaknesses become even more apparent, it no longer offers as compelling a model as it once did to excite the envy and admiration of the rest of the world. Instead of looking to the US as the cause of, or solution to, their problems, other nations are now looking more within their own traditions and experiences for ideas and innovations to confront the challenges they face. Today regional and international associations, far more daring than any envisioned during the Cold War, are being debated in every capital from Algiers and Bangkok to Penang and Cairo. Likewise, a wide variety of alternatives—from Muslim fundamentalism to Confucian democracy—are being presented as far more popularly based, socially cohesive, and morally centered than American or EC-style liberal democracy. These alternatives to the "American dream" may frighten and upset many, and Iran and Singapore may not represent a desirable future for most of the world's people, but the message is clear: the failures of the West do not represent the future either. The material abundance of the market economy, if accompanied by massive social inequalities and moral decay, cannot continue to claim the allegiance of the world's masses. Liberal, capitalist democracy itself must mutate or it risks becoming neither liberal, capitalist, nor democratic.

A New World Order?

The prevailing direction of the last decade of the twentieth century will be toward increasing the responsiveness of social systems to their citizens. Today, throughout the world, we can see political movements erupting like volcanoes from below the seemingly placid surfaces of nation-states. People are refusing to accept the leadership of elites whom they see as having too long acted in their own interest while neglecting popular needs and concerns. This grassroot populism, however, can move into fundamentally different directions. It can seek to create new societies and states through limiting the circle of citizenship and using force and intimidation to exclude everybody not within it; or it can attempt to draw the larger circle and forge new forms of regional and global interdependence. The former direction might be called "external," in that its concept of citizenship establishes an external relationship with non-citizens who must then be treated as objects to be coerced or manipulated to secure assent to the wishes of the in-group. This seems to be the dominant social pattern emerging in Yugoslavia, Afghanistan, Somalia, and other places where tribalism in on the descendant. If the general trend of global populism takes this direction, the Renaissance state link between citizenship and militarism will be retained and violent conflicts could spread to every society where people of different cultural and ethnic backgrounds share common nation-state borders.

A second direction that populism might take could be called "internal," in that the identity of the citizen is formed through constructing an awareness of common concerns with people of diverse cultures and traditions. Instead of externalizing others and trying to move them from the outside, this kind of populism would try to gain the cooperation of others through a reliance on mutually-shared experience and goals. Examples of such internal populism would be the peace cultures of Germany and Japan, the great nonviolent movements that liberated Eastern Europe, and the current UN plans for Iraq and Cambodia to consist of more loosely joined and federated politics than the traditionally conceived nation-state. If this form of populism proves dominant, a revised network of regional and global institutions could emerge which are much more flexible, streamlined, and efficient in meeting real world problems.

If "external populism" proves dominant, the threat of extended international anarchy would cause any attempts at international order to be based on force and coercive power. These would come from either the US, as the world's one remaining Super Power, or from an international force connected with the United Nations. Such a possibility has prompted critics like Noam Chomsky to declare that what some would call a "new world order" would actually be a "great-power order." With the self-interest of the great powers at heart, a US-led; great-power hegemony to ensure global stability would probably lead to a freezing of the present distribution of world economic resources and the continuing toleration of repressive regimes, provided they guaranteed cheap labour and resources to fuel the global economic engine. A future great-power axis might emerge stretching from Washington to Tokyo and Berlin (and perhaps including Moscow and Kiev) that would be dominated by international corporations and dedicated to the maintenance of the high standard of living current in the West and some nations of East Asia.

This scenario would, in effect, be "order" at the expense of most of the world. Predictably, such a vision was recently put forward in the first of the *US Defense Department's Planning Guidance for the Fiscal Years 1994-1999,* although it was later toned down under harsh foreign criticism. A key passage states: "We [the US] must account sufficiently for the interests of the advanced industrial nations to discourage them from challenging our leadership or seeking to overturn the established political and economic order."[22] The Pentagon scheme effectively demolished two principles at the heart of the UN Charter: that each nation should have an equality of rights and duties, irrespective of its wealth, power or status; and that no nation can take the law into its own hands or be the judge and arbiter of its own conduct in international affairs and in internal matters of international importance. As far as being a "new" concept of world order, the Pengaton plan hauntingly recalls Thucydides' description of the policy of the Athenian League in his account of the history of the Peloponnesian War.

Clearly this kind of arrangement as a response to the spread of external populism would dash the hopes of those who have envisioned a new global order which lessens the importance of state sovereignty and promotes the status of international law. But if "internal populism" were to triumph, the prospects for a world system that is truly "new" might dramatically increase. Given that such populism is based on an expanded sense of identity by the citizenry, such an order could give rise to a sense of international solidarity and allow the development of international standards or right and wrong that could then be used as a basis for conducting internal relations and subsequent resolutions of disputes and conflict.

The US might have a unique role to play in this process. The intense domestic scrutiny being given to the American system has become something of a mass phenomenon involving a huge percentage of the US population. All sorts of schemes have been proposed to bring together a nation now seriously disunited.[23] It is entirely possible that the US could soon rewrite its Constitution and restructure its political system, thereby extending participation in the system to large numbers of those now seriously dispossessed. Through the power of *nemesis,* this could positively affect other internal populist movements overseas. In addition, this process could also resolve the debate over "multiculturalism" within the US, producing a society in which an overarching framework of freedom could provide the atmosphere for immigrants and citizens of different cultures to work out their own vision of the future in a manner not allowed them in their native lands. Unlike the external populist solutions that stress division and "ethnic cleansing," however, the resulting mosaic of cultures within the US would still be arranged into a greater picture through toleration, civility, and interdependence.

Following America's successful use of the politics of reconciliation, an increased capacity for identification by citizens of one nation with those of many others could then more strongly link the idea of solidarity with that of "security," thus promoting the emergence of a principled basis for developing policies for the conduct of trade and the giving and receiving of resources between nations. Both richer and poorer nations would understand how their own fate was bound up with the welfare of others. This might be easier to achieve on a regional basis. It is more feasible for the nations of regions with similar psychological and sociological backgrounds to accept the idea of solidarity sufficiently to allow them to work out fair and suitable trade agreements and transfer resources within their own blocs. As such, arrangements prove successful and gain credibility, the citizens of these regions might slowly move toward a greater notion of identification and unity.

A key element in this type of plan would be a very flexible idea of "region," not necessarily geographically contiguous, and linked to collective security arrangements. As George Bernard Shaw once wrote, the practically of such a scheme would reside in "neither a single Spartan Superstate, nor a single obviously unworkable and unstable League of All Mankind from China to Peru...but several combinations, psychologically homogeneous within themselves, all equally interested in keeping the peace in their own way."[24]

Central to any such approach would be the international recognition of all national groups within each nation-state of the region. Indeed, recent events in Iraq, Yugoslavia, and Somalia have clarified more than ever the necessity that nation-states must not take the law into their own hands when dealing with nationalities, especially minorities like the Kurds. With international agencies guaranteeing the integrity of nationalities, most other economic and security arrangements could be handled by intraregional arrangements. If this were to occur, there would most certainly need to be a restructuring of the UN to provide effective representation to nationalities along with nation-states and a considerable strengthening of a peacekeeping force to protect them all.

What must be faced when developing any idea of international solidarity is that most people find little attraction in the idea of collective bonds based on superficialities of global homogenization.[25] Instead of having what was once called Westernization providing the key to world unity, what in fact has happened is that each cultural tradition of any depth has taken only what it values from the West and forsaken the rest, much to the consternation of theorists of global convergence, who are continually puzzled by questions like why are Americans so at odds with the Japanese. For a real feeling of global solidarity to exist, it must come from the strength felt by a cultural unit which in many cases transcends national boundaries and yet does not encompass the entire globe. In a truly new world order, regions might be defined more by cultural homogeneity than by geography, such as Islamic and Confucian, or by linguistic-ethnicity like Hispanic or Turkic or indeed by mostly language, like the Commonwealth and the family of French-speaking nations. Additional regional arrangements would be built on already existing cooperation over the administration of such regional resources as water or through efforts to develop environmental policy. Multiple allegiances and relationships would be developed for different needs and purposes, since each nation or nationality would simultaneously belong to different regional groupings.

International political parties might also assist this effort at developing basic concept of international solidarity. These could work at local, regional, and international levels to promote policies conducive to heightening the status of international law and reformulating the idea of state sovereignty, as well as dealing with the issues of poverty, environment, and weapons proliferation. Membership in these parties might or might not preclude belonging any other. Some people might prefer to act like the original Fabian Society in providing ideas and energy that all political parties and organizations would feel impelled to consider, if not adopt. Others might want to actively run for office or prefer to operate outside of national governments altogether and engage in nonviolent struggle. With the end of the Cold War and the more universal extension of democracy, such international parties have a greater likelihood of emerging than ever before.

A New Political Metaphysic

If the internal kind of populism that I have been describing proves ascendant in the next century, the world today will be seen in retrospect as poised at the beginning of a real future, rather than at the "end of history." The triumph of internal populism in most regions of the planet could result in bold social visions, employing a logic different from the one currently accepted in the West and provide the basis for new experiments in societal reconstruction and development. Each culture, each tradition in those neglected parts of the planet now meaninglessly called the "Third" and "Fourth" world have their own conceptions of space, time, deity, nature, and humanity—ideas that could prove vital in locating the key to unlock a radically new set of possibilities for the planet. It is no accident that these older traditions, whether of Siberian shamans or Chinese herbalists, native Amazonians or Turkish dervishes, are being turned to on a mass scale by those inhabitants of over-developed societies who only recognize that their own lives and the world system are wildly out of balance.

The most striking examples of an attempt to draw upon pre-industrial patterns of life as guides to the future have come through the Green movement. Using the findings of modern science, environmentalists have demonstrated the logic underlying many of the truths contained in the traditions of Third-and Fourth-World cultures like those of the Native Americans. No longer is a view of the natural world as sacred dismissed as "superstitious" animism. Today this belief is held to be an intuitive recognition of the intricate interdependence that exists between humanity and natural law. Some sense of order, and of balance, binds people and Nature together, and disregard for this order plays havoc with the entire global organism (which some environmentalists refer to as "Gaia," the ancient Greek word for Earth), injuring in turn the myriad forms of life which it supports.

The recognition that there are natural limits or restraints upon economic development has prompted keen interest in the ways of life practised by pre-industrial people. Accordingly, some of their practices are being revived by modern society as it seeks to develop a "post-industrial" order. The concept of the extended family, for example, is coming back into favour where it simultaneously meets the needs of a variety of unrelated people at different stages of life: young people who reject the roles offered them by industrial organizations; parents who want to work full-time and still raise their children; and the elderly who have either been discarded or disregarded by industrial organizations as unfit to work. Parents in such neo-extended families are increasingly employing the dissatisfied young as live-in housekeepers and handymen, and the aged as resident baby-sitters and counselors. In some cases, housing is being constructed according to new architectural designs which enable these generations to live together, or in close proximity, with a minimum of conflict—a return to a kind of tribal arrangement.[26]

A similar return to pre-industrial pattern is occurring in contemporary society's attitude toward time. Originally viewed in a linear manner, the stages of life were divided into clear-cut educational, productive, and retirement phases for the young, mature, and elderly, respectively. Today, however, the most innovative companies are providing employees with sabbatical, educational, and leisure activities during the work phase, while offering more work opportunities for the young and elderly.

Slowly, as more cyclical view of time is becoming accepted, in which people are seen as organisms who continually return to certain stages of the personal growth process, albeit at a different place or dimension.

In addition, the industrial age, which began by largely removing from the home such activities as work, education, health care and even, to some degree leisure, is ending by returning them home through the revolution in personal electronics. This has great implications for the vast populations which still live in pre-industrial social conditions. Instead of having to go through all of the destructive steps of migration to the cities, mass poverty, urban lawlessness and the rest, these people may become able to participate in an international economy as personal computers grow ever simpler and easier to operate. With wireless modems, for example, people could maintain social, economic, and political links with the larger life of their society while living in conditions as untouched by development as their choose. The greatest barrier to such developments would be the myopia of Third and Fourth-World political leaders who so often feel that economic growth lies in the same suicidal ways that the more advanced economies are already rejecting. To prevent this from happening, the leaders of the advanced industrial nations must be willing to transfer the latest technology to the least economically developed people, especially those methods which are most beneficial to the environment.

Now that the great-power world system, begun in Northern Italy and so well-described in the thought of Machiavelli, has ended, perhaps the thought of his contemporary, Pico della Mirandola, will come into its own. Indeed if one were to give a name to the new epoch that might await us, it should perhaps be taken after Pico's treatise, *Oration to the Dignity of Man,* in which he conceived of human nature in a strikingly different manner than that of the medieval theologians. Humanity, Pico believed, was like a "divine chameleon," an infinitely variable entity that could become like anything to which its attention was directed. Not confined to the medieval great chain of being, humanity could soar beyond the angels and touch the hem of deity, or sink below the most bestial of all creatures. Only the human will limits human achievement.

The key element in Pico's vision is complete and total non-attachment. Since only the human will is free, the key to its creativity is the ability to disengage itself from the forms or institutions it has created and construct new ones. All forms are bound by time. Looked at from the eye of eternity, they are useful only for a moment and inevitably begin to atrophy and decay. The free personality and the free society will ride the "crest of cycles" and seek ever more expanding allegiances in a variety of context and circumstances. It is through the realization of this outlook that a truly nonviolent new world order can begin to emerge.

What really gives cohesion and order to all societies is an internal awareness of some pattern or shape to daily life. Often reflected in such diverse cultural creations as drama, architecture, music, and painting, this order may appear balanced and harmonious as in ancient Greece, soaring and other-worldly as in the Gothic, or enclosed and in-bred as in the Byzantine. A new world order will also have a shape, but if it is to become Picoian, it must prove much more dynamic and flexible than any of its shapes in the past. Violence, as Gandhi knew, is intricately tied to rigidity, an absolutizing of relative truth. Most social systems that collapse in violence do so because they are insufficiently flexible to accommodate the new needs of their people. It could be, then, that the shape of things to come will no longer be bound to static notions of hierarchy, as in the Far East, or in monotheistic pyramids of order as in the West, but more like the vision of Nicholas of Cusa who saw God, the ultimate reality, as a circle" with circumference nowhere and center everywhere." If the notions of identity constructed by citizens of the future somehow can be linked to this image of dynamic order, nonviolence as a way of life may become the rule of life, the axial principle for the highest civilizations of the next century.

Notes and References

1. Reinhardt Bendix has studied the political development of five great power his *Kings or People* (London 1978). But while he attributes the formation of modern political and social institutions to the organization for war, he neglects the systemic impact of the rivalry for world domination.
2. See Noel Annan's discussion of this argument in his *Our Age* (London, 1991), Chapter 15.
3. The sorry story of how US intelligence agencies participated in this has been documented in Christopher Simpson, *Blowback* (New York, 1988). He exposes the fascist-inspired mind-set that dominated US foreign policy from as early as 1943.
4. Paul Kennedy, *The Rise and Fall of Great Powers* (London, 1989).
5. The vicissitudes of American intellectual life in the forties and fifties have been magnificently charted by Richard H. Pells in *The Liberal Mind in a Conservative Age* (New York, 1985).
6. Curiosly this repression by both sides of utopian thought within antifascist groups resulted in the triumph of the Universalist Catholic vision of the Christian Democrats in France, Germany, and Italy that we know today as the EC. See James Joll, *Europe Since 1870* (London, 1990), Chapter 15.
7. Richard H. Pells, *The Liberal Mind in a Conservative Age,* p. 41.
8. James Burnham, *The Machiavellians* (Chicago, 1960), Preface.
9. See Christopher Simpson, *Blowback.*
10. For a historical account of US military aggression in Central America, see Stephen Schlesinger and Stephen Kinger, *Bitter Fruit* (New York, 1984). The subversion of electoral politics by the US began in post-war European and was soon extended throughout the world by the military intelligence services. A broad overview was presented in Bill Mayer's PBS documentary, "The Secret Army." Of course the story of the intelligence agencies' manipulations of elections in the US

since the Kennedy assassination has never been fully told. One attempt was made in Gary Sick, *October Surprise* (New York, 1992). For a current example of how military intelligence still operators "off-shell" operations in the US, see John Connolly, "Badlands," *Spy,* April 1992.

11. Richard H. Pells, *The Liberal Mind in a Conservative Age,* p. 147.
12. Charles Reich, *The Greening of America* (New York, 1971).
13. Eric Hobsbawm, *The Age of Empire* (New York, 1989), p. 241.
14. The Renaissance connection between citizenship and warfare has been commented on by many historians of ideas, especially J.G.A. Pocock in *The Machiavellian Moment* (Princeton, 1975). However, he does not explore how this made possible the development of the warfare state with its tragic implications for world history.
15. This policy was extended over the years by the European trading powers until it finally appeared in the eighteenth century as the system we know as "mercantilism." According to C.M. Andrews, "it fomented war in provicing an economic struggle among the commercial and industrial nations for place, power, and wealth." See his *The Colonial Background of the American Revolution* (New Haven, 1967), p. 93. For a lively account of how the system provoked the eighteenth-century cycle of revolution, see Hugh Brogan, *The Pelican History of the United States of America* (London, 1986), Chapters 6 and 8. Even today a variant of this policy is often referred to as "managed trade" and criticized as leading to economic warfare. See especially the work of Chalmers Johnson on Japanese trading policy.
16. This application of the idea of Social Darwinisim to international relations was indissolubly linked to the idea of progress which meant superiority in science, technology, trade, and industrialization.
17. See J.M. Roberts, *The Pelican History of the World,* Book Five, (London 1988), Chapter 2.
18. For a lucid, well-written account of Gandhi's indictment of modern civilization, see R.N. Iyer, *The Moral and Political Thought of Mahatma Gandhi* (Santa Barbara, 1983), Chapter

2.

19. See Krisna Kumar, *Prophecy and Progress* (London, 1978), Chapter 4.

20. Korel van Wolferen in the *The Enigma of Japanese Power* (London, 1990), makes much of the influence of European fascist ideas on Japanese society, especially the system of economic planning. But he strangely neglects the clear thread that stretches from Saint-Simon through German capitalists like Walter Rathenau to the phenomenon of "managerialism" that was so popular a topic of analysis in the 1930s. According to writers such as James Burnham, all of these were responses to the dislocations and upheavals caused by industrialism. The Japanese system thus can be seen as an attempt at meeting the still unresolved contradiction within our industrial world.

21. For a fascinating account of the power of American popular culture over the world's imagination, see Pico Iyer, "The Selling of America," *Harpers,* December 1991.

22. *New York Times,* 8 March 1992. p. 4.

23. This theme has been pursued for the last few years in a series of essays by Gore Vidal.

24. George Bernard Shaw as quoted in Michael Holroyd, *Bernard Shaw: The lureof Fantasy* (London, 1991), p. 6.

25. See R.N. Iyer, *Parapolitics* (Santa Barbara, 1989), Chapters, 13 and 17.

26. For an intriguing discussion of the concept of locating the future within the past, see Krishna Kumar, *Prophecy and Progress,* Chapter 8.

Chapter-4

Nonviolence and the Case of the Extremely Ruthless Opponent

Ralph Summy

Chapter-4

ONE OF THE most common criticisms of nonviolent action—from academics, politicians, and general public alike—is its ineffectiveness against an extremely ruthless opponent.[1] As long as an opponent is willing and able to resort to acts of severe repression, a nonviolent response is considered not only instrumentally inappropriate, but possibly also the cause of inciting the degenerate and sadistic amongst the enemy's forces to even baser forms of brutality.[2]

Leaving aside the observation that similar reservations can be expressed about the appropriateness of a violent response in such circumstances, I shall attempt, in this paper, to examine critically—in terms of both a theory of power and the empirical evidence—the orthodox view concerning the limitations of nonviolence. Are the critics, it will be asked, posing the right question in assessing whether or not nonviolence "works." If not, in place of the ruthlessness factor, is there any question or series of questions highlighting other factors that might prove cogently sound in predicting the success or failure of a nonviolent strategy?

Since we live in a society steeped in utilitarianism, for the purposes of this paper, "success" will be measured at the instrumental level. This is the level at which the challenge is raised. Is the nonviolent method, in the face of extreme ruthlessness, an effective means of achieving a designated, tangible goal? What are the chances of a cost/benefit calculation working out favourably for the nonviolent proponent? Other interpretations of success are not germane to this inquiry. For instance, whether nonviolence offers intrinsic value to its practitioners, opens up avenues of expressive politics, cultivates a range of personal skills, or has long-term value benefits for society in which "right" means become "right" ends in the making, these sorts of criteria of "success" fall outside the bounds of the present exercise. Nevertheless, the exclusion of such criteria as a frame of reference does not imply that they lack significance beyond the narrow definition adopted by most of the critics of nonviolence.[3]

A second proviso also narrows the inquiry. It will be assumed—accepting the common assumption of the detractors of nonviolence—that the choice lies between violence and nonviolence. Yet in the range of real world conflicts this is clearly not so. A violent response may be manifestly imprudent and thus it may be ruled out by even the most ardent of militarists, or the cause of resistance may be better served by doing clothing or pursuing "conventional" means rather than by acting nonviolently.[4] This paper, therefore, examines the orthodox argument from the standpoint of one of its own highly arguable pre-analytical assumptions.

Thirdly, a distinction is made throughout between the spheres of "nonviolent politics" and "conventional politics." Apart from the latent violence structured into the state and many other institutions and norms, most political activity is nonviolent in generic sense that it does not directly involve killing, maiming, or physically coercing fellow human beings. Conventional politics is usually nonviolent in this limited sense. However, it lacks one or more of a number of other characteristics that distinguish it from nonviolent politics. ... the case of the latter, the action is always, by definition, physically nonviolent, and most of its votaries are conscious of—and seek to avoid—structural and psychological violence. A nonviolent action is also readily identified by the fact that it lies outside society's regularised patterns of political behaviour. It tends to be considered novel or unusual and as a weapon of... powerless. It sometimes is illegal. It always carries with it an element of risk (however small) for its practitioners, because it is seen by the authorities and their supporters as not only "different" but also as a potential challenge to the established way of conducting politics and hence to the security of their position. Paradoxically, nonviolent is often exercised as an alternative to violence in situations where the standard response might widely be expected to be the use or threat of physical force. Irrespective, however, of whether opponents might prefer and even acknowledge nonviolence as reasonable or legitimate under certain circumstances, they still are apt to respond with violent measures of their own. On the other hand, were the action to have been conducted in the conventional sphere of politics, a violent response, on the opponents' part, would constitute a rejection of their own system. To avoid this obvious contradiction, any violent response, if entertained at all, would most likely be confined to illegal and covert channels.

A fourth point also needs to be clarified at the outset. The analysis centres on the efficacy of nonviolence qua strategy. There can be no disputing the fact that in an immediate tactical situation, where an attacker is bent on violence and strikes swiftly, as in an assassination attempt or surprise armed assault, a positive nonviolent response is usually not a viable option for the targeted victim.[5] When such a situation arises or has been allowed to develop, then the practical option of survival for those under fire becomes the classic "fight or flight." However, what is being questioned in this article is the generalised belief that at the strategical level, a nonviolent campaign against a "no holds barred" opponent is destined to meet the same fate.

A final point concerns the use of the concept of "ruthless opponent." In this paper, the concept covers a wide sweep: from a regime that might sporadically apply extreme brutality or target only a small number of dissidents to one where there is a total clampdown on any internal opposition and borders are closed to the penetration of foreign media.[6] The latter, or a "totalitarian" regime, would generally be considered the "worst-case scenario."

The Orthodox Case

The subject of nonviolent politics is not extensively examined in the mainstream literature of political science,[7] nor is it given considerate thought by most politicians and defence analysts.[8] If it is raised at all, it tends to be misrepresented (e.g., equated with passive resistance, pacifism, direct action, or civil disobedience), or else perfunctorily and derisively dismissed as naive and unrealistic. Its major weakness is seen to be linked to the nature of the opponent's response. As long as the opponent lacks the will or capacity to inflict severe reprisals or abides by a moral or political code of self-restraint, nonviolent political action has a chance of being successful. But without those pre-consitions it will be crushed by the effective application of superior firepower, the *ultimate ratio* of conflict resolution.

This position was reflected in the reasoning of former Australian Defence Minister and political-science scholar, Kim Beazley, when he explained the Australian government's reluctance to embark on an investigation into the feasibility of civilian-based defence. He observed that "nonviolence proved effective for Gandhi in India's struggle for independence, because the British were relatively benign."[9] It is argued that against a power prepared to exercise its repressive force to the fullest, a nonviolent strategy is defeatist. At best it is limited to a declaration of popular sentiment that keeps alive the prospects of unified opposition by orthodox strong arm methods at a later date.

French sociologist Raymond Aron expressed similar reservations when responding to George Kennan's favourable reference to the potential of nonviolence in the latter's 1958 Reith Lectures.[10] As summarised by Aron, Kennan's "theory" could be reduced to the following proposition:" It is enough that a population, even without arms, be resolved to make a conqueror's life impossible, for the latter to discover, little by little, the vanity of conquest."[11] To Aron, such an assertion was seriously flawed, "*in so far as it claims to be realistic*" (italics in original). He insisted it was

> open to decisive objections, because it envisages certain facts and overlooks others. First of all, it assumes that the day of massacres or exterminations is definitively over, that a people which lays down its arms will be neither deported nor reduced to slavery nor simply exterminated. Unhappily, there is no reason for subscribing to this act of faith.[12]

He then went on citing a number of historical tragedies that befell peoples who failed to offer armed resistance, as, for example, the Jews under Hitler and the Incas and Aztecs at the hands of the Spanish invaders.

The Aron argument, despite its appeal to realism, suffers from at least three major flaws. Not only has he engaged in the logical fallacy of *post hoc, ergo prompter hoc* argument, since the mere sequence of the events does not establish any causal relationship between failure to resist violently and massacres that followed, but, more importantly, in all the cases he has cited, no concerted nonviolent campaigns, either spontaneous or planned, were conducted. Even if nonviolent campaigns had occurred, the ensuing calamities might have resulted from deficiencies in the way the campaigns were staged, and have had nothing to do with the intrinsic nature of nonviolence. Therefore, how can it be said that nonviolent politics is the cause of the disasters? Part of Aron's problem stems from his unstated assumption about the theory of power about which I would say something more later. Another problem can be traced to his misunderstanding of nonviolence which he equates with passive resistance. In making the same point as Beazley about British restraint in India (a claim of arguable historical accuracy[13] as well as dubious political science), he states that "the effectiveness of passive resistance, as practised by the Indians under the leadership of Mahatma Gandhi, is subordinate to the respect, on the part of armed men, for certain rules (my emphasis)"[14]

George Orwell, who considered Gandhi a "dangerous fool" in calling for nonviolent resistance to the tyrants of Europe, put his case as follows:

> It is difficult to see how Gandhi's methods could be applied in a country where opponents of the regime disappear in the middle of the night and are never heard of again. Without a free press and the right of assembly, it is impossible not merely to appeal to outside opinion, but to bring a mass movement into being, or even to make your intentions known to your adversary.[15]

Thus nonviolent resistance is considered "impossible" against the extremely ruthless dictator who presides over a totalitarian system. It cannot effect the downfall of such a regime. Indeed, political scientist Michael Walzer takes the argument one step further. He observes: "Nonviolence, under extreme conditions, collapses into violence directed at oneself rather than at one's murderers."[16]

Walzer seems more sensitively attuned to the complex dynamics of nonviolent strategy than the other critics—having taken the trouble to familiarise himself with some of the literature. Yet his basic response is confined to an enlargement of the same argument. Although his sympathies lie with the development of a nonviolent politics, he finds it wanting at the crucial point of "replace(ing) aggressive war with political struggle." In his words:

> [Nonviolence] cannot by itself determine the means of struggle. The invading army can always adopt the common methods of domestic tyrants, which go well beyond curfews, fines, and jail sentences; and its leader ... may well be tempted to do that for the sake of a quick "victory." Tyrants will not, of course, lay siege to their own cities or bomb or bombard them, nor will invaders who encounter no opposition. But there are other, probably more efficient, ways of terrorizing a people ... and of breaking their resistance.[17]

In a power relationship where one party does not need the other pany, and yet the other party needs it, the advantage in determining the outcome of a conflict heavily favours the first party. This is the endemic situation prevailing between ruler and most led. The latter have the option to act independently while the former is locked into a dependency relationship. Furthermore, those few amongst the ruled that are apparently isolated and powerless very often have avenues to explore that will reverse their predicament. Graphically, the interaction between ruler and ruled is represented by the lines numbered one and two in figure A.The ruler is either dependent and the ruled independent (Line 1), or the ruler is more dependent than the ruled (Line 2). If a third line were drawn that is confined solely to the independent quadrants, there would be no power exercised by either party over the other. Indeed, no form of governance would exist between the parties.

FIGURE A

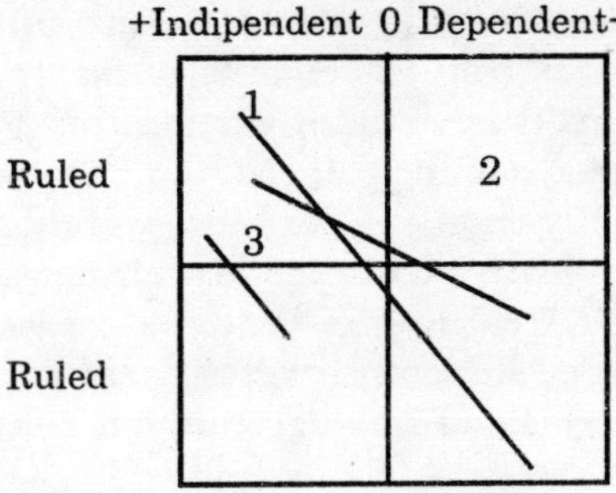

The conventional view of power is not perceived in this way. The routine obedience of subjects makes it difficult to imagine that it is actually the ruler who has the greater need for the ruled (and not vice versa). Despite repeated examples of the rules choosing to withdraw their support and their actions leading to the disintegration of the ruler's power, most people (even some sophisticated theorists like the orthodox critics of nonviolent resistance described above) cannot bring themselves to acknowledge fully the revolutionary implications of what follows from the simple preposition that no ruler exists without the willingness of his/her subjects to be ruled. Instead, they tend to long to the view that power flows from the top to the bottom as represented by the two dependency relationship lines in Figure B. It is thought that the subjects are not only dependent on the ruler for various benefits, but can be negatively dependent in the sense of facing very unpleasant consequences if they become disobedient. The possibilities of subverting the ruler are not explored.

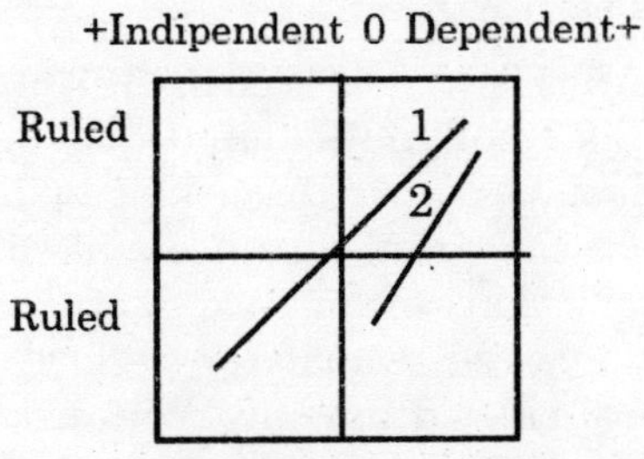

FIGURE B

In a totalitarian state, Walzer assets, the nonviolent leadership can be singled out for arrest, torture, and execution, and disappear without trace. A climate of fear pervades the populace. He opines: "It is virtually certain that the men and women of the occupied country—those who have been marked out for survival, at any rate, and perhaps even those who have been marked out for death—will yield to their new masters and obey their decrees." According to Walzer's assessment: "The country will grow silent. Resistance will be a matter of individual heroism or of the heroism of small groups, but not of collective struggle."[18]

Nonviolence, in other words, is reduced to a futile but heroic gesture against any opponent who wields power with consummate ruthlessness. The exception to this monolithic exercise of violence occurs when the opponent or his auxiliaries are restrained by a code of conduct similar to that of the nonviolent resisters. However, asserts Walzer:

> When one cannot count on the moral code, nonviolence is either a disguised form of surrender or a minimalist way of upholding communal values after a military defeat, Though civilian resistance evokes no moral recognition among the invading soldiers, it can still be important for its practitioners. It expresses the communal will to survive and though the expression is brief, as in Czechoslovakia in 1968, it is likely to be long remembered. The heroism of civilians is even more heartening than that of soldiers. On the other hand, one should not expect much more from civilians confronted with a terrorist or potentially terrorist army then brief or sporadic resistance.[19]

Walzer's position is summarised in the statement "nonviolent defence depends upon noncombatant immunity."[20] Such "immunity," he insists, is apt to be lacking in the case of a foreign occupation where the social distance and cultural differences between protagonists are often great or other concerns (like the invader's own perceived security or welfare) take precedence. The same general rule—I am sure Walzer would argue—also applies to the effectiveness of nonviolence in domestic conflicts.

Subjects without "immunity" will find collective nonviolent action an inappropriate form of resistance.

While the advantages of directly enjoying "immunity" from an opponent are indisputable, the efficacy of nonviolence, in my view, involves a political process that can extend beyond this single dimension, even in a totalitarian state. One can find the key ingredients to "success" by turning first to the theory of power behind the dynamics of nonviolence and bearing in mind the notion of strategic choice expressed in the following three quotes:

> The outcome of nonviolent struggles can only be examined in the light of the entire sequence of choices made by both protagonists and the effects that these choices have on their total relative power as the conflict unfolds.[21]

> You can erect a throne using bayonets but you cannot sit on bayonets for long. The days of the conspirators are numbered. I ask you not to carry out their decisions.[22]

> Strategy is to will something.[23]

Theory of Power

The nonviolent theorist begins with the proposition that governmental power is dependent and therefore potentially very fragile. No ruler, from the most despotic to the most democratic, can rule without the consent or compliance of a sizeable fraction of the populace. The dependency relationship can also extend to well-positioned minority groups. For example, if any group of key advisers, administrators, police, military personnel, and workers in vital areas such as energy supply, transportation, and communication refuse (or threaten not) to formulate policy and carry out their duties—and competent replacements cannot be found to fill the vacancies—the ruler's power is drastically undermined. More-over, a minority of outcast group that has no direct dependency relationship can still control the power wielded over it by mobilising the support of third and fourth parties that do have the capacity to exercise direct leverage over the ruler.

Notwithstanding the very real problems presented by extreme

ruthlessness, it is still necessary to refocus on the fundamental leverage of dependency that the ruled exercise over the ruler. Their obedience or compliance is required. Gene Sharp, the doyen of nonviolent scholars, makes this his central thesis. And there are many political theorists on whom he can draw for support, ranging from Machiavelli to Comet to Weber to Maclver.[24] As he conceives of power, it is something given to the powerholder and what can be given can also be withheld. There is a choice available.

> When people refuse their cooperation, withhold their help, and persist in their disobedience and defiance, they are denying their opponent the basic human assistance and cooperation which any government or hierarchical system requires. If they do this in sufficient numbers for long enough, that government or hierarchical system will no longer have power. *This is the basic political assumption of nonviolent action* (my emphasis).[25]

Sharp's view of power stresses the fact that it is fragile, nebulous, fluctuating, and easily destroyed. He calls his view "pluralist," because the loci of power are widely diffused. Power is not a monolith, flowing downward and held in the hands of one central authority, not even in a totalitarian society (which is theoretically a misnomer). Although the initiative in the power relationship of ruler/ruled rests with the latter, who can withhold consent, the ruler can, nonetheless, mobilize certain sources of power in order to obtain that consent. These sources Sharp identifies as "authority" (people's acceptance of the ruler's right to command and be obeyed without imposition of sanctions), "human resources" (number of people prepared to assist ruler), "skills and knowledge" (capabilities of these functionaries), "material resources" (ruler's degree of control over natural and financial resources and the means of communication and transportation), "intangible factors" (psychological, cultural, and ideological factors predisposing people to obey), and "sanctions" (use of "stick" against recalcitrants).[26]

However, against these sources a campaign can be mounted by the ruled. The power sources can be undermined as long as people appreciate the ephemeral nature of the sources and the reasons why the ruler has been obeyed in the past. Sharp notes that people's political obedience has various, multiple, and interrelated explanations. He cites seven major ones: (i) habit; (ii) fear of sanctions; (iii) moral obligation arising from considerations of the common good of society, attributing superhuman qualities to the ruler recognition of ruler's legitimacy, and conforming to commends as accepted norms; (iv) self interest in supporting ruler; (v) psychological identification with the ruler, (vi) zones of indifference about some laws and policies; and (vii) absence of self-confidence about some laws and policies; and (vii) absence of self-confidence among subjects.[27] Once people have become aware that sources of a ruler's power are not a fixed quantum, intrinsic to his being, but are dependent on people's obedience and assistance, they can set about designing strategies and tactics that strike at the ruler's points of greatest vulnerability. Grave social, economic, and political problems [that] involve at some point a serious maldistribution of power can be righted through the mobilisation of popular empowerment based initially on actions of noncooperation and defiance.[28] For the oppressed of the world, Sharp's focus on the privileged powerholders' dependency offers the hope of radical social change through weapons of nonviolence. He has catalogued in great descriptive detail almost two hundred methods of nonviolence that are at the disposal of people in overcoming a ruler's domination[29] and since the publication of his classic work, he tells me that he has discovered—or been informed about—approximately another two hundred methods. In other words, due to the dependency of the ruler's position, it is not necessary to overpower him (and it usually is a "him") with superior blocks of power but to actively deny him, through the four hundred or so methods, that which he cannot rule without, viz. popular support.

This dichotomic theory of power appeals in its simplicity. It also means that people have a choice. Voluntarism and bipolarity, however, minimize the complexities of social reality. Sharp does not sufficiently consider that structures such as capitalism, patriarchy, statism, bureaucracy, and technology (which also embody social relations) can impose barriers between the ruler-subject division, making it difficult for people to escape their regular patterns of behavior. Brian Martin sees these structures as not only possibly complicating the starkness of the Sharpian dichotomy but actually replacing it. In his words, many structures reflect" social interactions, so regular and entrenched that they take on a dynamic of their own."[30] When examining power in structural terms, nearly everyone is both superordinate and subordinate in different ways. Thus various systems of power must be taken into account when mobilizing any nonviolent action. An example given by Martin is the relationship of oppressed workers with the ruler. While in principle labour can be mobilized to walk off the job, in practice it is not quite that simple.

> The workers are likely to be divided along lines of status, skill, wages, gender and ethnicity; the mass media may provide little support or active disinformation; certain workers may have been tied to the regime by dispensation of special favours, being involved in corruption, or compromised by participating in repression of minorities; education in nationalism may make it easy for the ruler to raise the specter of foreign enemies, external agitators and hurting the national interest.[31]

Gaining unity and sustaining commitment is affected by a full range of interlocking structures. Also, to understand the dynamics operating in a society, a theory of power needs to incorporate the cultural dimension. Traditions of independence and opposition to authority, values regarding violence and attitudes to learning, beliefs about "chosenness" and approaches to conflict management, and, above all, the paradigms by which people process knowledge and experience, all significantly interpose themselves between the protagonists, so that at a particular moment in history, people may not be able to choose freely for nonviolent resistance. The problem is not the brutality of the opponent but the psyche within the resister. For example, an argument can readily be mounted to demonstrate that the

Palestinians would have had greater chance of success in securing an independent homeland if they had resorted to nonviolence. yet much more is involved in convincing them to adopt such a strategy than a simple reduction to the thinking of Western instrumentalism. It is interesting to note that the mainly nonviolent action of the *intifadah* sprang up spontaneously out of a visceral desperation at the grassroots and not as part of a planned strategy emanating from PLO leadership.

While not invalidated by a social analysis that looks at structural and cultural factors, Sharp's neoliberal picture of the ruler—subject dichotomy would be strengthened, in my opinion, if it were to feature in its theory a clear recognition of the numerous systems of power that intercede and pose problems for the Sharpian ideal functioning of nonviolence. How and whether these problems can be overcome needs to be addressed, in some form or other, whenever a nonviolent strategy is formulated. Nevertheless, the basic theory of the ruler's ultimate dependence on a significant section of the ruled is refutable and provides an important insight for nonviolent strategists. Their task is to being the conflict to the point where that dependency relationship comes to the fore. Dependence should be seen as representing the centre of gravity in effecting successful nonviolent action.

Although mobilizing resistance around the intrinsic relationship of dependence faces special problems in the totalitarian system, the task is far from impossible. In the first place, totalitarian control is an ideal that can never be achieved one hundred per cent in practice. There will always be chinks to breach in the monolith, even against a Stalin or a Hitler. The problem is to overcome the paralysis of fear, to use it creatively, to realize that "moments of profound doubt can give birth to new certainties." [32] With imagination and courage, people will discover, as Vaclav Havel points out, that "it is not only the struggle for human rights that has it sown peculiar power, but incomparably more innocent activities as well."[33] The "cultural activism" of artists and writers such as Milan Kundera, Ludvik Vaculik, Josef Skvorecky, and, of course, Havel of Czechoslovakia and Ariel Dorfman, Isabel Allende, Jose Donoso and Antonio skarmeta of Chile attests to the power of ideas penetrating the chinks of totalitarianism and commencing its demise. This process is facilitated in today's world by advances in communication technology which make it increasingly difficult for any society to remain closed within and sealed off from outside.

But Havel is saying more than this. He is revealing how, during the course of its existence, totalitarianism sows the seeds of its own destruction. In time, the process of mission prevails over fusion. It occurs because a new dependency relationship develops which is vulnerable to the initiatives of nonviolent resisters. The system, rather than the ruler, becomes the opponent. The system acquires an "automatism" more powerful than the will of any individual, including the secretary of the party. Everyone is infused to

> do what is done, what is to be done, what must be done, but at the same time—by that very token,—they confirm that it must be done in fact. They conform to a particular requirement and in so doing they themselves perpetuate that requirement...The real accomplice in this involvement, therefore, is not another person, but the system itself.[34]

Continuing, Havel explicates: "Only a very generalised view (and even that only appropriative) permits us to divide society into rulers and the ruled." With the evolution of the totalitarian system the real line of conflict "runs *de facto* through each person... what we understand by the system is not, therefore, a social order imposed by one group upon another, but rather something which permeates the entire society."[35]

The new dependency relationship is paradoxically both a source of despair and of promise and opportunity. There is despair because power has been appropriated from power, "as though it had become dictator itself." In this dreadful world it appears "that theory itself, ritual itself, ideology itself, makes decisions that affect people, and not the other way around."[36] People are afflicted with "living a lie." There is, however, also an opportunity for revolt which springs from each of us possessing "some longing for humanity's rightful dignity, for moral integrity, for free expression of being and a sense of transcendence over the world of existence."[37] The desire to "live within the truth" never completely dies. It poses an onging threat to the needs of that opponent called "totalitarianism" for the "living of a lie."

> If the main pillar of the system is living a lie, then it is not surprising that the fundamental threat to it is living the truth ... Truth plays a far greater. An above all a far different role as a factor of power, or as an outright political force ... The effective range of this special power cannot be measured in terms of disciples, voters, or soldiers, because it lies spread out in the fifth column of social consciousness, in the hidden aims of life ... in the strength of a potential which is hidden throughout the whole of society, including the official power structures of that society.[38]

By seeing the system as, in effect, the ruler—and not elite groups and leaders who are as much the system's ruled as the people—the focus then turns towards personal transformation and reaching depths of other "souls." Ideas, attitudes, and, above all, the human spirit, with its infinite possibilities, emerge as paramount in the nonviolent struggle. Johan Galtung illustrated how this can operate with the story of a Polish theatrical group dressed as pink panthers rushing into the street and forming a mock queue. The absurdity of the parallel with their daily lives was not lost on the cheering audience.[39] For the same reason, the "cultural activism" of rock singers is perceived as a threat by autocratic regimes—to wit, the crackdown by the former Czechoslovakian government against the perceived subversion of the "plastic people of the Universe" and the recent banning of a "hard metal" group in Malaysia.

The Empirical Evidence

Whenever nonviolent action has been instrumentally successful—whether against a despotic, totalistic, or democratic regime—the core element can be traced to the existence of a dependency relationship. It is the necessary, though not sufficient, part of a successful calculus. There are many examples of brutal tyrants and totalitarian systems capitulating to improvised nonviolent action and in every case a dependency relationship either existed between the protagonists or was established indirectly through third parties. There are two kinds of dependency relationship:

(a) direct dependency; and
(b) indirect dependency.

Direct Dependency

Anotable example of the first category of a direct relationship is the nonviolent campaign against the Shah of Iran during the upheavals of 1978-79. Basically the revolution (or overthrow) was conducted nonviolently as only relatively minor acts of violence contributed to the downfall of a highly autocratic regime. Despite possessing enormous military capability—the Iranian government being backed by one of the best equipped armies in the world and allied to the world's most lethal military machine—the Shah and his immediate successor Bakhtiar were unable to govern a country where the overwhelming majority of people refused to accept their authority. No degree of brutality, assassination and torture carried out by the Savak, or secret police, could blunt the people's revolutionary fervour. To paraphrase an apt metaphor of Gandhi's: It was as if the Shah and his underlings were continually striking their swords upon a body of water. Their arms became exhausted and their strength was rendered powerless.

The Ayatollah virtually used the same metaphor. The only difference is that he substituted the word "blood" for "water." "Blood," he proclaimed, "will achieve victory against the sword."[40] At the height of the uprising he importuned: "People of Iran, sacrifice your blood to protect Islam and overthrow the tyrant and his parasites."[41] To shoot down people who were shouting "Praise be to Allah," gave to the victims an etemal salvation while bringing down on the Shah and his subordinates the damnation of an entire nation. The turning point of the revolution is said to have occurred on 8 September 1978 when a large crowd, led by teenagers and veiled women, was raked by automatic gunfire, leaving between two and three thousand dead in Teheran's Jalih Square. From that moment on, Iranians across the political spectrum, including members of the armed forces, were dedicated to the Shah's demise. Cries of "Death to the Shah" became common.

The Ayatollah scarcely followed the Gandhian tradition. But he utilised effectively one of the same political stratagems—that of "moral *jiu-jitsu.*" This term was first used by Richard Gregg to describe the process whereby nonviolent activists disarm an extremely ruthless opponent with his own weapons system.[42] He is thrown off balance. The exposure of his violence against nonviolent protesters casts him in an extremely bad light, may lead to shifts in opinion, and then may reshape power relationship favourable to the nonviolent group. As Sharp explains:

> Cruelties and brutalities committed against the clearly nonviolent are likely to disturb many people and to fill some with outrage. Even milder violent repression appears less justified against nonviolent people than when employed against violent resisters ... Thus, wider public opinion may turn against the opponent, members of his own group may dissent, and more or less passive members of the general grievance group may shift to firm opposition.[43]

Sharp calls this process "political *jiu-jitsu,*" because he is interested in changing power relations. He believes that its effects—as noted above—may be registered on functionaries of the ruler, on third parties outside the immediate conflict, and on the aggrieved group itself. It can both widen the number and deepen the resolve of the resister. A case in point, cited by Sharp, occurred in Czechoslovakia during the uprisings of 1989.

> On November 17, 1989, Czech riot police brutally suppressed nonviolent demonstrators demanding free elections and democracy in the streets of Prague. These beatings galvanized political opposition to the hard communist regime. Czechs and Slovaks erected shrines at the main sites of the beatings, raising those injured to the stature of heroes. Hundreds of thousands took to the streets daily following

the police actions. As one student put it, the beatings were "the spark that started the whole movement." Within four weeks the Communist hard-liners were forced to resign, and the Communist party had to relinquish its majority of Cabinet positions.[44]

There were many other incidents of violence against nonviolent dissidents rebounding to the advantage of the nonviolent forces during the events of Eastern Europe in 1989. The key component was that people began to lose their fear and thus were able to build a movement to the point that the leverage of dependency could be exercised to telling effect. Despite beatings, imprisonments, torture, and executions, people refused to submit. When this sort of defiance is waged on an extensive scale, no system, brutal or beings, can long survive. Violent sanctions, by themselves, will not induce obedience; they must incite fear. "Importantly," notes Sharp, "when fear of punishment does not control the subjects' minds, repression is unlikely to succeed. As in wars, the prospects of physical injury and death do not cause soldiers at the front to flee or to surrender." Similarly, if nonviolent proponents "believe in their cause sufficiently, they are likely to continue the struggle regardless of the danger to them individually."[45]

The nonviolent resistance movement against President Pinochet in Chile began to make headway as soon as the individual resisters came to terms with personal fear. "This was our first, but most important step," observed a Chilean woman whose son was amongst the *desaparecidos.*[46] This did not mean that the resisters exposed themselves to unnecessary danger. They proceeded carefully in small groups that operated underground. In the open, they often resorted to symbolic protests such as the "cold-shoulder" treatment, and social ostracism. In responding to decrees and orders they feigned misunderstanding; in the workplace they made use of "quiet mistakes" in the obstructionist manner of the good soldier Schwik.[47]

Latin Americans have a long history of nonviolent action— or *brazos caidos* (literally, fallen arms)—against ruthless dictators. Much of it has been successful, in the sense that the dictator was deposed. According to Patricia Parkman, "the existence of such a tradition ... has been visible throughout the region (in Brazil and Haiti, as well as in the Spanish-speaking republics) at least since the early years of this century."[48] Between 1931 and 1961, eleven Latin American presidents left office in the wake of civic strikes.[49] With the exception of two of these man, their record of human rights abuses was legendary. Another four civic strikes during this same thirty-year period were unsuccessful. The *Latinos* themselves refer to all such insurrections as the *huelga general* or general strike, a term borrowed from the labour movement. However, researcher Parkman believes that this term "obscures the distinctive cross-class character of the civic strike," which she defines as "the collective suspension of normal activities by people of diverse social groups united by a common political objectives."[50]

One of the most notable of these "total" civic strikes was mobilised against strongman Maximiano Hernandez Martinez of El Salvador in 1944. He had been in absolute control of the country since 1932, initially consolidating his power with a massacre estimated to number between eight and thirty thousand in a country that, at the time, had a population of about one million. The successful peaceful uprising twelve years later was preceded by a about armed uprising. Indeed, the ruthlessness the way he dealt with the hapless insurgents is what provoked a broad cross-section of the population to engage itself in a series of "national shutdowns." The success of their action then inspired attempts to unseat the governments of the other three Central American dictatorships, also by nonviolent means. However, only one of these proved successful—the one against Jorge Ubico of Guatemala. One of the more ironic historical footnotes to Martinez's downfall is that a national day is now celebrated in El Salvador to commemorate the heroic patriots who failed in the earned insurrection, while the success of the nonviolent civic strike is left to the reflections of a handful of scholars.

The ultimate test for the efficacy of nonviolence is usually posed in the form of the question; "Yes, but what about Hitler or Stalin?" Although nonviolence was not tried on a large scale against either of these tyrants, there are cases where it was improvised and it met with successful results. Some of the most dramatic episodes occurred in Norway against the Nazi puppet Vidkun Quisling. After the German invasion in April 1940, an underground resistance sprang up. Some violence was displayed but the major response was nonviolent. Indeed, entire campaigns were conducted nonviolently—exploiting the government's direct dependence on the cooperation of the citizenry. Far from the "individual heroism" to which Walzer restricts nonviolent action, large segments of the society challenged nonviolently the radical restructuring policies which the Nazis sought to impose through their agent, Quisling. Sporting associations, the clergy, the justice system, railway workers, and teachers refused to cooperate and obey the directives handed down by the conqueror.[51] The teachers are a prime example. When Quisling ordered the teachers to introduce a curriculum promoting the ideas of the fascist" corporate state," some 8,000 to 10,000 out of a total of 12,000 immediately sent in letters of resignation.[52] Their defiance led to the arrest of hundreds and their internment in a concentration camp under conditions of torture and starvation. Yet very few yielded. At home, parents protested the government's action and those "teachers not arrested refused to be intimidated," so that "eight months later the teachers were released."[53]

In due course, Hitler intervened and ordered that the experiment of the "New Order" be abandoned.[54]

Resistance against the Nazis was also waged with a modicum of success in Denmark and Holland. As in Norway, violence characterized some, but by no means all, of the actions. In the first three years of Denmark's occupation, the resistance was almost purely nonviolent. The Nazis were severely harassed and their objectives remained unfulfilled by a combination of strikes, demonstrations, boycotts, delaying tactics, and symbolic actions. Illegal underground newspapers were printed, and evacuation routes were organized that enabled approximately seven thousand Danish Jews to flee to neutral Sweden. "All [these actions] contributed to the effective resistance in Denmark against the German occupation."[55]

The Nazis' inability to deal effectively with nonviolent resistance in Denmark, Norway, and Holland—and to a lesser extent in France and Belgium—was a major finding of British military historian, B.H. Liddell-Hart who interrogated German generals after the war. In his words:

> They [the Nazis] were experts in violence, and had been trained to deal with opponents who used that method. But other forms of resistance baffled them—and all the more in proportion as the methods were subtle and concealed. It was a relief to them when resistance became violent and when nonviolent forms were mixed with guerrilla action, thus making it easier to combine drastic repressive action against both at the same time.[56]

A partial explanation of the success of nonviolent resistance against the Germans in the northern European countries can be attributed to the fact that the Nazis regarded the inhabitants as fellow Aryans. An image of the "self in the other" restrained their behaviour. A sense of co-humanity established a bond of moral dependency, so that they were not free to deal with these people as they were with Jews, Slaves, and Gypsies. A dependency of interest also existed as they needed their support in order to effectively prosecute the war, maintain standards at home, and realize wider objectives like the One Thousand Years Riech. Yet there is evidence that the Nazis were even thwarted in their genocide of the "subhumans" (*untermenschen*) in some areas of their conquest, because they were dependent on the support of the very population they planned to exterminate. Despite moving into Eastern Europe to gain *lebensraum* for the German *volk*, they soon discovered that they required the cooperation of their intended victims. A leading German military administrator in Byelorussia is reported to have admitted in 1942 that "German forces could not exercise effective control without enlisting the population."[57] The same author cited a statement issued by German military commanders in the Soviet Union in December 1942, deploring "the seriousness of the situation [which] clearly makes imperative the positive cooperation of the population. Russia can be beaten only by Russians."[58] Another German commander, General Harteneck, wrote in May 1943: "We can master the wide Russian expanse which we have conquered only with the Russian and Ukrainians who live in it, never against their will."[59]

Hard-line Soviet communism, too, faced nonviolence resistance on a number of occasions. The 1968 nonviolent response of the Czechoslovakians to the Warsaw Pact invasion of their country is well-documented. For eight months, the occupying forces were unable to gain control. The death-knell of communism finally sounded throughout eastern Europe in the last quarter of 1989 when, with few exceptions, it was the method of nonviolent popular action that toppled government after government. Nonviolence was that to another severe test, this time within the Soviet Union itself, when the Russian people successfully thwarted the attempted coup of August 1991. Whilst asserting the multiplicity and complexity of the causes behind these successes, Adam Roberts contends:

> The whole chain of events in eastern Europe and the Soviet Union could be seen as a triumph of civil resistance [a movement that is nonviolent and whose goals are widely shared by the community], validating the proposition that all government, even totalitarian governments, are based on the consent and cooperation of the ruled: take that away, and the regime must collapse (my explanation in brackets).[60]

A less famous case of nonviolence, at the height of Soviet power, occurred in remote Siberia. In 1953, a strike of 250,000 inmates at the Vorkuta labour camp was instigated, mainly by the state's political prisoners.[61] Although some of the strike leaders disappeared and others were shot, the prisoners continued their strike against their poor conditions for over three months. In the end, food and fuel shortages forced them to capitulate, but when they went back to work they were granted some of their demands.

Indirect Dependency

The gains achieved from the Vorkuta strike came about to

some extent because the prisoners were able to win the sympathy of their Russian guards, who slipped in supplies and spread leaflects between the camps. When the Russian soldiers where replaced by non-Russian-speaking Asians from far eastern republics, the strike eventually collapsed. Thus a third party played an important role in sustaining the strike and therefore in heightening the tension between protagonists.

There are other occasions where a third party or series of other parties go beyond this role of merely assisting in the mobilization of the nonviolent action and actually form the dependency linkage with the opponent. If an aggrieved party has no, or a weak, dependency relationship, a third party on whom the opponent is dependent may act as surrogate. The strategy of nonviolent protesters, who cannot directly utilise a dependency relationship with their opponent, is clear: appeal to or coerce a third party that has both linkage to you and to the opponent. Galtung calls this mechanism of operation, "the great chain of nonviolence."[62] He stresses the "self-other gradient," which, if it is too steep, forces the oppressed to look for "third-party intervention (or better, intercession) from somebody closer to the oppressor ...".[63] Yet the problem need not be a lack of dependency caused by social distance or dehumanization but rather the lack of dependent interests. A ruler can be just as ruthless in dealing with a group of subjects he does not need anything from as he can be with subjects he considers to be subhuman. In most cases the brutality reflects both a lack of strong material need and an image of subhumanity.

Such a case inexemplified in the brutal response of the US administration and its straps to the Vietnamese people. The communists and the people they led had no relationship of any kind with their US opponent. What they were able to do was link up with American "doves," including combat soldiers and draft resisters, thereby vicariously exerting pressure on the American "hawks" and forcing their withdrawal. Whether the nonviolent intervention was induced out of compassion for the two million Vietnamese killed is problematic. But whatever the motivation, the end result was effected by the converging of a number of third-party dependency factors. The American leadership was dependent on the voters at home; it depended on a drug-free army on the battle front; it depended on a middle-class younger generation integrated into its value system; and it depended for its survival on the capacity to control and direct the many upheavals threatening the social order at that time. Thus the course of the war, despite its extremely cruel nature, was drastically affected, indeed concluded, by the nonviolence of an intervening third party.

The same "great chain of nonviolence" operated in the case of the US civil rights movement. The southern blacks had only a minimal dependency relationship with the Southern white power structure and absolutely none with the "red neck" constituency. Interceding on their behalf were the liberal white community of the North and the Northern blacks who were in a position to exercise leverage on the national leadership. In turn, the national leadership, through civil rights legislation and the enforcement of Supreme Court decisions, was able to bring pressure to bear on a reluctant South. This process began with the nonviolent actions of the Southern Christian Leadership Conference under Martin Luther King and those of the Student Nonviolent Coordinating Committee and the northern-based Congress on Racial Equality—the latter group having a long history of commitment to nonviolent struggle. These groups through the process of moral *jiu-jitsu* were able to bring to the surface the injustice and violence of Southern racism which horrified many Northerners to the extent that they insisted that American liberal values be applied universally throughout the land. The murders and beatings administered by Southerners to "uppity" nonviolent blacks rebounded against the brutal bigots because a communication network existed to trigger a third party into action.

Even against one of the most inhumane acts of this century—the Holocaust—there are examples of nonviolence proving successful through the intervention of third parties. Indeed, one can argue that it was not the ruthlessness of the Nazis that led to the Holocaust but the ubiquity of the Jew's marginalization.

Where the Jews were not marginalized by tho roct of the society, as in Denmark and Bulgaria, they survived "the Final solution." One can even point to isolated acts of nonviolence within Germany "working" against the Nazi policy of genocide. A famous case occurred in Berlin on 27 February 1943 when the Nazis rounded up Jews married to non-Jews, as well as their children, and processed them for shipment to Auschwitz. The German spouses responded immediately, demonstrating outside the Gestapo headquarters in Rosenstrasse, shouting for the return of their husbands despite the threat of being machine-gunned. The amazing thing is that the protest succeeded, inasmuch as thousands were released.[65] A tragic sequel to the event is that some of the husbands, who did not then go into hiding, were later rounded up one by one and shipped off for extermination. This time the Gestapo realized how to prevent any collectively organised protest. Only the husbands that went underground survived.[65]

The dynamics behind the positive response of the Gestapo to the women's collective protest is instructive. As long as the dependency relationship activated by the third party takes precedence over the lack of concern for, or interest in, the oppressed people, the nonviolence of the interceding group will "work." The extreme ruthlessness of the ruler toward the intended victims is overridden. Explains Galtung:

> In other words, over a small gap in social distance, with less dehumanization in, nonviolence worked—even a simple, primitive type of nonviolence measured by Gandhian standards. The "Aryan" wives bridged the gap, being the Self in the Other to the Nazis and the Other in the Self to their husbands. Without that bridge it would not have worked.[66]

The Gestapo was presented with a moral dilemma by the German spouses. Here were females of "good" German stock protecting their homes. The women wee displaying the nobility of womanhood and the courage associated with the true "Aryan spirit." Also, the wives enlisted, through their demonstration, the sympathy of other Germans. On the other hand, when the husbands could be picked off separately and the Nazi leadership could avoid facing the contradiction in their ideology and the outrage of other Germans, no amount of individual nonviolent protest could save the doomed husbands.

Many other cases can be cited to show that nonviolence has "worked" in the past, either directly or indirectly, through the rallying of third-party support.

Conclusion

On the basis of both the theory of power and the history of nonviolent actions, nonviolence does work against extremely ruthless opponents. As Kenneth Bounding was fond of saying, "what exists is possible." The key question to ask in determining the efficacy of nonviolence is not how ruthless is the opponent (although this is an important consideration in designing a nonviolent strategy and selecting the appropriate techniques), but rather, does a dependency relationship exist, either on the basis of interest or morality, between the protagonists directly or through "the great chain of nonviolence" that can be utilized to the advantage of the ruled?

The existence or establishment of a dependency relationship does not ensure success, but it is a necessary, if not sufficient, condition. The only exception would be the opponent's collapse due to his own complete shortcomings or the independent actions of other parties. But to effect changes with input from the nonviolent actor, a dependency must be evoked somewhere along the line.

Some of the other strategic principles that nonviolent proponents should consider and act upon, to enhance the prospects of success, include:

(i) development of a strong organizational network that is decentralised but bound together by a communication system allowing for constant consultation and the fostering of integrated action;

(ii) challenging the societal myth(s) that lie behind a problem;

(iii) building of solidarity and morale;

(iv) training of nonviolent activists;
(v) planning of strategy and tactics:
(a) choosing wisely between dispersion and concentration
(b) choosing the right mechanism of change
(c) selection of key targets to focus on
(d) maintenance of initiative
(e) flexibility
(f) looking for legitimacy;
(vi) consistency (no waxing and waning0 and persistence (over time);
(vii) selection of a compelling issue;
(viii) obtaining clarity and unity over objectives amongst nonviolent actors;
(ix) exhausting of conventional alternatives before engaging in nonviolent action (as long as such methods are clearly not futile and only serving to prolong oppression); and
(x) taking steps to secure the outcome:
  (a) negotiating effectively
  (b) seeing to replace necessary functions that the defeated adversary performed
  (c) preventing third parties from replacing the defeated adversary and undermining recently achieved gains
  (d) preparing to re-initiate struggle if the opponent reneges on negotiated settlement.

If the nonviolent strategist wisely integrates the above ten supportive principles (which are by no means exhaustive) with the necessary condition of dependency, then the chances for success improve tremendously. However, as with violent politics, there can be no guarantees of success. All one can say with certainty about nonviolent politics is that it will not succeed without the ruler's dependency.

Aristotle recognized this insight when he pointed out that a tyrant "wants his subjects to have no mutual confidence, no power, little spirit."[67] Reverse the situation—that is, make them dependent on him in a dominating relationship—and the can rule indefinitely. In practice, however, subjects do display from time to time qualities of what we now call "empowerment"—leading Aristotle to observe: "Still, oligarchy and tyranny are shorter-lived than any other constitution."[68] If hegemonic control, in Weberian terms, is suffused throughout the society's values, structures, and practices, a new *Weltanschauung* may need to be forged in order to cast off the dependency. It is far easier to mobilize resistance against the exercise of overt violent power where the issues of dominance and dependency are visible and unequivocal for all to behold. Thus in situations where nonviolent proponents seek very radical structural changes, it can even be asserted that nonviolence is apt "to work" better if the opponent is extremely brutal.

Hitler may not have read Aristotle or weber. But he was aware of the vulnerability of dictators when the populace was of an independent mind. He and his generals recognised where the power of nonviolence was rooted. In a conversation in May 1943 with ... Rosenberg, reported by the latter, the Fuehrer observed:

> Ruling people in the conquered regions is, I might say, of course a psychological problem, One cannot rule by force alone. True, force is decisive, but it is equally important to have that psychological something which the animal trainer needs to be master of his beast. They must be convinced that we are the victors.[69]

That any government is founded ultimately on consent—and not on brutal force—was unequivocally acknowledged by Hitler. "For, in the long run," he wrote, "government systems are not held together by the pressure of force, but rather by the belief in the quality and the truthfulness with which they represent and promote the interests of the people."[70]

If Hitler admitted that nonviolent defiance could threaten a government and suggested that it could work under conditions of severe repression, a *prima facie* case exists for extensively investigating its dynamics. It certainly behooves students of political science to understand far more clearly both the limits of nonviolent sanctions and their potential. Adam Roberts, commenting on the aftermath of the collapse of communism, wrote:

> What can be asserted is that nonviolent methods have a greater importance than has been allowed for in many philosophies, whether of Left or of Right.[71]

Notes and References

1. In tabulating a wide range of "arguments" and "actions" in support of "social defence," Brian Martin also notes that the question of "severe repression ... is one of the most challenging ... and also one of the most common" questions to be raised. See his" Social Defence: Arguments and Actions," in Shelley Anderson and James Larmore (eds.), *Nonviolent Struggle and Social Defence* (London: War Resisters' International, 1991), p. 99.
2. For a discussion of this latter point, see Marie B. Byles, "Light from Japan on Nonviolence," *Gandhi Marg,* Vol. 9, No. 4, October 1965, p. 290. See also L.H. Pelton, *The Psychology of Nonviolence* (Elmhurst, N.Y.: Pergamon Press, 1974), pp. 22-23.
3. A substantial body of literature has developed which focuses on the non-instrumental aspects of nonviolence. See, for example, Joan V. Bondurant, *The Conquest of Violence: The Gandhian Philosophy of Conflict,* (Berkeley: University of California Press, 1965); Joanna Rogers Marcy, *Despair and Personal Power in the Nuclear Age* (Philadelphia: New Society Publishers, 1983); B. Harding, *The Healing Power of Peace and Nonviolence,* (Middlegreen St. Paul Publications, 1986); J Kovel, *Against the State of Nuclear Terror* (London: Pan Books, 1983), esp. pp. 170-192; R. Bollton, *People skills* (Sydney: Prentice-Hall, 1986); and Virginia Coover *et al, Resource Manual for a Living Revolution* (Philadelphia: New society Publishers, 1985).
4. The need to examine each case separately and recognise its complexity is argued effectively by Steven Duncan Huxley

in his, *Constitutional Insurgency in Finland: Finnish "Passive Resistance" against Russification as a Case of Non-Military Struggle in the European Resistance Tradition* (Helsinki: Finnish Historical Society, 1990).

5. Christopher Krueger and Patricia Parkman essentially make the same point about not confusing tactics with strategy. "On a tactical level", they declare, "superior armed force can control many, if not al situations. Any act of resistance that is limited in time and place can be negated by sufficiently ruthless opponents. On the strategic and political levels, however, the probable effects of violence become less easy to calculate." (See his "Identifying Alternatives to Political Violence: An Educational Imperative," *Harvard Educational Review,* Vol. 55, No. 1, February 1985, p. 110).
6. The distinction is also drawn in terms of "limited repression" and "massive repression." See Anders Bosserup and Andrew Mack, *War Without Weapons: Nonviolence in National Defense* (New York, N.Y. Schocken, 1975), p. 68.
7. For a critical review of the paucity of material on nonviolent politics in the standard political-science texts and some of the blatant miscomprehensions when it is mentioned, see Leonard Gambrell, "Understanding Political Power: The Contribution of Nonviolent Resistance Studies," *Civilian-Based Defense,* Vol. 2, No. 3, February 1985, pp. 1-4.
8. Only a few politicians, as far as one can gather from their statements and writings, appear to understand the nonviolent theory and dynamics behind the success of the new social movements, and only a few European governments have incorporated a civilian-based defence component into their defence policy or even bothered to investigate its feasibility.
9. Kim Beazley, Paper presented at a conference on "Alternative Defence Strageties for Australia", University of queensland, 4-7 July 1984.
10. Kennan has also shown an interest in nonviolent defence on other occasions. In particular, see his review of Gene Sharp's book *Making Europe Unconquerable: The Potential of Civilian-based Deterrence and Defence, in New York Review of Books,* 13 February 1986, pp. 3-4. This review was

subsequently included as a foreword to a later edition of the book.

11. Raymond Aron, *Peace and War: A theory of International Relations* (New York: Doubleday & Co., 1966), pp. 630-31.
12. *Ibid.*, p. 631.
13. For a counter to the assumption that Gandhi faced a relatively humane and civilised antagonist in the British, see Johan Galtung, *Nonviolence and Israel/Palestine* (Honolulu: University of Hawaii Press, 1989), pp. 21-22. See also Rajiv Vora and Rakesh Bharadwaj, "Uncivilized Civility and Civilized Satyagraha," *Gandhi Marg*, Vol. 3, No. 5, August 1981, pp. 266-79.
14. See Raymond Aron, *Peace and War: A Theory of International Relations.*
15. George Orwell "Reflections on Gandhi," in *The Collected Essays: Journalism and Letters of George Orwell*, Vol. 4 (in Front of Your Nose) (Harmondsworth: Penguin, 1970), p. 529.
16. Michael Walzer, *Just and Unjust War: A Moral Argument with historical Illustrations* (New York: Basic Books, 1977), p. 332.
17. *Ibid.*, pp. 331-32.
18. *Ibid.*, p. 333.
19. *Ibid.*, pp. 332-33.
20. *Ibid.*, p. 334.
21. Christopher Kruegler, "Why Nonviolent Sanctions Fail: Typical Strategic Blunders and Their Antidotes," paper presented at a seminar on "Nonviolent Sanctions" held at Harvard University on 24 September 1986.
22. Boris Yeltsin, quoted in David Remmick, "For Citizens: A Crucible of Conscience," *Guardian Weekly*, 1 September 1991.
23. Johan Galtung's lecture delivered at the University of Queensland on 3 July 1991.
24. Niccolo Mchiavelli says: "The Prince who has the public as a whole for his enemy can never make himself secure; and the greater his cruelty, the weaker does his regime become. In such a case, the best remedy he can adopt is to make the populace his friend." (See The Discourses on the First Ten

Books of Livy," *The discourses of Niccolo Machiavelli* (Routledge & Kegan Paul, London, 1950, Vol. 1, p. 254). August Comte says: "Thus authority is derived from concurrence, and not concurrence from authority ...so that no great power can arise otherwise than from the strongly prevalent disposition of the society in which it exists." *The Positive Philosophy of August Comte* (trains. H. Martineau, George Bell & Sons, London, 1896, Vol. II, pp. 222-23). Max Weber says: "If the state is to exist, the dominated must obey the authority claimed by the powers that be" ("Politics as a Vocation," in *From Max Weber: Essays in Sociology* (trains. eds., H.H. Gerth and C. Wright Mills, Galaxy Book, N.Y., 1958, p. 78). Robert M. Maclver says: "Social power is in the last resort derivative, not inherent in the groups or individuals who direct, control, or coerce other groups or individuals. The power a man has is the power he disposes; it is not intrinsically his own. He cannot command unless another obeys. He cannot control unless the social organisation invests him with the apparatus of control" (*The Web of Government,* Macmillian, New York, 1947, pp. 107-108).

25. Gene Sharp, *The Politics of Nonviolent Action* (Boston: Porter Sargent Publishers, 1973), p. 64.
26. *Ibid.*, pp. 11-12.
27. *Ibid.*, pp. 19-24.
28. Gene Sharp, *Social Power and Political Freedom* (Boston: Porter Sargent Publishers, 1980), p. 312; and chapter 12, "Popular Empowerment,"
passim.
29. Gene Sharp, *The Politics of Nonvilent Action,* pp. 117-445.
30. Brian Martin, "Gene Sharp's Theory of Power," *Journal of Peace Research,* Vol. 26, No. 2, 1989, pp. 214-15.
31. *Ibid.*, p. 216.
32. Robert Elias, "Scenes from `Absurdistan," *The Humanist,* January-February 1992, p. 21.
33. Vaclav Havel, "The Power of the Powerless," in Jan Vladislav, ed., *Vaclav Havel: Living in Truth* (London: Faber and Faber, 1989), p. 75.

34. *Ibid.*, pp. 51 and 53.
35. *Ibid.*, p. 53.
36. *Ibid.*, p. 47.
37. *Ibid.*, p. 54.
38. *Ibid.*, p. 57 and 58.
39. Johan Galtung, "Europe 1989: The role of Peace Research and the Peace Movement," Public Lecture Series, University of Queensland, 10 July 1991.
40. Quoted by Mohammed heikel (former Cairo editor and confidant of Egyptian President Anwar Sadat), "Iran: A Nation Ready to Die," *The Courier Mail,* 24 December 1979.
41. "Iran Erupts Again," *Newsweek,* 11 December 1978.
42. Richard Gregg, *The Power of Nonviolence* (New York, N.Y: Schocken, 1966), 2nd rev. edition, pp. 44-46.
43. Gene Sharp, *The Politics of Nonviolent Action,* pp. 657-58.
44. Gene Sharp, *Civilian-Based Defense: A Post-Military Weapons System,* (Princeton: Princeton University Press, 1990), pp. 58.59.
45. *Ibid.*, p. 28.
46. *People Power* (viodeo, 53 mins, english version), Icarus Films International, 123 West 93rd St., Suite 5B, NYC, N.Y., 1990.
47. See the novel of Jaroslav hasek, *The Good Soldier Schweik and His Fortunes in the World War,* trans. Cecil Parrott, Penguin, Harmondsworth, 1974. This is a reprint of the posthumously published work which Hasek had not completed at the time of his death in 1923.
48. Patricia Parkman, *Nonviolent Insurrection in El Salvador: The Fall of Maximiliano Hernandez Martinez* (Tuscon: University of Arizona Press, 1988), p. 2.
49. Patricia Parkman, *Insurrectionary Civil Strikes in Latin America 1931-1961* (Combridge, Mass.: The Albert Einstein Institution, 1990), Monograth No. 1. This paper was first presented at the 1989 AGM of the American Political Science Association. The eleven Latin American presidents overthrown by nonviolent insurrection were: Carlos Ibanez del Campo (Chile 1931); Gerardo Machado (Cuba 1933); Maximiliano Hermandez martinez (El Salvador 1944); Jorge Ubico (Guatamala 1944); Elie Lescot (Haiti 1946); Arnulfo

Arias (Panama 1951); Paul Magloire (Haiti 1956); Joseph Nemours Piere Louis (Haiti 1957); Frank Sylvain (Haiti 1957); Gustavo Rojas Pinilla (Colombia 1957); and Joaquin belagure (Domini-can Repubic 1961).

50. *Ibid.*, p. 1.

51. M. Skodin, "Norwegian Nonviolent Resistance During the German Occupation," in Adam Roberts (ed.), *Civilian Resistance as a National Defence* (Harrisburg: Stackpole Books, 1968), pp. 144-50. See also Ernst Schwarcz, "Nonviolent Resistance Against the Nazis in Norway and Holland During World War II," in robert L. Holmes (ed.), *Nonviolence in Theory and Practice* (Belmonst, CA: Wadsworth Publishing Co., 1990), pp. 185-87.

52. Lanza del Vasto, *Warriors of Peace; Writings on the Technique of Nonviolence* (New York, N.Y. Alfred Knopf, 1974), p. 210.

53. Gene Sharp, *Civilian-Based Defense,* p. 67.

54. Lanza del Vasto, *warriors of Peace: Writings on the techniques of Nonviolence,* p. 211.

55. J. Bennet, "The Resistance Against German Occupation of Denmark 1940-45," in Adam roberts (ed.), *Civilian Resistance as a National Defence,* p. 155. See also Kruegler and Christopher Patricia Parkman, "Identifying Alternatives to Political Violence: An Educational Imperative," pp. 113-14.

56. B.H. Liddell-Hart, "Lessons from Resistance Movements: Guerrilla and Nonviolent," in Adam Roberts (ed.), *Ibid,* p. 205. See also B.H. Liddell-Hart, *Defence of the West: Some Riddles of War and Peace* (London: Cassell, 1950), pp. 53-57 (Chapter VII, "Were We Wise to Foster `Resistance Movements'"?)

57. Alexander Dallin, *German Rule in Rusia, 1941-45: A Study of Occupation Policies* (New York: St. Martin's Press, 1957), p. 218.

58. Quoted in *ibid.*, p. 497.

59. Quoted in *ibid.*, p. 550.

60. Adam Roberts, "Civil Resistance in the East European and Soviet revolutions," Paper Presented at an International Conference on "The Soviet Union in Eastern Europe, 1945-89," Norwegian Nobel Institute, Oslo, 28 February-1 March

1992, p. 1.

61. See joseph Scholmer, "Vortuka: Strike in a Concentration Camp," in Molford Q. Sibley (ed.), *The Quite Battle: Writings on the theory and Practice of Nonviolent Resistance* (Garden City, N.Y.: anchor Books; 1963), pp. 187-204.
62. Johan Galturng, *Nonviolence and Israel/Palestine* pp. 13-33.
63. *Ibid.*, p. 26.
64. Gene Sharp, *The Politics of Nonviolent Action,* pp. 89-90. See also John Galtung, *Nonviolence and Israel-Palestine,* pp. 22-23.
65. For an account of one of the surviving husbands, see Heinz Ullstein, *Spielplatz Meines Lebens,* (Munich, Kindler, Verlag, 1961), pp. 338-40. A section of this passage has been reprinted in Theodore Ebert, "Effects of Repression by the Invader," *Peace News,* 19 March 1965.
66. Johan Galtung, *Nonviolence and Israel/Palestine,* p. 23.
67. Aristotle, *The Politics* (trans. by T.A. Sinclair, rev. by Trevor J. Saunders), (Harmondsworth; Penguin Books, 1983), p. 227.
68. *Ibid.*, p. 353.
69. Hitler to Rosenberg, July 1943, cited in Gene Sharp, Exploring Nonviolent alternatives (Boston: Extending Horizons, 1971), p. 43.
70. Adolf Hitler, *Mein Kampf* (New York: Reynal and Hitchcock, 1941), p. 338.
71. Adam Roberts, "Civil Resistance in the East European and Soviet Revolutions," p. 1.

Chapter-5

Recalling the Christian Church to Its Pacifist Faith

Lance Robinson

Chapter-5

THE ATTITUDE of the Christian Church in its various manifestations is important for a consideration of the theme of peace and security in Asia Pacific and that is so for the following reasons.

First, in nearly the whole of the Pacific region, the Church's religion is a predominant one, and therefore what the Church believes and teaches about peace and war will influence the attitudes of Christian people in those countries. Political leaders, if the are Christian, may be influenced directly themselves, and in any case the beliefs of a substantial proportion of their populations will certainly affect public policy.

Secondly, in most of the Asian region, the Christian faith is a minority faith but not an insignificant one. The way states treat minority groups is watched carefully by other states and affects international attitudes. Should the Christian minority become a Christian Pacifist minority, this might well have a profound effect not only on how that minority is treated but also on the philosophic and the practical popular response to its stand. Public policy would have to address these changes. Christianity is a world religion.

Thirdly, members of all Christian Churches, even of those Churches with the most congregationalist of teachings and structures, believe the Christian faith to be of universal applicability, and see their unity with all other Christians irrespective of nationality as a significant part of their faith. This has important implications in two major ways. First, the peace and security of the Asia Pacific region has been, is, and will be much affected by the attitudes and actions of others beyond that region. In a great number of these states, the Christian faith and the Christian Church occupy a significant place in their philosophies and social structure. A strong pacifist attitude among Christians in those countries would inevitably have its effect upon national policies. Secondly, policies of those states within our region where there are Christians would be likely to be affected by the existence within their populations of a resolute group that saw their international security as of profound importance and who at the same time had renounced all dependence upon, or participation in, war as a means of settling disputes. To sum up, these arguments for the relevance of the subject to our theme, I may suggest that we should consider again the likely effects should the Christian Church again become universally or even largely Christian Pacifist in its belief, practice, and discipline.

Christian Faith as Originally Pacifist

My claim is that the Christian faith was originally pacifist. Perhaps it is necessary first to define the word "pacifist." In the English language the word was originally "pacificist" but in the manner of those, like me, of Anglo-Saxon background, it was lazily shortened to its present form. But the original word indicates the meaning "peace-maker." In the context of Christian theology, the word has the connotation of one who repudiates war, as well as all participation in it. To quote from the declaration made by the members of one of the Church pacifist groups, "we ... renounce war and all preparation to wage war, and to work for the construction of Christian peace in the world."

What is the evidence, then, that the Christian faith was originally pacifist. Let us look first at the New Testament. there are scriptures written by Christians within the fellowship of the Church in the first hundred years or so of the Christian era, and eventually accorded the distinction of being made part of the Holy Scriptures, and used and reserved as such ever since.

Peace resounds through the New Testament Gospels from the reputed song of the angel at the birth of Jesus to the greetings of the risen Christ to his disciples. I shall refer here to some of those passages that give the strongest evidence for pacifism. Jesus did not, as far as we know, leave any written work, and the record of what he said has all the possibilities of error of any such record. But while I would contend that much of what is attributed to Christ is authentic, that exercise is not necessary for our present purpose, since I am seeking to investigate the belief of the early Church with respect to peace and war, and the New Testament Gospels written, compiled, and selected by the early Church are clearly important evidence.

Significant events having relevance to our purpose would include the following. In the story of Christ's temptation in the wilderness we read that when he is tempted to seek the power and glory of worldly states (using their commonly employed means) in the fulfilment of his mission, he rejects the idea as devilish. When offered political leadership (probably by the zealots, the Jewish Freedom fighters under the Roman domination of the day), he declines it. In the striking, well-prepared, and crisis-provoking event of the first, Palm Sunday, while verbally defending the enthusiastic crowd's right to acclaim him as the messiah, he chooses to enter the holy capital riding a donkey, with clearly intended reference to the writing of the passage in the Old Testament prophecy of Zechariah which speaks of the Messiah as one under whose sway, the war horse, the chariot, and the battle bow will be done away with. When at the time of his arrest in the garden of Gethsemane one of his followers draws a sword and begins to lay about him, he is commanded to desist by Jesus who adds the words "he who takes the sword will perish by the sword." Later that night or early in the following morning, while being interrogated by the authorities on the nature of the "Kingdom" and his Kingship, he says: "My Kingdom is not of this world. If it were, my servants would fight." When in the course of that same encounter tries to have the crowd choose Jesus as the prisoner who was by custom released by the authorities during the time of the Passover feast, the crowd chooses Barabbas, one of the zealots, the freedom fighters of the day. This, together with the refusal of leadership of this group when offered to him and referred to earlier, shows that the early Christians saw the war of liberation not to be sanctioned even against the arrogant, often cruel and certainly idolatrous Roman empire.

Let us turn now to the reported sayings of Christ. We begin

the so-called "sermon on the mount," that collection of sayings describing life lived within the Kingdom of God, that is, in obedience to the rule of God, following the will of God. Here we find the injunction not to resist evil, but should anyone strike you on the right cheek, turn the other also. Some commentators have made something of the fact that a blow on the right cheek might well be received by a subordinate as one in authority uses the back of his hand. On the other hand, in a situation of a generalized disturbance, crowd riot, military police or the like, a blow might of course easily be sustained on either side of the face. However, in either situation the command not to retaliate in kind is clear. But this is not an unprincipled subservience, but a disciplined, determined concern to defend principle with dignity, but with no resort to violence, no retreat in the face of danger. We are told to go the second mile when commanded to carry baggage, be it, say, the mails or a soldier's pack as he returns to camp. So there is to be no general noncooperation and indeed a selfless willingness to be helpful in nonviolent situations, and even in excess of what the Roman decrees demanded.

The "love your enemies" text reads in full thus: "You have heard that it has been said, `you shall love your neighbor and hate your enemy,' but I say to you love your enemies, pray for those who persecute you." Now Judaism did not say hat a private enemy should be hated. So the saying is dealing with the enemy ... without. Such an enemy is to be loved. What does that mean? Much has been written about the use of the word *agape*, translated as "love," and the corresponding verb. The eminent New Testament scholar, C.H. Dodd, has summed up his view of this word's New Testament meaning as "to seek the welfare of the beloved, no matter what the cost." So, far from desiring or acting to bring harm to the enemy, one is to act so as to further his well-being, that is, pacifism.

Something should be said here about the view sometimes put forward (as, for example, by Debeluis) that those sections of New Testament that are called eschatological should be interpreted so as to counter the nonresisting or pacifist view. If the early Church supposed that the day of the Coming of the son of man was to dawn very soon, then the disappointment of that hope should mean a re-enactment of the morality which would have been very much an interim one, with the idea that the resultant hardship and suffering would be short-lived and that divine intervention would soon end it. However, the texts I have quoted do not appeal to an expected early intervention but to the nature of God. The disciple is indeed "to be perfect, even as his Father in heaven is perfect." Moreover, he is to "be merciful, as his father is merciful," and so to imitate the mercy and not the wrath of God, for "vengeance is mine, I will repay, saith the Lord."

Before we leave the Gospel passages that give evidence of the pacifism of the early church, mention must be made of the beatitudes, that of short aphorisms placed at the beginning of the Sermon of the mount in the Matthew version and in probably a more primitive form in St. Luke. Here we find the reported saying of Jesus "blessed are the peacemakers for they shall be called Sons of God." Bainton makes the interesting point about this passage when he points out that elsewhere in the Roman Empire of that day those to be called Sons of God because they were peacemakers were the emperors themselves. They were the supporters of the Pax Romana and indeed the very word "eirenepoios" (peacemaker) is to be found among certain of the emperors' aims. But the methods to be used by Jesus' followers where to be quite different from those of Emperors, as different indeed as were the notions of "peace" they entertained. This is shown in the way the beatitudes continue, for they go on to speak of the blessedness of those persecuted for righteousness sake, and of his followers when they are generally reviled, hated, and slandered "for my sake." Such an attitude contrasts strongly of course with those of the emperor and his armies.

The peacemaking methods of the Christians were to be, such as could be, summed up in Jesus' exhortation to them "follow me." The main point of the incident about taxes, as reported in Mark 12 is to emphasize that while civil authorities had a legitimized authority and therefore merited a corresponding obedience, the fuller and superior authority is that of God.

Turning now to the epistles, I may say that many of them were written before the compilation of the Gospels, but in the knowledge of the living and tradition of the words and works of Jesus. Many nonpacifist Christians appeal to those passages in the writings of St. Paul which they see as supporting their view. Well-known among those passages are "the powers that be are ordained of God," and "the power bears not the sword in vain; for he is a minister of God, to execute his wrath on the wrongdoer."

But there is a good deal to be said on the other side with respect to this passage. The first and perhaps the main point is that St. Paul had stated in the passage immediately preceding the one in question (*Rom* 12[17-21] which is climaxed and summed up in the words "be not overcome of evil, but overcome evil with good." The writer then goes on to apply this principle to the relationship of the Christian to the State. He is concerned with supporting the teaching of Jesus about the natural place of the state, and concerned both to urge cooperation with it in conscience, where that is possible, and to ensure that unnecessary conflict between Church and State not be stirred up. G.H.C. McGregor, in discussing this, notes Paul's attitudes to the imperial idea. He boasts of his Roman citizenship (Acts 22), he saw the State of his day as a restraint against super evils, and he uses the system as a basis for spiritual metaphor. One of th emain goals of his mission efforts isto take the Gospel to Rome and he uses his Roman citizenship to get him to that city, appealing to Caesar when those same missionary efforts lead to his arrest and his arraignment before local authorities. And McGregor also speculates as to whether St Paul would have written in the same terms at the close of his life or at the opening of a general prosecution of the Church. The argument, however, is basically to emphasise the might of the State to assist as a natural (and therefore God-given) part of the creation of humans and human society. It would certainly justify what we should nowadays call police action, but certainly not that any action taken by any power is to be regarded as having divine sanction. An antipacifist interpretation of the passage proves too much. For, if it sanctions the use of force at all, it is the kind of force with which Paul's readers were familiar, and force which included wars of aggression, the enslavement of captives, and the martyring of Christians.

Finally, we should note the concluding verses for the very next section of this epistle. Love does no wrong to a neighbor and love is therefore the fulfilment of the law. Moreover, Pau's own life and very probably his death shows his clear readiness to disobey the State in the case of a conflict of loyalties to it and to God, just as truly as did the apostles Arraigned as recorded in Act 5: "We must obey God rather than Men." Before we leave St Paul, we should refer to the parallel he draws between the Christian life and soldierly life, or, more precisely, between the resources available to the Christians in their struggle against evil and the equipment of the Rome soldiers of Paul's day (Eph 6). In a telling and sustained analogy by contrast, Paul says that the fight is "not against flesh and blood." Paul is deliberately using the figure of military warfare to emphasize that the "warfare" of Christians is something entirely different.

The book of Revelation is sometimes also used by those who take a nonpacifist view. Its lucid presentation of prophecies of war mirrors Christ's prediction of wars and rumors of wars in the apocalyptic passages of the synoptic Gospels. Referring to the Revelations passage, G.J. Hearing gives us this summary of his and other's views "Christian apocalyptic was built up in the first century on the Jewish model, and largely out of Jewish materials of which the revelation of St John is the biblical example... No apocalyptic eschatology preserves traces of the warlike Messiah by taking them over to its portrait of Jesus. One notices that the warlike element is wholly confined to the apocalyptic eschatology, and does not extend to the figure of Christ outside it. And as the Messiah of apocalyptic fights with Angels at his side, and not with men, this action in no way affects the example with the Christ of the gospels has left behind. Heavenly beings and superhuman powers now we war on God's behalf. when Men fight, they are doomed to destruction; only the Devil lets Men fight for him. The Author of the Apocalypse is convinced of that."

One line of enquiry into whether or not the early Church was pacifist asks the question "did Christians serve in the army?" Up to 170 AD there is no evidence whatsoever of Christians in the military service. In 173 AD there is no evidence whatsoever of Christians in the military service. In 173 AD there is evidence of Christians serving in the Thundering Legion under Marcus Aurelius, and from that time evidence for some Christians serving in the ranks increases. Nevertheless at this time Celsius, a critic of Christianity, was writing: "If all men were to do the same as you, there would be nothing to prevent to King from being left in utter solitude and desertion, and the forces of the Empire would fall into the hands of the wildest and most lawless barbarians." Le Clercq and Cadoux have compiled lists of burial inscriptions of soldiers who were Christian. Le Clercq's total of 176 contains many names from post-Constantinian times, However, and probably only eight are incontrovertibly from earlier times, however, this evidence also shows that they were by Christian communities which did not prohibit such records on their tombs.

Bainton attempted to classify the inscriptions geographically and concluded that pacifism flourished best in the interior of the empire and less near its borders, although six pre-Constantinian inscriptions come from Rome, a centre of the faith that was among the first to relax a rigourist approach on other issues also. Christians in North Africa were divided on the issue. The eastern frontier reveals the greatest Christian participation in war, though at the same time protest by ascetic or monastic groups is also recorded. However, the overwhelming testimony of Christian writings of the period supports the contention that the received position of the church was pacifist. Here is a list of such writings, and I am largely indebted here to Clive Barrett for its compilation.

JUSTIN MARTYR (writing c.138): "You can be convinced that this happened... We who used to kill one another, do not make war on our enemies. We refuse to tell lies or deceive our inquisitors: we prefer to die acknowledging Christ."

"We, who were filled with war and mutual slaughter and all wickedness, have each and all throughout the earth changed our instruments of war, our swords into ploughshares, and our spears into farming tools, and cultivate piety, justice, love of humankind, faith and the hope which we have from the Father, though 'the Crucified One."

IRENAEUS (c.130-c. 200) describes Christians as peoples who "have made their warlike lances and swords into ploughs and changed them into sickles which he gave for reaping corn, and now do not know how to fight, but when struck offer even the other cheek."

CLEMENT OF ALEXANDRIA (c.150-c.215): "We Christians are a peaceful race ... bred not for war but for peace."

In a passage appealing for equal treatment for women: "We do to train women like Amazons to be manly in war, since we wish even men to be peaceable."

TERTULLIAN (c.160-c.225): "The Lord's capacity for suffering was wounded in Malchus, and so he cursed the works of the sword for ever."

"Christ, in disarming Peter, ungirt every soldier."

There is evidence that from 170/180 a few individuals tried to combine being soldiers and being Christians. Tertullian rejects this way absolutely upholding the pacifist position always assumed by the Church. He asks in amazement:

"Shall the Son of Peace, for whom it is unlawful to go to law, be engaged in battle?"

"How will a Christian take parting war, nay, how will he serve even in peace?"

"If we are enjoined to love our enemies, whom have we to hate? If injured, we are forbidden to retaliate. Who can suffer injury at our hands?"

ORIGEN (c. 185 c. 254) "Nolonger do we take the sword against any nation, nor do we learn war any more, since we have become sons of peace through Jesus who is our author."

Jesus "taught that it was never right for his description to go so far (the king of human life) against a man, even if he should be very wicked."

"It was impossible for Christians to follow Mosaic law in killing their enemies."

With Origen we have some of the clearest evidence for the orthodoxy of Christian pacifism. He had to face severe criticism from pagans on the Christian tradition of refusing military service. He acknowledge and affirms the tradition by replying simply: "We defend the empire in a better way."

CYPRIAN (d. 258): "God has willed that iron be used for tilling the teeth; therefore he has forbidden its use for taking human life."

"The hand that has held the Eucharist must not be stained with blood and the sword."

He denounces war: "Murder, which in the case of an individual is admitted to be a crime is called a virtue when it is committed wholesale."

LACTANTIUS (c.240-c.320): "It will not be lawful for a just man to engage in warfare ... It is the act of putting to death itself which is prohibited. Therefore, with regard to this precept of God, there ought to be no exception at all, but that it is always unlawful to kill a man, whom God willed to be a saved creature."

"How can a man be just who hates, who despoils, who puts to death? And they who strive to be serviceable to their country do all these things."

He condemns any form of retaliation—the sort of motive upon which modern policies of deterrence are based. "For, he who endeavors to return an injury, desires to imitate that very person by whom he has been injured. Thus he who imitates a bad man can by no means be good."

At the end of the third century, a number of soldiers were put on trial for laying down their weapons when they were converted to Christianity...

MAXIMILIAN (martyred, 291): "I cannot be a soldier. I cannot do evil. I am a Christian."

Tarachus : "Because I was a Christian, I have now chosen to be a civilian."

MARCELLUS (martyred, 298): "I have thrown them (his weapons) away, for it is not fitting that a Christian who fights for Christ his Lord should be a soldier according to the brutalities of this world."

There are various examples of the Christian language of spiritual warfare being contrasted with the physical warfare which is unacceptable to Christians.

One of the most famous soldier-converts lived in the following century.

MARTIN (316-397) also left the army after being converted: "I am a soldier of Christ: it is not lawful for me to fight."

He rejects accusations of cowardice: "I will take my stand unarmed before the line of battle tomorrow, and in the name of the Lord Jesus, protected by the sign of the Cross and not by shield or helmet."

VITRICIUS , a priest and another former soldier, was told by Paulinus of Nola (353-431): "You have thrown away the arms of blood and, as it were, put on the arms of peace. You have scorned to be armed with the sword because you were armed with Christ."

Pacifism, Just War, Crusade

From the time of Constantine, the pacifist period in the history of the Church comes to a rapid close. It should be remembered that Constantine came to power over the empire as a whole only after some twenty years of internal conflict. The place of Christianity was one f the issues before the contestants in the struggle. With the acceptance of Christianity as the official faith by the emperor and the empire, there grew a fusion in the popular mind of the empire and the Kingdom of God as opposed to the barbarian and pagans without. Moreover, the great persecution of the Church in the preceding period had links with half-barbarian provinces. With the restoration of *Pax Romana* by Constantine, the religion of one God and life in the empire under one emperor were seen as congruous.

Eusebius of Caesarea and the eastern Theologians Diodo of Tarsus and to some extent Chrysostom said much the same thing as did Ambrose and Prudentius.

So far their process of change did progress that by the early fifth century only Christians could serve in the army. But the change was not complete or absolute. In nearly all cases, the clergy did not bear arms and there is the well-known case of Martin of Tours who refused to join battle saying "I am a soldier of Christ; I cannot fight," and other similar instances. The main upholders of the nonviolent tradition were the monks. Their withdrawal into separated communities meant also withdrawal from the army and Chrysostom applauds their vocation in this respect by saying "the monk fights for the religion and the true worship of God, the king to capture booty, being inspired by envy and the lust for power." The link between Christianity and pacifism was not dead. The pagan emperor Julian the Apostate rejected Christianity partly on the ground that he saw it as inculcating pacifism.

The theological justification for participation in war took the form of the development of the doctrine of "the just war." We may note Ambrose's use of Cicero's writings in this work "On the Duties of the Clergy," taking over the concept of the just war in which good faith is observed with the enemy, and suppliants spared. He had recourse to many Old Testament examples of wars fought in the name of God. He relegated pacifism to the private sphere and to the clerical life, but the did furnish two aspects of the just war theory—that the conduct of warfare should be just and that priests and monks should abstain. Ambrose had been a pretorian prefect in northern Italy, but Augustine was from Africa, with a deep sense of the wrongs of the conquered. Change can be seen in his own views. He once wrote of the teachings of the Sermon on the Mout that "we believe them to have been fulfilled by the Apostles," but later his view was that "they should be obeyed as perfectly as they were fulfilled by the Apostles." Augustine demands that not only the cause fought for must be just, but that the authority going to war must be the recognised ruler. Medieval writers, including St Thomas Aquinas, built their theory further on this basis. The principles set forth dealt with two main aspects—the reasons for going to war and the conduct of the war itself. Both had to conform to certain standards. A Roman Catholic writer, Stratman, writing earlier this century, summed up the condition a just war must fulfil—according to St Augustine, the Thmists, and Francis Victoria as follows:

(i) Gross injustice on the part of one, and only one, of the contending parties.
(ii) Gross formal moral guilt on one side—material wrong is not sufficient.
(iii) Undoubted knowledge of this guilt.
(iv) That war should be declared only after every means to prevent it has failed.
(v) Guilt and punishment must be proportionate. Punishment exceeding the measure of guilt is unjust and not to be allowed.
(vi) Moral certainty that the side of justice will win.
(vii) Right intention to further what is good by the war, and to show what is evil.
(viii) War must be rightly conducted: restrained within the limits of justice and love.
(ix) Avoidance of unnecessary upheaval of countries not immediately concerned, and of the Christian community.
(x) Declaration of war by lawful authority exercised in the name of God.

In justification of this theory, which by and large was taken into the Churches of the Reformation without much modification, theologians had looked back to classical, especially Gnostic writings and to the Old Testament texts. From the New Testament they cited the incidents of the Cleansing of the Temple, the "Render unto Caesar" passage, and the passage from *Romans* 13 referred to earlier, and the Lukan reference to buying a sword.

This last in later times received three kinds of interpretation:

(i) The coercive power of the state was ordained by God because of sin and should therefore not be administered by Christians. Obedience was required except when against conscience. This was the position adopted by the Anabaptists.

(ii) Luther's view that though Christians would not need the state, they should accept office.

(iii) The state was ordained not only because of sin, but also to set forward righteousness and faith. It was a Christian version of the Old Testament's idea of Theocracy and it was taken up by Calvin.

This leads us to the *Crusade* idea which developed after barbarian invasions of the empire and when breakdown of governments meant that the theory of the just war could not be applied. Nevertheless, participation in war carried for the laity a moral taint up to the very time of the Crusades. A council at Winchester in 1076 exacted that he who had killed a man during the Norman conquest should do penance for a year. In this same century, the great truce of God and Peace of God covenants greatly limited the scope and practice of warfare. But Bishops were also often Princes, and so when those who took such oaths failed to keep them, they were often enough punished by the secular arm. Peace was to be enforced. Implied in this is the idea of the Crusade—that is, a war conducted under the auspices of the Church for a holy cause, the cause of peace. Soon enough, failure to live peacefully at home was put forward as a reason for shifting warlike attitudes into the realm of overseas adventure. The restrictions of the just war were largely disregarded, and the well-documented cruelties of siege, crucifixion, and torture and wholesale slaughter became commonplace and accounts of these were given with self-righteous relish.

The Bysantine attitude was, by and large, quite different and the resistance to the Turks lacked among them the religious fanaticism of the West. Even the monasteries were infected, and military monastic orders, Templars, Hospitalers, and Knights of St John, established.

The Theologians accommodated the crusade to the just war because at any rate initially, the fighting was not to covert the unbeliever, but to protect the rights of pilgrims. But there was a fundamental difference. This was a war of faith to vindicate a right of religion under a foreign ruler.

Soon enough, this motion was seen to be explicitly religios when it was used to suppress heresy at home.

The Cathars, a sect originating among disillusioned crusaders, were violently put down with vigour, lack of discrimination, and "with unspeakable joy." The inquisition was set up shortly afterward to deal both with those who had survived and with members of other heretical groups which had come into being.

The Crusaders evoked a revulsion against their methods and there are recorded criticisms against them. The only one that came near to a pacifist position was that of the Franciscans. They had a fine reputation for bringing peace between feuding Italian cities, and some among them wanted the entire crusading enterprise replaced by missionary endeavour, but others preached crusades. St Francis himself, while he went in person to interview the Sultan, did not denounce the fifth crusade which he accompanied.

Pacifism can be found among the medieval sects also. The Waldensians and the Franciscan Tertiaries gained exemption from military service and papal support for their claims. Wycliffe, the translator, was a non-absolutist pacifist, and the Hussites gave rise to two wings, one pacifist, one crusading.

Following the Renaissance and the Reformation came the growth of nationalism, the "wars of religion," the industrial revolution, imperial colonialism, and the Churches' worldwide missionary endeavour. These three positions have been held by in various measures and at different times by a variety of groups.

In recent times, the doctrine of just war has been defended by people like Reinhold Niebuhr on the basis of the "lesser of two evils" argument. This is really just a restatement of those among the principles included in the just war theory that state that the end sought must be just and that the means used must not be such as to cause more suffering or injustice than the regime which the war is fought to overthrow. It is argued that no human action, even that of the most devout, is ever wholly sinless in a world where human beings, groups, and states are all interdependent to a great degree and where actions have both good and bad consequences and choice between evils is necessary and indeed inevitable. In certain cases, and Niebuhr would have cited the allies side of the Second World War a Christian should choose to support a war.

The problem with this approach is that it involves a choice between evils, a balancing of the unweighable, and a measuring of the unmeasurable. Not only are the probable consequences of actions to be guessed at (and how often is history predictable?), but ... are various forms of evil and suffering to be weighed for purposes of comparison? Moreover, much of the information which might be thought necessary to begin such a weighing will not be available, and much false information is likely to be purveyed by all parties to disputes. The first casualty in war is after all truth.

The development of weapon construction following the industrial revolution and the tremendously rapid expansion of scientific discovery and technological skill as applied in this field have not had a profound effect upon the way Christians (but not only Christians) have regarded war. I remember hearing Neimoller, by that time a pacifist, addressing a gathering largely composed of pacifists, saying that he had been brought up as a Christian in the Prussian militaristic mould. In the first World War he saw his captaincy of a U-boat as part of his Christian discipleship. His opposition to Hitler before and during the Second World War was not from a pacifist point of view. It was Hitler's internal policies and his philosophy that he opposed. At the collapse of Hitler, he was still not a pacifist. When the war in the East ended with the dropping of the A-bombs he was shocked, but was still not a pacifist. It was only with the development of the H-bomb and his realisation of the effects of such a weapon if used in war, that he was constrained to look again at the theology of the just war which he had all along accepted, and indeed at the whole of Christian teaching in this regard. His conclusion was that the just war theory was no longer tenable and his rethinking of his theology led him then to a firm Christian pacifism.

That the war situation has been changed in degree vastly by the development of modern technology is beyond question. In the Second World War, step-by-step escalations of the scale of what became known as "total war" took place and often received sanction by Christians. When toward the close of that conflict in the West, Bishop Bell of Chichester spoke out against the block-bombing of German cities, it was the earlier words of Churchill who said that "there are no lengths of violence to which we will not go" that won popular approval. But the Bishop's stand is a testimony to the endurance of the just war theory at that time, as well as to some Christian sensitivity.

At the height of the Cold War (and even now despite lessened tension the possibility persists), there was a real danger that if an all-out nuclear war broke out, the combined effect of flash blast, fire radiation, fallour and the nuclear winter effect could result in the destruction of a large part, possibly all, of the human race. With the increased likelihood of nuclear proliferation at present, the future possibility of catastrophe is still very great. Such a situation, where human beings have the capacity to destroy the human race, had not existed in human history before the atomic terror. The possibility has brought before the conscience of people and groups, including Christians and the Church, the need for the banishment or war itself as well as the urgent necessity for nuclear disarmament.

Other weapons of mass destruction, chemical and biological weapons, have also been developed to presumably a high level of technical efficiency.

Perhaps we are less active and concerned about the threat of these weapons only because there has been no case where they have been used on a sizeable scale, although there have been accusations concerning their alleged use in some comparatively localized conflicts.

The pacifist doctrine is in no way undermined by these developments. From the pacifist point of view, they give a horrifying and cosmic-scale twist to Christ's statement "he who takes a sword will perish by the sword."

But the just war theory and the crusade idea are both much affected in their application by technological developments. Both assume that the "right" side can and will win. It is commonplace now to say that there will be no winners in a full nuclear conflict. The just war theory required moderation in method and control of the scope of the suffering involved, and this has traditionally involved concern for non-combatants. That idea is blown up by the bomb. The likelihood that the suffering brought about by the conflict should be less than that threatened by the persistence or even the spread of the "enemy" form of government and administration is hardly feasible when one considers the likely effects of nuclear war. Yet such likelihood is a part of the application of the just war theory. In the face of these possibilities, there has grown up the idea of "limited war" and even "limited nuclear war." The Gulf War was a "limited" one in terms of time and in certain other respects, but the application of technology to war-making was carried to unprecedented lengths in terms of the intensity of aerial bombardment and the precision of delivery of "smart" missiles. We have yet to her fully the extent of suffering caused by the war. How was it possible, before the war was joined, to know the degree of suffering caused by the Iraqi invasion of Kuwait and to compare it with the suffering likely to be caused by the war? It was repeatedly defended by leaders in the US and Great Britain, however, as a just war. The unwillingness of the US and others to submit the issue to wide agenda meeting to discuss Middle East issues seemed also to contravene the requirement to use all avenues of negotiation before the war was declared.

Before leaving the issue of the effects of technology on considerations of the morality of war, mention should perhaps be made of the use of television and satellite communication not in the weapons but in the reporting of thoir use. In the case of the Vietnam war, this had a profound effect upon public opinion.

The realities of the conflict and its effect both on the local population and upon the US itself and other foreign troops were brought into people's living rooms. When the just war theory talks of limitation of suffering etc., realism about what is actually happening is essential to its application.

That experience probably led to the strict military censorship of most of the material which came on to our screen in the Gulf War. Nevertheless, despite that, things shown sometimes with a sense of boasting—the pinpoint accuracy—but in one case to hit something being used as a public shelter, or the annihilation of a routed remnant of Iraqi military—these things helped people realize more fully the terror and suffering and slaughter of modern war.

Some Modern Statements

We would now deal with some modern Christian statements on peace and war. My hope is to indicate that among leaders and groups there is a realization of the need for a theology of peace, rather than a theology of war. The number of statements is immense and my knowledge of these is in any case limited. However, I would refer to the famous encyclical *Pacem in Terris* issued by Pope John XXIII in 1963; for, it has been formative of much in the great number of later statements by Roman Catholics and others, to some statements from the World Council of Churches; and because I know it best, some statements of the Lambeth Conferences of Anglican Bishops.

Pacem and Terris: The whole encyclical is worthy of careful study, but I will refer to certain sections of this first Papal Encyclical to be addressed "to all men of goodwill" as well as to the Chruch.

From Part I in the official English version:

"Peace on earth, which men of every era have most eagerly yearned for, can be firmly established only if the order laid down by God be dutifully observed."

"The fact that one is a citizen of a particular state does not detract in any way from his membership of the human family as a whole, nor from his citizenship of the world community."

"The right of every man to life is correlative with the duty to preserve it."

From Part II

"Those therefore who have authority in the state may oblige men in conscience only if their authority is intrinsically related with the authority of God and shares in it."

"... If civil authorities legislate for or allow anything that is contrary to that (the moral) order, and therefore contrary to the will of God, neither the laws made nor the authorization granted can be binding on the consciences of the citizens, since "God has more right to be obeyed than men."

From Part III

"The same moral law which governs relations between individual human beings serves also to regulate the relations of political communities with one another."

This Part III includes a section on disarmament. I summarize points from it. Note is taken with sorrow of the enormous stocks of arms, and the vast use of intellectual and economic resources on arms developed nations. Their peoples are burdened; others are deprived.

A balance of arms is alleged as necessary to preserve peace. As a consequence, there is constant fear.

The arms race should cease. Stockpiles should be reduced equally and simultaneously. Nuclear weapons should be banned, general agreement should eventually be reached about progressive disarmament and control.

The fundamental principle on which our present peace depends must be replaced by another which declares that the true and solid peace of nations consists not in equality of arms, but in mutual trust alone. We believe this can be brought to pass!

Quoting Pius XII: "Nothing is lost by peace, all may be lost by war!"

Then, this is important in its relevance to the just war theory.

"Men are becoming more and more convinced that disputes which arise between states should not be resolved by recourse to arms, but rather by negotiation."

"It is true that on historical grounds this conviction is based chiefly on the terrible destructive force of modern arms; and it is nourished by the horror aroused in the mind by the very thought of the cruel destruction and the immense suffering which the use of armaments would bring to the human family; and for this reason it is hardly possible to imagine that in the atomic era war could be used as an instrument of justice."

From Part IV

This part argues for a form of public authority to be established which is in a position to operate in an effective manner on a worldwide basis.

It must be set up by common accord and not be imposed by force.

"The difficulty is that there would be reason to fear that a super-national or world-wide public authority, imposed by force by the more powerful political communities, might be or might become an instrument of one-sided interest."

From Part V

Arguing against revolution and for gradualism, and quoting Pius XII again, this part asserts: "Salvation and justice are not to be found in revolution, but in evolution through concord. Violence has achieved only destruction, not construction; the killing of persons, not their pacification; the accumulation of hate and ruin, not the reconciliation of contending parties. And it has reduced men and parties to the difficult task of rebuilding, after sad experience, on the ruins of discord."

Perhaps it is worth adding here words of a later Pope, John Paul II, spoken in Hiroshima in 1981:

"War is the work of man.
War is destruction of human life.

War is death.
To remember the past is to commit oneself to the future.
To remember Hiroshima is to abhor nuclear war.
To remember Hiroshima is to commit oneself to peace."

The first assembly of the World Council of Churches (WCC) was held in 1948. Its statement "War is Contrary to the Will of God" begins strongly with the words "War as a method of settling international disputes is incompatible with the teaching and example of our Lord Jesus Christ."

It goes on to ask the question "can war now be an act of justice?," reports three conflicting broad positions that are maintained, and acknowledges a deep sense of perplexity in the face of them:

(i) Though entering a war may be a Christian's duty in particular circumstances, modern warfare with its mass destruction can never be an act of justice.

(ii) In the absence of impartial supranational institutions, military action is the ultimate sanction of the rule of law, and citizens must be distinctly taught that it is their duty to defend the law by force, if necessary.

(iii) Military service of all kinds is refused, in the conviction that an absolute witness against war and for peace is the will of God. The Church should speak to the same effect. From the time of the second assembly held in 1954, just two years after the development of the H-bomb, the Council became increasingly forthright in its opposition to nuclear weapons.

In 1981 the WCC's appropriate unit and the Churches commission on International Affairs jointly orgnized an International Public Hearing on Nuclear Weapons and Disarmament. The report provides a great amount of information and analysis. The Hearing group drew particular attention to the following statement in the report:

"We believe that the time has come when the Churches must unequivocally declare that the production, deployment, and use of Nuclear Weapons is a crime against humanity and that such activities must be condemned on ethical and theological grounds."

The most recent assembly of the WCC met while the Gulf War issue was a hot one.

Unanimity was not achieved in any statement on that war, some Anglicans from Britain being among those supportive of the coalition forces' initiative.

Before going on to consider Anglican statements, however, mention should be made of the Kairos Document, a study paper put out by some Churchmen of various persuasions in South Africa. It deals with the issues of racialism, apartheid, and the Christian response. It was, as stated above, a discussion paper, and contained contributions which were not always in full agreement with each other. However, on balance it was strongly critical of those who in the name of reconciliation advocated submission to the injustices of apartheid. Most of the contributors would have supported the armed struggle against the government of South Africa.

Mention should also be made of the work of the Pacific Conference of the Churches on the tissues of the nuclear threat and of world peace.

They produced clear high-quality educational material and strong statements in favor of a free, independent, and nuclear-free Pacific.

I turn now to the statements of the Lambeth conferences of Anglican Bishops. When the Conference met in 1930, the resolutions included the statement that "war as a method of settling international disputes is incompatible with the teaching of our Lord Jesus Christ." This statement has been reaffirmed by every Lambaeth Conferences since, in 1948, 1958, 1968, 1978, and 1988.

In 1978 the Bishops also included the following in their resolution on "wars n violence." "Jesus, through his death and resurrection, has already won the victory overall evil. He make evident that self-giving love, obedience to the way of the Cross, is the way to reconciliation in all relationships and conflicts. Therefore the use of violence is ultimately contradictory to the Gospel."

They went on to call Christian people everywhere to (a) re-examine their own attitude toward, and their complicity with violence; (b) to take with utmost seriousness the questions which the teaching of Jesus places against violence in human relationships and the use of armed force by those who would follow him, and the example of redemptive love which the Cross holds before all people;(c) to engage themselves in nonviolent action for justice and peace and to support others so engaged, recognizing that such action will be controversial and may be personally very costly; (d) to commit themselves to informed disciplined prayer not only for all victims of violence, especially for those who suffer for their obedience to the man on the Cross, but also for those who inflict violence on others; and (e) to protect in whatever way possible at the escalation of the sale of armaments of war by the producing nations to the developing nations, and to support with every effort all international proposals and conferences designed to place limitations on, or arrange reductions in, the armaments of war of the nations of the world.

Earlier in the same resolution are the words, "we further declare that the use of the modern technology of war is the most striking example of corporate sin and the prostitution of God's gifts."

It should be noted that this last quoted statement makes it hard, though perhaps not impossible, to hold that modern war can be the lesser of two evils, and strikes at the idea that a modern war can be just war.

Furthermore, the statement at the beginning of their section three as quoted is one which pacifists would acclaim, perhaps only quibbling that instead of saying that "the use of violence is ultimately contradictory to the gospel," it would be clearer and better to say "always contradictory to the Gospel." But the placing of the doctrine of the Cross at the heart of the issue is to e supported and applauded.

These statements have been from large Churches or groups of Churches which therefore are concerned to draw all their people with them, and which also have sometimes been very conservative or very divided on issues of pubic policy and morality. It is perhaps true to say that conferences of bodies are sometimes more radical that those same bodies are in the back home situation, and also that the common attitudes of ordinary Chruch people would lag far behind those quoted, and that efforts to inform, educate, and move the whole of any Church is a massive and often slow undertaking.

Perhaps that is why a smaller group, the Society of Friends, the Quakers, has such a fine pacifist record in many countries in their "peace testimony" as they call it. Being the body without formulated agreed statements of belief, their peace work is undertaken directly from the base of religious experience. It has three traditional aspects: to take no part in war removing the causes of war; and the promotion of peace and brotherhood and the healing of wounds. That such a small body can successfully accomplish the things it does accomplish is a source of inspiration to pacifists in the larger Churches, despite their covert longing that their Quaker friends should come to know the added graces of credal forms, liturgy and sacrament; and that we might share more fully their graces of silence, consensus, and their special sort of bloody minded ruggedness.

Christian Pacifism Restated

This brings us to the final section of this paper, covered with an attempt to make a modern statement of the Christian pacifist paper suggests.

As indicated just above, we must start with the work of Christ in overcoming evil in his life of self-giving love, and in his death of self-giving love. Thus Christ met evil with love, and it is the Christian joy and Gospel that he was victorious. The non-Christian may see Christ's life and death as but the sad, if poignant, case of a good person, in the end martyred for a cause which would have been magnificent were it not hopeless. But the Christian Church is the community which sees much more in the Christ even than this. Christians are convinced that the life of Jesus of Nazareth, his coming, his living and his loving, his serving and his suffering, his dying and his rising from the climax and focus for all human history, and both declare and show the nature of God, and human nature fully developed and unspoiled.

But that is not all, the fact and sacrifice of Christ are allied to the call of Christ. He said "follow me" and went on to spell out the implication "take up your Cross, and follow me." The proclamation of the Cross must be accompanied by obedience to the way of the Cross, for faith without work is dead. Evil must be overcome by good, hate by forgiving love. We must follow. Many modern Christian theologians (e.g. Brunner and for that matter a New Zealand Bishop in my hearing) acknowledge that Christ's way was the full way of self-sacrificial love. They indeed acknowledge that he was a pacifist. But they go on to say that Christ is, after all, a special case. Christians have always believed Jesus to be sinless, and certainly none of the rest of us is. So while his example is clear, it is unrealistic and wrong to suppose that ordinary mortals tread that same high pathway.

All that sounds good and humble. After all, each of us, and also all the churches, are conscious enough of frailty in faith, and brittleness of discipleships. However, the argument is a cop-out. What sounds like humility is actually an excuse for lack of faith. The church has always taught that the guidance, the strength, and the enabling power is available to Christians and to the church as they accept the challenges of the Christian faith and set themselves to respond to them. Christ promised the gift of his own spirit, the Holy Spirit of God, to those who seek it within the fellowship of the church. Christians rejoice in that gift, and it is part of the universal ongoing Christian experience, expressed in all sorts of different ways, but acknowledged by the whole body of Christ. Therefore the line of argument that says that pacifism was all right for Christ but not for us is in fact heresy. It is making, to use traditional forms of expression, one member of the trinity superior to another. It is saying that God the Holy Spirit is not capable of enabling the church and Christians to follow the precept and example of God the Son.

To look at the same scene from the standpoint of the doctrine of the nature of the church is also to expose the falsity of the view described. The church is described as the body of which Christ is the bead, and all Christians its members. It is a strange and indeed sad body which is in the situation of not being able to respond to the messages and motivations of the head. Such "contrite" theology is indeed, as Sidney Hinkes, General Secretary of the Anglican Pacifist Fellowship described it, properly to be seen as "decapitationist theology," separating the head from the body.

But such a theological approach, though central, essential, and primary, will probably not be enough to convince most church people—and they still remain to be convinced. They will say, in the immortal song of Eliza Doolittle in *My Fair Lady,* "Don't tell me, show me."

Thus the Christian pacifist, in his endeavor to recall the church to its pacifist faith, must live out his or her pacifism in its fullness. That fullness of commitment to the cause of reconciliation will be a costly thing by its very nature. But it is the only way. May I conclude by quoting T.S.K. Scott-Craig who, writing as long ago as in 1938, said, in words which ring frighteningly but inspiringly true today:

> This is not teaching for the world, which has not accepted Jesus, nor for a church which requires a basis in civilization if it is to continue its historic work. It is teaching for the radical disciples of Christ; but is their very own, their glory and their trial, their confident martyrdom. When the clash comes, the lesser values must for them sink into the background; family, property, culture, nation, race. These are all subordinate to the god of the kingdom of love, which is already God's kingdom. And if it appears to be conquered by the world, if its members are nailed with their Incarnate

Lord to a Cross, it rises triumphant into that transcendent order where God is all in all.

Chapter-6

NONVIOLENT STRATEGIES FOR CONFLICT RESOLUTION IN THE POST-COLD WAR ENVIORONMENT: A VIEW FORM JAPAN

TAKESHI ISHIDA

Chapter-6

THE JAPANESE DIET recently passed legislation to allow the dispatching abroad of the Self-defence Forces which are equivalent to military forces under the "peace" constitution, to cooperate with United Nations' peace-keeping operations. This dramatic change in defence policies from the pacifist principle in Japan shows that the end of the Cold War does not necessarily lead to a favorable condition for nonviolent strategies for solving international conflicts. In the post-Cold War period, there is an imminent threat of international "police action" In order to cope with the possibility of international "police actions," by strong powers, including the use of military forces, under the banner of the United Nations. Because of the absence of East-West confrontations, there is no longer a serious disagreement among the members of the Security Council to deter such "police action." voluntary international corporations, like nongovernmental organisations (NGOs), must be developed to seek nonviolent solutions for international conflicts. This presents the new theoretical challenges to expand the idea of nonviolent strategies for conflict resolution beyond the border of nation states.

The legislation which allows the Japanese "self-defence forces" to join the United Nations Peace Keeping Operations (PKO) was passed during the Diet session of 1992. The Japanese "self-defence forces" were created in 1950 in order to replace the US military forces which were sent from Japan to the Korean peninsula under the banner of the United Nations. Despite Article 9 of the post-war Japanese constitution which prohibits the possession and use of military power for setting international disputes, the Japanese "self-defence forces" were in fact the equivalent of the military forces and have been expanding ever since with the total military budget being ranked third in the world. The existence of military power under the "peace constitution" has become an accomplished fact, and it has been a major concern among the Asian nations which were occupied by the Japanese Imperial Army during the Second World War.

The passage of the legislation which enables the Japanese "self-defence forces" to operate abroad has heightened the concern and anxiety among the people of Asia. The legislation can be seen as a way of legitimizing the existence of the "self-defence forces" because the military threat from Russia has been reduced remarkably. It can also be interpreted by Asian neighbors as a way for the Japanese government, which has accomplished economic status in the world, to increase its voice in international matters by sending military organizations abroad.

Major shifts in the Japanese defence policy are the result of various domestic factors, including the long-term one-party dominance in the post-war Japanese politics which effectively reduces the chances for the opposing opinions against the government policies to be represented. However, instead of discussing the domestic factors, I would like to concentrate on the more general issue of changing international environment after the end of the Cold War. In particular, I would like to examine the effect of the end of the Cold War on the nonviolent strategies for conflict resolution. I will argue that the end of the Cold War increased the possibility of nonviolent strategies but also significantly reduced the deterrent function of the United Nations to eliminate the use of violent strategies.

The end of the Cold War indeed significantly reduced the danger of nuclear war between the Super Powers and expanded the possibility of using nonviolent strategies for conflict resolutions among the other nations. More importantly, many revolutionary changes in East European nations took place in a peaceful manner without the use of violence, and these changes provided excellent examples of the use of nonviolent strategies is international politics.

However, at the same time, it cannot be denied that the end of the Cold War created conditions which are unfavorable to the development of nonviolent strategies. One is that there is an increasing tendency on the part of the Super Powers to sell arms to other nations in order to improve the trade balance.

Following this tendency, regional conflicts moved to the centre of the international scene. The other condition, which is more important, however, is the imminent threat of international "police action" by strong powers, including the use of military forces, in order to maintain the new "international order" in the post-Cold War period. Because of the absence of East-West confrontations, there is no longer a serious disagreement among the members of the United Nations Security Council to deter "police action" by strong nations. The tone of the argument found in newspapers of Asian nations suggests that the above-mentioned legislation, which was passed in the Japanese Diet, would promote the role of the "self-defence forces" to help the United States exercise to "police actions" under the banner of the United Nations.

There are two basic ways to prevent military interventions by strong states under the banner of the United Nations. One is to propose reforms within the United Nations and the other is to influence the United Nations from outside through the activities of the non-governmental organizations (NGOs). The first is to build a mechanism within the United Nations General Assembly so that the opinions of the smaller nations, which do not belong to the Security Council, will be reflected in the decision-making process. Furthermore, with regard to the international peace-keeping operations, there should be a way to clearly distinguish the cases which require the exercise of military power and those which do not. Peace-keeping operation activities by civilian organizations are helpful for solving international conflicts, while violent activities by military organizations are likely to hinder peaceful solutions, even if done by the United Nations' peace-keeping operations. If the use of military power becomes truly unavoidable, the military forces should comprise members of the neutral small nations, rather than members of the strong states.

The reforms within the United Nations to prevent military interventions by strong nations have an obvious limitation. Since the United Nations is composed of independent nation-states including those which are politically and economically subordinate to the strong nations, it is difficult for these smaller for these smaller states to resist the will of the strongs states.

Instead of simply relying on the United Nations, we could use international public opinion with the help of the nongovernmental organizations to prevent the domination by the strong states. There are already good examples in the cases of human rights and environmental protection. It is possible for the nongovernmental organization in strong states to affect policy-making in the respective nations, and international public opinion may play a major role in preventing arrogant behavior of strong states. What is important in the activities of nongovernmental organizations is that their nonviolent endeavour in many countries contributes to the development of nonviolent strategies for conflict resolution. Some nongovernmental organizations have been active in assisting the sick, the wounded, and the poor, who were the victims of military conflicts. In addition some other non-governmental organizations have been trying to eliminate the causes of violent conflicts and they help improve living conditions, defend human rights, and promote mutual understanding between different ethnic and religious groups. These activities constitute one of the most important means to prevent violent conflicts and to promote nonviolent strategies for conflict resolution and should be promoted worldwide.

In the past, nonviolent strategies for conflict resolution have been discussed within the context of a particular nation-state and in terms of reactions to the invasion of other state or to domestic dictatorial rule. *Civilian-based Defence* by Gene Sharp, for example, highlights these two points. However, today nonviolent strategies for conflict resolution must be seen as strategies, across the national boundaries and as preventive, rather than responsive, strategies. In order to cope with the possibility of international "police action" by strong states, we must consider the nonviolent means of conflict resolution within the international context. We should also consider ways to prevent conflicts, rather than simply responding to conflict situations. It is, therefore, necessary to accumulate case studies which go

Chapter-7

INTRODUCTION

THE POST-COLD WAR WORLD has proven a difficult place for pacifists and advocates of nonviolence, particularly for those in Western Europe. For years we campaigned against the nuclear threat and the old Super-power rivalries that fed the arms race. As part of a strategy of "citizen's diplomacy" and grassroot peacemaking, links were established with peace and justice/ human rights groups in Eastern and Central Europe. Then, in 1989, the old authoritarian systems of actually existing socialism began to crumble—in part due to mass civilian—based nonviolent resistance. "People's power"—nonviolent action for change-was in the ascendant. The mood of pacifists and nonviolent activists in the West was ebullient. There was a glimpse of a new order emerging in Europe, based on vibrant civil societies constituted by citizens having experience in organizing themselves for defending their rights and for bringing about change in the domestic and international arena.

Now, in the mid-1990s, those days of hope seem to belong to a different age, dimly perceived through the lens of ethnic conflicts and rival nationalisms that besmirch so much of the world today. As those of us who are committed to nonviolence cast our gaze around the world, we begin to understand some of the despair and frustration expressed by the British pacifist Sybil Morrison during the Second World War.[1]

> There was nothing pacifists could do in 1939 but standstill and say, if they were allowed to say anything at all, that Hitler might be a worse evil than war, but that to try to overcome one evil with another evil was not only normally intolerable but could lead to even greater evil.

Afghanistan, Angola, Burundi, Georgia , Kashmir, Liberia, Nagorno-Karabakh, the Middle East, Northern Ireland, Somalia, Sri Lanka, Sudan-in all these places the conflict and the killing continues. What can we do? We dream of transformative action, the kind of intervention that can create the environment for peace and reconciliations in these conflict zones. But whilst we proclaim the efficacy of nonviolence as a mode of action and philosophy of life, we find it difficult to come up with realistic and workable nonviolent responses to the bloody conflicts burgeoning in many regions of the world.

For many advocates of nonviolence, particularly those in Europe, the most difficult situation has been the ongoing nightmare of former Yugoslavia and Bosnia-Herzegovina. On the day I started writing this essay, my monthly copy of the pacifist publication *Peace News* arrived. Amongst the contents was a letter from a life-long pacifist who confessed: "Right now I feel pacifism has nothing to offer to the people of Bosnia-Herzegoivna. I have lost faith in pacifism."[2] In the same issue of *Peace News,* Howard Clark of War Resisters' International acknowledged.[3]

> Many pacifists have questioned their own long-held beliefs in considering how the war in Bosnia-Herzegovina can be stopped. This situation confronts even the most knowledgeable of us with dilemmas and uncertainty. It is one of those times when there is no clear cut strategy which would quickly and decisively end the violence and aggression. Yet all the while we are witnessed to a suffering which cries out "something must be done."

What can be done by concerned activists, peace groups, and nongovernmental organizations to intervene as unofficial third-party peace-makers in conflict situations beyond the boundaries of their own countries? This is one of the most pressing issues that confronts advocates of nonviolence as we move toward the end of the century. In this article I want to develop some thoughts on this question and, in particular, attempt to widen our understanding of nonviolent intervention beyond the limitations of what has been termed unarmed interpositionary peace forces.

UNARMED INTERPOSITIONARY PEACE FORCES

This type of intervention involves concerned individuals trying to interpose their bodies between the direct parties to a conflict, in the hope that they might thereby prevent or bring a halt to the conflict. Thomas Weber has traced the history of such efforts, starting with the attempt by the British pacifist Maude Royden in the early 1930s to organise a "peace army" which would be prepared to intervene as a human barrier between combatants in armed conflicts and war situations.[4] Weber's historical overview concludes with the Gulf Peace Team which succeeded in establishing a multinational peace camp near the Iraqi border with Saudi Arabia for a few weeks during December 1990 and January 1991 in a vain attempt to prevent the outbreak of the most recent Gulf War.

Whilst acknowledging the bravery and commitment of the participants in such efforts at nonviolent intervention, Weber concluded that their effectiveness was extremely limited. In his view.[5]

> It is doubtful whether independent interpositionary peace-keeping ventures would ever be able to command the economic and logistical resources required and, more importantly, raise enough volunteers to achieve a critical mass that would make a difference in terms of preventing or stopping hostilities. The attempts at interpositionary peace-keeping were well-intentioned but naive in their optimism as to resources and likelihood of outcome. The analysis of their experience suggests that perhaps the approach should be modified and that other variations on the theme, such as small-scale tactical intervention, should be explored more thoroughly.

Whilst such a cautious evaluation of past efforts to interpose an unarmed presence between combatants in conflict around the world confirms what many peace activists have long left, the point needs to be made that such instances of physical intervention constitute on one type of third-party action to bring about change in a conflict situation. Indeed, by its very nature, such an extreme form of what might be called "sacrificial nonviolent action" can only be enacted by a minority of committed "missionaries." It requires a degree of commitment and courage possessed by only a few "truc believers." To the extent that activists confine their efforts to such forms of physical intervention, they unintentionally contribute to the sense of helplessness felt by the bulk of concerned people who feel the need to "do something" but who cannot—for one reason or another—bring themselves to "lay their bodies on the line" in such a fashion.

In fact, there are a whole range of ways in which concerned individuals and groups can intervene, directly and indirectly, in conflict situations beyond their borders. In what follows I want to try and indicate the nature of these different forms of intervention. I would then try to present some tentative observation about the relative effectiveness of the different forms of intervention based on my own research on unofficial nonviolent intervention in the Israeli-Palestinian conflict.

TOWARD A TYPOLOGY OF UNOFFICIAL NONVIOLENT INTERVEN-TIONARY ACTION

The typology of forms of nonviolent third-party intervene outlined below is based on a set of three criteria—the geographical location where the action takes place, the style of the action, and the goals which inform the action.

Direct and Indirect Intervention

Third parties can be said to intervene directly whenever the action entails the physical presence of the activists in the zone of conflict. By contrast, indirect intervene takes place when third parties try to influence the process and outcome of a conflict through action taken within their own national boundaries, by means of actions which do not involve their physical presence in the immediate zone of conflict.

Nonviolent Direct Action and Conventional Political Action

Whilst types of intervention can be distinguished according to their location, they can also be categorised according to the style of the action. Here it seems appropriate to distinguish in an ideal-typical fashion between nonviolent direct action and more conventional forms of action for change.

Within the tradition of nonviolent direct action, as it has been practised in the West, it is possible to identify two schools of thought and practice. On the one hand, there has been the "civil disobedience school," where the defining characteristic of direct action was deemed to be its unconventionality and the risk of sanctions incurred by the activists, whether this be the sanction of ridicule, public censure, arrest, or physical injury. According to this perspective, the key feature of direct action is that it involves some kind of challenge to established methods of exercising pressure and working for change. It follows, therefore, that whether an action can be said to be direct or conventional depends on the political context within which it takes pace. Thus street marches are commonplace in liberal democracies and are recognized as legal and legitimate forms of articulating interests. As such, they do not constitute direct styles of action. On the other hand, to participate in some form of street politics under a repressive and authoritarian political regime, which operates a ban on demonstrations and marches, would be a direct style of action.

Another approach to direct action emphasizes a somewhat different aspect. This is what we might call the "do-it-yourself" school.[6] Within this perspective direct action can be distinguished from more conventional modes of articulating interests and exercizing pressure by its *directness*. That is, actions for change can be depicted as direct in so far as the change is sought through the direct and unmediated effect to the activists' own actions. By contrast, in conventional political action people typically seek change by asking or expecting others to bring about the desired change. People vote or write letters to the press hoping to pressurise politicians and opinion leaders to act on their behalf.

The ideal-typical direct style of action embodies in itself the potential to bring about the desired end, as direct consequence of the action itself-always assuming, of course, that sufficient numbers of people with appropriate levels of commitment are prepared to engage in the action. Thus, when activists engage in "direct disarmament" by destroying nose-cones of missiles, they also engage themselves in nonviolent direct action in so far as the direct effect of their actions-if they succeeded in disabling all missiles—would be the disarmament that they seek. Similarly, to the extent that people try to live their lives in close accordance to their ideals, their actions can be characterized as a sustained form of direct action. For such people, "the personal is political," and if enough people were to follow their example, then the changes embodied in their own lives would bring about the desired transformation at the macro-level.

On the basis of the above criteria, a distinction can be made between direct and conventional styles of third-party nonviolent intervention according to the degree to which the modes of action display the core features of unconventionality/risk-taking and/ or "directness."[7]

The Objective of the Action

Types of "unofficial" intervention can be distinguished by a third criterion: the prime goal and purpose of the action. However, it needs to be emphasized that such distinctions can be made with confidence only at the analytical level. In the real world, people and groups engage in peace actions for a variety of reasons and with an amalgam of short- and long-term objectives. Thus, short-term "practical" goals can be located within a longer-term utopian project of bringing about a demilitarized "world without weapons." As Bob Overy has remarked:[8]

> Many actions of peace movements are prophetic rather than immediately practical. Peace movements tend to be concerned with what is possible for the future, rather than what is possible now. The dilemma between doing what can be done and attempting to do what needs to be done is an acute one.

Despite such cautions, it would appear that with regard to

the more immediate and tangible goals that underpin particular forms of inteventionary action, there are four main ideal-type objectives:

(i) *Protest:* This is an action which aims to register concern about a particular conflict situation, including protest against the actions of one or more parties to the conflict, seeking by such intervention to help bring the conflict to an end and/or bring about a change in the prevailing situation in the direction of a less violent and more just condition. Protest actions can be targeted not just as core parties to the conflict but also at "parties concerned" such as one's own government or intergovernmental organizations like the United Nations.

(ii) *Support and Solidarity:* This is an action which aims to provide moral or material support to individuals, groups, communities and organisations which are indigenous to the zone of conflict and are direct parties to the conflict. Such efforts can represent the obverse of protest and propaganda work, inasmuch as support for one party to a conflict invariably involves some kind of negative stance vis-a-vis others. As with protest action, support and solidarity action can be targeted at one's own government or other parties concerned which are considered to have a potential role in extending support to one or more parties to a conflict.

(iii) *Humanitarian Relief:* This action aims at alleviating the suffering of those caught up in a conflict. In practice, such types of intervention invariably embody a certain degree of symbolic protest against those parties to the conflict, which are deemed responsible for the suffering and hence have an element of solidarity with the victims. Within this category should be included efforts to persuade one's own government and other agencies to initiate and participate in relief work of one kind of another.

(iv) *Reconciliation:* This includes actions intended to promote or facilitate dialogue and processes of conflict resolution and reconciliation between parties to a conflict. The role of outsider who seeks to aid reconciliation between parties to a conflict can range from that of "go-betweens" seeking to facilitate dialogue between the parties to a conflict to a more active mediatory role in a structured encounter focused on practical obstacles to the peace-making process. Such efforts can be oriented toward the grassroots level of everyday citizens from different communities, or targeted at more politically influential groups right up to decision-making elites drawn from the core parties to a conflict.

On the basis of these distinctions, it is possible to construct a matrix of 16 deals-typical forms of third-party interventionary action, represented schematically in the diagram below.

Types of Nonviolent Interventionary Action

Location of Action	Direct Intervention		Indirect Internention	
Style of Action	Direct	Conventional	Direct	Conventional
Objective of action				
Protest	P_{DD}	P_{DC}	P_{ID}	P_{IC}
Support	S_{DD}	S_{DC}	S_{ID}	S_{IC}
Relief	R_{DD}	R_{DC}	R_{ID}	R_{IC}
Reconciliation	Rn_{DD}	Rn_{DC}	Rn_{ID}	Rn_{IC}

TYPES OF UNOFFICIAL THIRD-PARTY INTERVENTION IN THE ISRELI-PALESTINIAN CONFLICT

In this section the aim is to use the framework presented above in order to illustrate the many different ways in which "outsiders" can intervene in a conflict by brief reference to some of the relatively recent instances of third-party nonviolent intervention in the Israeli-Palestinian conflict. Before doing this, however, a general observation needs to be made. The most common forms of intervention in this conflict, and others, are conventional styles of indirect intervention. Within most democratic states concerned, people have available a whole range of legitimate and legal means of articulating their concerns about events taking place *beyond* their borders—whether their concern be to.

(i) voice their protest,

(ii) express their solidarity with one or more parties to the conflict,

(iii) seek support for humanitarian relief efforts direct towards the victims of the conflict, or

(iv) try to promote constructive dialogue and processes of reconciliation between the antagonists.

Amongst the standard means available are the following:

— symbolising one's stance vis-a-vis a conflict by all the conventional means such as lapel-badges, displaying bumper stickers, and the like,

— talking about the issues with friends and acquaintances,

— raising the issues in different organizations such as peace groups, political parties, trade unions, community groups, and other voluntary associations,

— Seeking to raise issues in the media by all legitimate means such as writing letters to the press, submitting news items, participating in "access" programms on the radio and television, and so forth,

— networking with contacts around the world, including those directly involved in the conflict, by means of electronic mail and other more time-worn modes of communication,

— lobbying national politicians and "opinion leaders" in general,

— writing letters and communicating the nature of one's concern to representatives of the direct parties to the conflict,

organizing meetings, debates, film-screening, and social evenings and other public events to raise public awareness about the conflict,

— participating in marches, pickets, petitions, and other conventional forms of "street politics,"

— boycotting certain products/preferential purchasing of others in an effort to exercise consumer pressure on parties to the conflict.

— fund-raising, whether this be by means of street collections, "bring-and-buy" sales, selling (and buying) "movement" publications, or by means of that wonderful balm of the middle-class liberal's conscience, the regular banker's order or financial donation to the worthy cause, and

— forming "twinning" arrangements between communities, institutions, and groups in one's own country and those located in the conflict zone.

All these methods of trying to influence developments in a conflict are unremarkable extensions of the normal means of articulating interest and exercising pressure within one's own political community. Participants are unlikely to incur any unforeseen costs or sanctions. Furthermore, they are aimed invariably at affecting in one way or another the activities of governments, organizations, and agencies more directly involved in the conflict. As such, they constitute what can be termed conventional modes of indirect interventionary action.

Protest

Whatever the type of nonviolent interventionary protest action engaged in by concerned individuals and groups, they are invariably informed, either explicitly or implicitly, by the notion of what has been called "the chain of nonviolence." This is the idea that by nonviolent interventionary action one might touch the conscience of the public, "bystanders," and more immediate parties to the conflict, thereby acting as a catalyst for their subsequent mobilization to effect changes in the outlook and stance of other groupings with which they have contact, so that eventually the impact of the original action might reverberate along the links in a chain leading to political elites and key policy makers. As a part of this process, groups throughout the world have engaged in the full range of conventional modes of indirect intervention referred to above—publishing newsletters, organizing petitions, lobbying politicians, organizing marches and demonstrations, and so forth-in order to register their protest against different aspects of the conflict in the Middle East between Israel and the Palestinians. Often the immediate targets of such indirect interventionary actions are domestic public opinion and national governments. These constitute the first link in a chain of influence which, it is hoped, will eventually lead to the core parties to the conflict. In addition, a number of more direct forms of nonviolent intervention have been initiated. Here I want to make reference to just two relatively recent examples for illustrative and comparative purposes.

"1990: Time for Peace"

The first took place in Jerusalem toward the end of December 1989s. This was the "1990: Time for Peace" international rally. The idea behind the rally was to mobilise Palestinians and Israelis, with the support of a sizeable international presence, in a joint nonviolent demonstration in favour of a just peace to the conflict. The original initiative came from the Italian Peace Association and was taken up by other nongovernmental organizations concerned with the question of Palestine.

In preparing for the rally, the Europeans were determined to involve "Peace Now," the mainstream Israeli peace movement. Although not a membership organisation as such, those who are drawn from a broad band of the liberal Zionist political spectrum. As such, they were perceived as a vital link in the chain of nonviolence reaching into the heart of Israeli decision-making circles. After a lot of negotiation and dialogue between the Europeans and the Israelis, Peace Now agreed to participate. In part, this was due to the credibility and prestige of the Italian Peace Association and the representatives of the European Peace movement involved in the negotiations-many of them had been involved in promoting dialogue between Palestinians and Israelis for a number of years. In addition, Peace Now had finally decided that the time had come to call for official Israeli recognition of the PLO, and as such was prepared to participate in a joint rally with Palestinians calling for "two states for two peoples."

As the events unfolded at the end of 1989, it embraced a range of conventional and more direct styles of action in which several hundred overseas participants took part alongside Israelis and Palestinians. Friday, 29 December was devoted to women's actions. It started with a conference, then some 3,000 women joined the weekly Friday vigil of Women in Black at one of the main intersections in West Jerusalem. There then followed a women's peace march of about 5,000 participants who walked across the "border" from Israeli West Jerusalem in the heart of Palestinian East Jerusalem. The following day some 30,000 engaged in a direct style of action when they formed a Human Peace Chain around the walls of the Old City of Jerusalem. Surrounding the demonstrators was a ring of some 2,000 Israeli police and paramilitaries who could not resist practising their crowd-control techniques of teargas, water cannons, and rubber bullets and clubs upon those who had the temerity to be chanting "we want peace"! By the end of the day, some fifty demonstrators had been arrested and similar number seriously injured.

After the two days of street demonstrations, the rally continued with a series of smaller-scale events including a series of workshops and meetings where Israelis, Palestinians, and participants from overseas joined together in discussion and debate about different aspects of the conflict and the necessary steps to be taken for peace.[9]

June 1992: Walk for a Peaceful Future in the Middle East

This instance of direct intervention was planned as an exercise in direct action, and all the participants knew beforehand that they risked sanctions of one kind or another. The initiative originated with a group of people who had participated in the Gulf Peace Team and the peace camp of December 1990. They had realized that a lasting peace in the region required a solution to the Palestinian question. To further this end, they had attempted to organise a peace walk between Jerusalem and Amman, the capital of Jorden in June 1991. Planned at short notice, the walk failed to attract the support of the mainstream Israeli peace groups and received only token support from prominent Palestinians. It aroused little interest and was aborted after the Israeli authorities halted the march once it had left Jerusalem.

Undeterred, the organizers planned another march to coincide with the 25th anniversary of the June 1967 War and occupation of the West Bank and Gaza Strip. Consultations were held with Israeli and Palestinian human rights groups, and support solicited from international peace organisations and pacifist networks such as War Resisters' International and the International Fellowship of Reconciliation. Eventually somewhere in the region of 150 participated from overseas-predominantly drawn from western and northern Europe and from North America. After a few days spent in nonviolent training and preparation, they set off on the first leg of what was planned to be a one-week march from Israel into the occupied territories, ending with a demonstration in Jerusalem. Enroute it was planned to hold solidarity demonstrations outside Israeli prisons which held Israeli draft-resisters and Palestinian political prisoners. On the second day of the march, they approached the green line which separates Israel from the occupied territories, where the police and border guards prevented them from proceeding any further. The marchers sat down in the road and refused to move, and 120 of them (including 16 Israelis) were arrested. After 48 hours in detention, the overseas participants were required to leave the country after the Israeli authorities cancelled their tourist visas.[10] One event that did take place, however, was an international vigil outside the jail in Ashokelon where Mordecai Vanunu remains imprisoned in solitary confinement.

I have presented about a brief description of these two examples of direct interventionary protest action with regard to the Israeli-Palestinian conflict because they represent two contrasting cases. The differed in two significant aspects, the immediate targets of the action, and the political context within which the actions took place. The 1990 Time for Peace rally was targetted primarily at the mainstream of liberal Israelis and it sought to touch these people through the involvement of Peace Now. The Walk for Peace, on the other hand, failed to obtain the support of Peace Now and consequently failed to connect with a vital link in the chain of nonviolence. With regard to the political context, the Time for Peace rally took place at a time when the Israeli peace movement was in the ascendant, with Peace Now having just declared its commitment to a twin-state solution to the conflict. The rally also coincided with a decision by the Palestinian leadership within the occupied territories, buoyed by the success of the *intifada,* to prioritize the promotion of dialogue with mainstream Israelis. As such, the rally complemented the projects of peace-seekers on both sides of the conflict and was thus able to attract considerable support from both constituencies. As a participant in the rally, there was about those days in Jerusalem a sense of community, of people from diverse backgrounds coming together for a common purpose. It was an experience that exercised a powerful impact on the many thousands who participated.

By contrast, the Walk for Peace took place at a time when the priority of most Israeli "doves" was with the upcoming general election, which resulted in the defeat of the right-wing. Likud bloc and the victory of a Labour-led bloc that professed its commitment to exchanging land for peace. In addition, few members of Peace Now could accept the legitimacy of the kind of civil disobedience that the Walk for Peace appeared to entail.[11] Furthermore, for most Palestinians within the occupied territories their priority was to survive the unprecedented economic and material hardships that were visited upon them during the Gulf War and the post-war period. Thus the march took place within a political context that was not supportive of the initiative. Apart from the publicity surrounding the arrests at the "green line," the impact of the march on Israeli and Palestinian public opinion was minimal.

Support and Solidarity

As with interventionary protest actions, aimed at extending support and solidarity to one or more parties to a conflict can be distinguished according to the location where they take place (home or away from home), and according to their style direct or conventional. As was detailed above regarding protest actions, the most common forms of intervention in relation to the Israeli-Palestinian conflict have been indirect and conventional in style. Types of direct intervention that have been undertaken include fact-finding educational/solidarity tours of the conflict zone by sympathetic third parties and the placement of volunteers to work with peace-oriented groups and projects within the occupied territories and Israel.

An idea of the range of support actions, involving direct and indirect forms of intervention, is indicated in the following list of suggestions of "How to Help" adapted from *Educational Network,* the newsletter of an international network of people concerned about the future of Palestinian education in the occupied territories.

(i) Link your teachers' union with a teacher's union in the occupied territories.

(ii) Get your union to actively support the rights of Palestinian teachers in the occupied territories to form unions.

(iii) Establish a scholarship fund for one or more Palestin ian students to study either in Palestine or abroad.

(iv) Reproduce and publish information about Palestinian education.

(v) Send delegations of teachers to visit the occupied territories.

(vi) Sponsor Palestinian teachers to visit your city for an

educational tour.

(vii) Establish teacher-exchange programme.

(viii) Send an experienced educator to the occupied territo ries to give workshops on innovative teaching techniques.

(ix) Set up a pen-pal programme with a Palestinian school in either English or French.

(x) Set up a sister-school programme with a Palestinian school.

(xi) Keep the Educational Network informed about important educational conferences so that we can send a Palestinian teacher to attend.

(xii) Send to the Educational Network articles or other writings or books dealing with innovative approaches and ideas in the field of education.

(xiii) Support an educational development project in the occupied territories.[12]

Humanitarian Relief

With regard to the Israeli-Palestinian conflict, tens of thousands of individuals around the world have intervened indirectly with the express aim of relieving the suffering of its victims—through contributing in one way or another to charities and international humanitarian organizations.

Others have intervened in a more direct fashion by spending time working with the victims of the conflict in Israel and the occupied territories. This can be of a relatively short-term nature—such as groups of medical personnel spending their vacation time assisting with health care and educational work in the occupied territories.

Frequently such short-term projects are part of a longer-term involvement by organizations and agencies. One examples of such a sustained form of direct intervention for the purpose of relieving suffering has been the one pioneered by organizations like Medical Aid for Palestinians (MAP). MAP was founded in 1984 after the Israeli invasion of Lebanon and the massacres of Palestinians at Sabra and Shatilla in Beirut. Since the outbreak of the *intifada* in December 1987, it has concentrated on sending medical supplies and trained personnel to medical institutions and health care programmes within the West Bank and the Gaza Strip. Frequently such volunteers publicise the conditions they have experienced when they return to their home countries. In so doing they draw upon the legitimacy provided by their professional standing to add strength and credibility to their advocacy of Palestinian human rights and their criticism of Israeli occupation policies. In this way, third-party intervention motivated primarily by humanitarian concern, can embrace other dimensions of protest and support/solidarity.

Reconciliation

The most common form of intervention to promote reconciliation between Israel and the Palestinians has aimed at facilitating meetings for dialogue wherever Israeli Jews and Palestinians can be persuaded to meet together. A particularly significant role in this process of "detente from below" has been played by peace groupings and non-governmental organisations who have created the context for such meetings by inviting representatives from both sides of the conflict to attend their conferences and gatherings. In the "safe" and supportive surroundings of such occasions, nominal enemies have been able to relax together, exchange views, and establish network of communication and friendship.

Academic institutions and research centers have also carved out an interventionary role with regard to promoting reconciliation by inviting representatives from different sides of the conflict to participate in problem—solving workshops based on a belief in the efficacy of unofficial "track two" diplomacy. As a general rule, it would appear that the greater the status of the sponsoring institution, the greater the political influence of the representatives prepared to participate.

At times, the distinction between unofficial "track two"

diplomacy and the official process of peace negotiations an become blurred. Thus, in August 1993, it emerged that informal negotiations had been taking place in Norway which were of far greater significance that the official process being acted out in Washington and elsewhere. Although the Norwegian government played a vital role in facilitating the secret meetings of the Israeli and Palestinian officials, the initial breakthrough was brought about by the intervention of an unofficial third party—the director of a Norwegian research institute who had been involved in a survey of living conditions in the Gaza Strip. This initial humanitarian involvement gave him access to representatives from all sides of the conflict, whilst they in turn had ample opportunity to judge his caliber and trustworthiness as a mediator and go-between.

OBSERVATIONS ON THE EFFECTIVENESS OF UNOFFICIAL THIRD-PARTY INTERVENTION

The mix of goals, both short- and longer-term, pursued by peace groups and others who seek to intervene unofficially in conflict situations beyond their borders makes it difficult to evaluate their effectiveness. A protest action that attracts media attention might be considered a success by the participants, even though it failed to make any observable impact on the conflict situation itself. In similar vein, actions that appear to exercise no immediate impact on a conflict can be deemed a success by participants because they resulted in a heightening of morale amongst the participants and the establishment of new networks involving the forging of new links in the chain of nonviolence. Pacifists and others might deem their interventionary action a success in so far as they created an opportunity to bear witness to their values and beliefs, without any particular thought to the practical outcome of their actions. Most antagoniists make sense of their actions in terms of a long-term scenario consisting of a sequence of actions which, cumulatively over time, might exercise an effect on the process and outcome of act conflict. Many of us who have engaged in different forms of interventionary action comfort ourselves with the analogy of the stone thrown into the lake: you can never tell how far the ripples of our action might reach in the long run.

Despite such problems a number of tentative observations do suggest themselves.[13]

(i) The impact of any interventionary protest action depends upon the context within which it takes place.

Protest activity typically aims at arousing public opinion either at home or in the region of conflict, in the hope that public pressure might be mobilized to influence either the policies of one's own government or the political elites of the core parties to the conflict. whether interventionary protest actions are direct or indirect, they invariably seek to address publics as links in a chain of influence leading to key decision-makers. However, whether or not publics respond to the prompting of peace and protest groups would seem to depend on factors beyond the control of the interventionists. Only rarely do peace groups initiate moral crusades, although they can certainly be on hand to guide and service them when public concern reaches a critical pass. By way of an illustration, reference can be made to the findings of Charles Chatfield on the impact of antiwar protest in he United States during the Vietnam war. He has argued that the US government only sought to disengage itself from the war when the public began to withdraw its support from the war effort in growing numbers after 1968. Rather controversially, he suggests that this swing in public opinion was due not so much to the efforts of the peace groups as such, but to the fact that the public began to see the war and the organized antiwar protest as threatening the established social order.[14] Whether or not one accepts such a conclusion, it would seem incontrovertible that without the backing of significant sections of the public, the activities of peace and protest groups have no immediately observable impact on governmental decision-making in the realm of foreign affairs, and have even less direct impact on the policies of the core parties to a conflict.

At the same time, the longer-term (and therefore virtually unmeasurable) influence of peace and protest groups should not be dismissed. Activists who insist on responding to the promptings of their beliefs play a vital role in refusing to allow us to ignore or forget the barbarism of violence and bloody conflict at home and abroad. Moreover, they can also exercise a kind of veto power—acting as watchdogs and ready to arouse public awareness whenever political elites attempt to initiate policies that contradict proclaimed commitments to furthering peace and justice.

(ii) The more modest the goal of inteventionary action, the greater is the likelihood of success.

Following on from the above, this seems an obvious point but it is still worth making. To the extent that a group restricts its aim to indirect intervention by influencing a specific aspect of their government's policy toward a particular conflict, the greater the chances of success. Almost by definition, when a group adopts the role of a conventional pressure grouping within the political domain, it chooses to operate within the parameters of what is "realistic" and possible. In the process the group might lose sight of its ultimate ideal, but such groupings do perform a vital function in widening the terms of political debate, maintaining issues on the political agenda—and they do stand a chance of achieving something tangible. As an activist with Peace Brigades International has observed:[15]

I believe we best promote the cause of nonviolence worldwide by working harder than ever for change in our own countries and by offering what support we can to our sisters and brothers working in much more difficult circumstances, rather than by rushing around trying to prove nonviolence is just as good as violence when it comes to sorting out somebody else's conflict.

(iii) The impact of any interventionary action is dependent to a significant degree upon the status of the intervener.

In general, the greater the prestige and standing of the individual, group, or organization that intervenes in a conflict situation, the less easy it is for the targets of the action to ignore the intervention. As a corollary of this general observation, it would appear that the closer the sense of identity between an intervener and the target of the intervention, there greater is the impact of the intervention. When concerned Jews from around the world express their collective concern about Israeli occupation policies, their voice can be heard right along the chain of influence leading to the Israeli political leadership.

(iv) To enhance its effectiveness, wherever possible, interventionary action should be oriented toward supporting the work of indigenous peacemakers.

There is a real danger that third parties motivated by genuine concern will seek to intervened in conflict situations in ways that are inappropriate, insensitive, and counter-productive. One way to avoid such mistakes is for third parties to subordinate their interests to those of peacemakers and activists indigenous to the zone of conflict who are working for peace and reconciliation. A noteworthy example of such work is that of the volunteers of Peace Brigades International (PBI) who spend time in conflict areas, escorting local peace activists whose work incurs the risk of physical attack. In their role as an international presence/observer alongside such people, the volunteers act as a deterrent against potential attackers and thereby help to widen the political space within which indigenous peace workers can operate.

The real strength of such efforts lies in their "modest" purpose and the acceptance of the essentially "service role" to be played by third-party activists. By restricting their aim to that of supporting and servicing the needs of peace—makers and activists living and working in the midst of the conflict, third-party activists avoid the danger of trying to impose their own priorities and schema upon the people embroiled in the day-to-day violence and horror, taking their cue from the people who, at the end of the day, carry the responsibility for resolving the conflict. This point has been made very strongly by Tim Wallis:[16]

> However difficult it may be for us in the peace movement to accept we may have to admit that we cannot stop the bloodshed in Bosnia, or in Somalia, or in Angola. The best we can do is to support those Bosnians, Somalis, or Angolans who may be resisting, or who would resist if they could, the

war and violence around them. In that case the "proof" of the efficacy of nonviolence is not to be found in our own acts of nonviolent intervention in conflicts, but in the nonviolent action of the people who live and struggle in the midst of those conflicts.

(v) The more constructive the interventionary action, the more observable its impact.

In his approach to nonviolent action, Gandhi emphasized the twin dimensions of satyagraha: the "negative" resistance to evil and the "positive" response of undermining the basis of injustice by embodying truth in one's individual and collective life. This became known as the Constructive Programme and it was Gandhi's great strength as a political organizer that he was able to devise campaigns that combined political protest with constructive action to meet people's basic needs. Thus he combined that campaign against foreign cloth with the constructive work of khadi—home-produced cloth. He defied the British and their salt tax and urged people to make their own salt.

The most effective forms of interentionary action are those which share some of the characteristics of the Gandhian approach to satyagraha: intervening to assist those in the conflict zone who are engaged in the struggle to promote a just resolution to the conflict, intervening to help the victims of the conflict, offering one's services to facilitate dialogue between "enemies." Such constructive modes of intervention, whether they be direct or indirect, lack the drama and publicity-potential of some of the more protest-oriented forms of intervention. But their impact on the conflict situation is invariably more substantial.

CONCLUSION: BREAKING THE LIMITS OF NONVIOLENCE

This essay started off with a reference to the limited impact of interventionary actions carried out by unarmed interpositionary peace forces. The participants in such ventures have usually been "true believers" in the efficacy of nonviolence as a functional alternative to violence. If we are to develop the potential of nonviolent intervention by third parties to affect the process and outcome of conflicts around the world, then we need to move beyond the narrow focus on interpositionary peacemaking. In the process we also need to face up to two harsh realities.

First, we need to recognize that some conflicts are not amended to resolution or management through third party intervention—whether such intervention be by violent or nonviolent means. This does not mean that we should not try to intervene in the various ways outlined above. But it does mean that we should not get disheartened at our "failures." To modify the old adage of Gramsci, we need to infuse our hopes with a dash of skepticism that comes from an intellectual analysis of the degree to which conflicts are susceptible at any particular state to resolution by the intervention of any kind of third-party action.

Secondly, we need to move beyond the notion of nonviolence as a functional alternative to violence, the conviction that whatever claims are made by the advocates of violent and armed intervention can be matched by nonviolent means at much less human cost. So long as we hold on to this notion, we will continue to feel frustrated at our inability to come up with nonviolent alternatives to armed intervention in regional conflicts. To put it simply, nonviolence is not a functional alternative to violence, if by that we mean a straightforward substitute for violence. Certain ends can be achieved by violence which nonviolence by its very nature cannot achieve. It might be possible to impose a cessation of open hostilities on a region by threatening intervention. You can "pacify" a people by shooting and bombing them into submission. There are no nonviolent alternatives to such forms of military intervention.

To acknowledge these limitations does not mean that nonviolent intervention can have no effect on a conflict. As I have tried to show in this article, there are a whole range of ways in which nonviolent intervention by third parties can contribute to a reduction in the level of conflict and the amelioration of suffering, and, in the process, lay the basis for a more cooperative future. A key task for peace researchers and nonviolent activists, as we move toward the next century, is to study and practise way in which nonviolent intervention can be rendered more effective. The starting-point for this must be to acknowledge some of the limitations of nonviolence as a means of intervention and then strive, in a true utopian fashion, to break beyond these limits.

Notes and References

1. S. Morrison, *I Renounce War* (London: Sheppard Press, 1962), p. 45.
2. H. Gieschen, *Peace News,* March 1994, p. 13.
3. *Ibid.*, p. 3.
4. Thomas Weber, "From Maude Royden's Peace Army to the Gulf Peace Team: An Assessment of Unarmed Interpositionary Peace Forces," *Journal of Peace Research* (Oslo), Vol. 30, No. 1, 1993, pp. 45-64.
5. *Ibid.*, p. 62.
6. I am grateful to Howard Clark for suggesting these distinctions.
7. In this sense nonviolent direct action is being used as an open-textured concept. That is, whilst acknowledging that there were cannot be an exhaustive specification of "direct action" in all its manifestations, there remain certain core characteristics common to all forms of action to which the concept is applied. See M. Taylor, *Community, Anarchy, and Liberty* (Cambridge: Cambridge University Press, 1982), pp. 2-3.
8. B. Overy, *How Effective Are Peace Movements?* (London: Housmans, 1982), p. 1.
9. For a discussion of "the great chain of nonviolence," Johan Galtung, *Nonviolence and Israel/Palestine* (Honolulu: University of Hawaii Press, 1989), p. 19 and also Andrew Rigby, *Living the Intifada* (London: Zed Books, 1991), pp. 167-168.
10. For a fuller account of the rally, see Howard Clark, *WRI Newsletter*, January 1990. See also Andrew Rigby, *Living*

the Intifida.

11. In 1988 Mordecai Vanunu was sentenced to 18 years' imprisonment in a secret trial after being found guilty of disclosing Israeli nuclear secrets to the *Sunday Times,* Since that time he has been kept in solitary confinement at Ashakelon prison, south of Tel Aviv.

12. Taken and amended from "How to Help Palestinian Education," *Educational Network,* No. 11, April 1993, p. 11.

13. I am very aware of the dangers of generalising from a single case study. Like any other conflict, there are aspects of the Israeli-Palestinian conflict which make it unique. Despite such reservations, I offer the same observations in the form of hypotheses to be tested against experiences in relation to other conflicts.

14. See Charles Chatfield's concluding "Reflections" in C. DeBenedetti, *An American Ordeal: The Antiwar Movement of the Vietnam Era* (Syracuse: Syracuse University Press, 1990).

15. Tim Wallis, "Intervention from Within," *Peace News,* January 1994, p. 10.

16. *Ibid.*

Chapter-8

Reflections on the Future of Nonviolence

Jan Oberg

Chapter-8

WHAT IS THE PURPOSE OF NONVIOLENCE?

THE ANSWER SEEMS to be self—evident. We want to prevent, reduce, and successively abolish violence wherever it occurs in human society and between humans and Nature.

Violence—structural as well as direct—occurs in situations of conflicts, when attitudes, behavior, or interests clash. If we define violence as a situation in which potentials are prevented from being utilized or realized—or, where the level of realization of human, social, and natural potentials is sub-optimal—we have to admit that we see violence almost everywhere. Violence is itself a conflict between what could be and what is—" the life not lived," as Erich From said.

Can we hope to *abolish* or just *reduce* violence? Is violence, as defined above, a *sine qua non* of development in the sense that development is the realization of potentials were they have not already been realized? Is violence, again in the above sense of under-realization of potentials, in some sense necessary for human affairs to develop, a kind of paradox or existential dilemma? Is development simply the opposite of violence?

If we take it to be true that there is violence everywhere and we commit ourselves undeterredly to struggle for nonviolence in general human affairs, are we not simply asking for the moon? Is our definition of violence for too broad and non-operationalizable? Is violence really so widespread and the world so mad?

I adhere increasingly to the view that working for a more nonviolent world is an absurd activity that has, anyhow, to be carried out because the world—or even existence itself—*is* absurd and that *that* is the only thing that makes sense to do under such circumstances.

Absurdity is not the same as meaninglessness but rather a

recognized lack of sense of community or connectedness, a situation in which things do not readily make sense. Absurd theater, a special genre that I strongly believe has a message to anyone working for peace, does not *represent* an image of life or existence, it *is* the absurd itself. Absurdity implies a lack of commonly agreed rules of the game, language, norms, and shared meaning of things. Thus communication between actors becomes meaningless, nonsensical. I act into the world and get a response which is totally different from what I had reasons to expect that it would be.

By way of illustrating my point, compare the figures of Charlie Chaplin and Mohandas Gandhi. These are perhaps not the first two figures of "modern times" (one title of one of Chaplin's films) you think of as being fairly similar, but I think they are. We find them in different settings—in films and in politics—but they display the fundamentally tragic human condition. Man is small and disconnected. Each of us attempts to do good and be good (nonviolently), but the response that we get from the world around, from Reality, is the opposite. We constantly get into new troubles (conflicts), we are constantly tempted to "fall" and to compromise with ourselves to become part of a common, shared world. We are punished—or at least threatened—by more powerful actors, be it individuals, politics as such, or the mighty forces of Western civilization, dictatorship, or technology.

A question is met with an answer to something else, if at all. Words are out of context. All we can do is to go on, to experiment (with truth), to live with the tragic facts of modern life, or—as Gandhi increasingly did towards the end of his life—contemplate death and accept our own death as a better outcome than any other compromise offered.

Both figures, in acting out *that* attitude vis-a-vis alienation of modern civilization, offer the rest of us a kind of transcendence, a way out, a way of living with satisfaction in the midst of the struggle knowing that have—the I"—would never succeed.

Peace, also with oneself, is the road, not the goal. It is the

Chaplinesque and Gandhian insights into the (absurd) human condition and their ability to find happiness (and not only despair in knowing that it has to be like that) which makes them such toweing figures. The pervasive sense of (black) humour combined with stubbornly keeping on doing what they think is right is another striking similarity between Gandhian and Chaplin. It further emphasizes their fundamentally dark vision of the human condition.

The use of violence has always been a challenge in the struggle for nonviolence. Perhaps we are now facing also a challenge from *the post-modern ways in which various old and new types of violence are readily accepted.* This is what I shall turn to in what follows.

THE CONFLICT WITH THE POST-MODERN WORLD

The contemporary post-modern world presents us, it seems, with a new problematique. Any viewpoint or interpretation of the world can be presented with an impressive amount of arguments and supported by analyses based on fact. Individuals can freely subscribe to one set of norms and values in one situation and another in another situation and defend their positions with conviction. This is something fundamentally different from the principled actor who, like Gandhi, constantly tries to adapt and refine a principle (or, rather, a set of principles) to changing circumstances throughout his life. The principled actor acknowledges that there is a kind of shared Reality, the post—modern actors say "no, there is no such thing, there is a multitude of realities and no truth (and certainly no Truth/Satya) possible."

In his thought-provoking book, *Reality Isn't What It Used to Be,* Walter Truett Anderson elaborates on the fundamental characteristics of the post-modern world in this manner:

> In recent decades we have passed, like Alice slipping through the looking glass, into a new world. The post-modern world looks and feels in many ways like the modern world that preceded it: we still have the belief systems that gave form

to the modern world, and indeed we also have remnants of many of the belief systems to pre-modern societies. If there is anything we have plenty of, it is belief systems. But we also have something else: a growing suspicion that all belief systems—all ideas about human reality—are social constructions. This is a story about stories, a belief about beliefs, and in time-probably a very short time—it will become a central part of the world view of most people. It will be core of the first global civilization.

But it is not yet a core. It is more a seed of discontent. It fills our daily lives with uncertainly and anxiety, renders us vulnerable to tyrants and cults, shakes religious faith, and divides societies into groups contending with one another in a strange and unfamiliar kind of ideological conflict—not merely *conflict between beliefs,* but conflict *about* belief itself.

Politics has always rested on the construction and maintenance of social reality, but until recently we didn't talk much about that. The deep issues concerning the nature of human truth were left to the philosophers. Most of the conflicts that tore the now-endings modern era were between different belief systems, each of which professed to have the truth: this faith against that one, capitalism against Communism, science against religion. On all sides was the assumption that somebody possessed the real item, a truth fixed and beyond mere human conjecture.

The modern era brought us into a world with multiple and conflicting belief systems. Now the post-modern era is revealing a world in which [....] a post-modern culture based on a different sense of social reality is coming into being—and it is a painful birth.

This is a challenging statement on our time. I do not want to discuss whether it is true(!) but what this type of post-modern thinking may imply for the nonviolent "project." I think the statement (and the book) immediately catches the attention of the peace thinker because it says something fundamental about social cosmology, about conflict, about emerging global civilization, about truth (and the possibility of "experimenting with Truth" in a Gandhian sense), and about beliefs, and also because it says something important about our individual and collective existence as well as the nature of politics.

It is nothing new that reality—or its interpretation—is, at least to a certain extent, socially constructed. That happens through formal and informal education, media, being together with others, social myths, etc. The new thing seems to be that it is socially constructed to such an extent that Reality disappears altogether.

If there is no common reference to something that we can agree to call Reality, communication becomes almost meaningless. We live in different worlds, not in the same. In this post-modern world, you have a project, an action that for some reason you want to, or *have* to carry out. You act, you play the role of the actor following a text, you perform. The script is given, you do not search for what is right to do from a series of beliefs or ethical norms, you choose the act itself first and then you choose the text that can deliver the legitimation and explanation of the act for yourself or some kind of audience.

Truth, then, becomes circumstantial. What is true is that my act is acceptable, legitimate, all right within the framework I choose; but that I choose because it legitimates what I do. This implies that individual freedom expands to the extent that each of us dissociates from the straitjacket of single principles (which are predicated on the existence of some kind of shared, single reality) and thinks and acts as if there were only socially constructed and subjectively interpreted multiple realities. In the eye of the spectator, what is right equates with who performs most convincingly according to the text. What the (real) Reality is plays no important role any longer. The criterion of something being true or right is: who chose the best manuscript and who performed his role better and who marketed his performance most effectively.

If we call this post-modern believing, and beliefs can change from one day to the next, truth being circumstantial, then, there are no criteria, no norms, and so shared community and no dialogue possible any longer. In short, social existence becomes absurd and only within some kind of personalized world in which the "I" or small—or sub—group "we" rules independently can the world make sense to me.

If the argument is chosen after the acting, we might raise a moral critique. If the arguments are not socially constructed in the old general social-science sense but manufactured through electronic media and other sophisticated means of transmitting power and power as such has hardly changed a bit from the modern to the post-modern world—moral criticism becomes irrelevant. There is nothing to argue against—or for—as long as the acting is performed as an excellent play and the movie is promoted in the world market in such a way that everybody hears about it, talks about it, and wants to see it.

So, value, positions, norms and legitimations become consumption goods, following patterns of supply and demand and being influenced by what is, today and tomorrow, fashionable or socially correct living. Ways of living of coming to terms with existence itself, becomes "life styles" and can be changed as frequently as you see fit or socially correct. The persons who searches for a philosophy and identifies a set of basic principles to live his or her life and by sticks to this as a belief is simply "out of touch" or "old-fashioned" in the contemporary post-modern world. Instead, we must create, trade, exchange, and mix "realities," and Reality becomes, for better or worse, democratized.

Truett Andreson says: "Individuals feel free to create new identities for themselves, and entrepreneurs of reality dabble gaily in the creation of new history, new science, new religion, new politics." Nothing, in other words, has any permanent value and values have no permanence. Thus there is nothing to stick to through a lifetime. Sticking to basic life principles becomes old-fashioned, if not ridiculous.

If all this is true, those of us sticking to nonviolence as a belief, a principle underlying the good society, are out of touch, and so are all those who used to believe in something. Truett Anderson makes the important distinction between the "constructivists" and the "fundamentalists." The first say that we live in a symbolic world in multiple realities, that it is all socially constructed and, yet, experienced as an objective, real world. The fundamentalists think that all this is socially dangerous because they believe that social order is impossible without a fundamental agreement that certain things are not just socially true but by God cosmically true, true for everybody and for all time.

This is obviously too pointed, if not a false, a distinction for two reasons. One, is pretty obvious that many adhering to the constructivist view point argue as if there is no longer any objective, real world (and how could there be, if we have become creators of our own personalized realities and these realities keep changing constantly?). Second, fundamental principles do not have to be God-given or true for all, or for all time. All it takes is a belief that there are basic principles and things to believe, and that they maintain some kind of permanent value over time at least for some of us.

At this point this whole reasoning can be refuted on the following grounds:

* The post-modern view of reality being constructed into multiple realities is obviously a belief in and to itself, as good as any other basic belief, and as such, it can be disputed. Thus it does not present us with a conflict about believing but, simply, with another belief.
* The post-modern worldview has appeared in a political era that has declared "the end of ideology" (Fukuyama) which, I would argue, is nothing but a thinly veiled legitimation of the modern Western, democratic, market-capitalist ideology attempting to dominate the emerging global civilization in spite of the fact that it is possible only as a belief system and ideology precisely of the world's few.

So why take the post-modern "multiple really" view with its

implicit negation of the existence of basic values and beliefs seriously? I think we must, because:

(i) It lumps all values and beliefs into one category. Obviously, some values are more important than others. It is fairly unproblematic that we can go in and out of subcultures or enjoy the freedom to move rapidly between cultures and learn a bit here and there. But there is reason for deep concern, should we equate this diversity with the demise of all lasting or existential principles in our individual and collective lives.

(ii) By ignoring existential values and basic societal principles, it legitimizes the search by elites for very unified and "fundamentalist" projects having to do with power on the top. Thus while any particularistic vision is now permitted for the individuals and the regions of Europe, power-Europe strives to arrive at a situation in which all "speak with one voice." This is ideology to me, and authoritarian ideology at that!

(iii) All types of parochialism, ethnocentricity, authoritarianism, nationalism, anti-semitism, anti-women policies seem to thriev and find legitimacy in the post-modernd worldview which, in effect, seems to say that" anything goes" as long as it serves an immediate purpose. We are constantly presented with the view that the world is becoming one and that we are increasingly becoming interdependent and integrated into one system. This trend, if at all true, is obviously counteracted by very strong centrifugal, particularistic forces.

NONVIOLENCE: ON MEANS AND ENDS ONCE AGAIN

I think we are constantly thrown back to the issue of means and goals. The post-modern world also negates the principle that there must be a fundamental correspondence between means and ends. As we have seen repeatedly in international affairs, "peace" is created by non-peaceful means, international law is preserved, or so they say, by interventions which violate the most basic norms of international law; and now Europe is bent on using the largest military apparatus, NATO (turned obsolete and irrelevant by the demise of the Warsaw Pact and the Soviet Union) into what is euphemistically called "peacekeeping forces."

I tend to think that the fundamental inseparability of means and ends—and of form and content—must be emphasized anew in our search for a more nonviolent world. In research, teaching, and policy-oriented activity, we must increasingly raise the simple everyday-oriented questions such as:

—Why do we see an increasing acceptance worldwide of the false distinction between "good" and "bad" violence? The act does not count, only the actor does (the Gulf War or Yugoslavia).

—Why are strength, courage, statesmanship, determination, and effective politics so readily equated with threatening and actual use of violence?

—What makes otherwise sensible people so susceptible to violence—promoting perspectives even to the extent of using violence themselves?

—Why is the media world so central in legitimizing violence worldwide? Why is "post-modernity" so isomorphic with the cultivation of (entertainment) violence and violence against?

—Does teaching—form, content, subjects—itself promote violence?

—Why do we that make comparative studies and teaching of violence and nonviolence in history, sociology, and political science? Why does even a major part of peace research refrain from systematic studies on nonviolence?

—Or, to pose the opposite, why, in many circumstances, would we actually not dream of using nonviolence to achieve our goals? And what generalized learning can we derive from that?

And, then, how do we live as peace researchers? Do we always practise what we preach? How do we organize ourselves as professionals in associations and institutes? Do we speak and write to be of service to the local and global community or is the career, income, competition, and influence of higher importance? How do we relate to our students? How do we present our views—from the point of view of what we love and the constructive values we want to promote in the world? Or do we spend our energies on what we do not like, on attacking those we consider our "enemies," and on negative, critical analysis stating only the problems? Are our ways of living and our households environmentally sustainable? Do we practise the principle of "what millions cannot have I should not have?"

The more nonviolence is understood as a basic attitude or social cosmology in life and to life, the more demanding it becomes to make means "ends—in—the—making." On the other hand, nonviolence should never be watered down to just implying some kind of tool kit that can be tried here and there.

My own answer is that I would probably not pass many of the more serious tests of nonviolent living and thinking and being only motivated by serving others. Western man is not exactly known for humility and self-sacrifice, and I am one of them.

NONVIOLENCE AND CONFLICT RESOLUTION

Possibly with the exception of the IPRA Study Group on Nonviolence, it was a long time since I saw a solid scholarly and policy-oriented analysis which applied the principles of Satyagraha to conflicts in contemporary international system. In discussing the future of nonviolence, I think we must admit that the study of conflict resolution is relatively underdeveloped, particularly when it comes to theory, conceptualization, and operationalization. A kind of Bondurant study applied to the contemporary world is highly needed. This touch upon the "translation" problem that I shall take up later.

During the last few years, together with my colleagues, I have conducted conflict-mitigation work in all parts of ex-

Yugoslavia. The points I want to make are not very sophisticated nor theoretical. They revolve around issues I have come across time and again there and do not think any of us has any viable answers to a fact which causes death and human suffering even while we sit discussing it.

There is still so much to learn about (a) conflicts and (b) conflict resolution. Thus, for instance, can we learn and can we teach:

— that conflicts are essentially something good but enigmatic which help us preserve diversity and pluralism?

— that wars and other types of violence are indicative of negative or inefficient conflict resolution, no matter how successful they appear?

— that violence is a sign of powerlessness, no matter whether committed by "strong" or "weak" actors?

— that violence never solves a conflicts, although it may seem to manage it momentarily?

— that the use of violence is a sure method of letting all other options slip out of one's hand, i.e. a reduction in freedom of choice.

— that means and ends are inseparable and, therefore, violent methods will lead to resolutions based on, or imbued with, new or recurring violence?

— that positive or efficient conflict resolution takes place when the parties redistribute or share power in the sense of increasing the combined ability to getting things done in ways which are compatible with satisfying their needs in non-conflicting ways?

— that conflicts and ways of living with them and solving them are culture-specific?

— that nonviolence can be a universal norm, although we want cultural and political pluralism; and that there are basic values, although we are said to live in a post-modern world in which there are no general values, no common interpretation, and no truth (and certainly no Gandhian Truth) any more?

— or will we stay forever "conflict illiterate"?

Can nonviolent conflict resolution be taught or must it be learnt by doing? Does it demand a special personal transformation? The propensity to accept violence—threats as well as actual use—does not seem to vary with the level of formal education of the person. There is violence of the highly educated and the uneducated and there is nonviolence of the highly educated and the uneducated. What we do know is that it is countries with the most highly developed formal education which have committed the most structural and direct violence in history and are committing it right now.

My personal belief is that we can teach nonviolence, but we can be sure that people will learn it and practise it unless. I can best express what I think—and hope—about the future of (working for) nonviolence by referring to a statement by one of Europe's towering figures, Milovan Djilas, the first real dissidant who witnessed the breakdown of the Yugoslavia he devoted his life to. Milovan Djilas, whose main inspirations were Gandhian and Leninist, once, said, without any bitterness, about the guerrilla struggle in Yugoslavia against Hitler's Germany: "Had we known that what we did was impossible, we would never have succeeded."

Although it often looks to be the case, we cannot know that a nonviolent world is impossible. For me, that is where hope lies for our own small projects in peace research, education, and action, and for the world at large.

Chapter-9

Practical Nonviolent Responses to new Forms of Violence

A.T. Ariyaratne

Chapter-9

THE INTERNATIONAL HUMAN rights enumerated in the International Covenants of Civil and Political rights and of Economic, Social, and Cultural rights cover a very broad sweep of human life. In certain respects, they highlight the advances in human thinking about the conditions necessary for human beings to live a more truly human life. One has only to compare, for instance, the content of the present-day human rights covenants with the Code of Hammurabi in Babylonia or accounts of the amphitheater of the ancient Romans where the general public came to witness the most cruel killings of other human beings as a source of legitimate pleasure to see the immense progress that has been made in what humanity has now generally come to consider to be the ideal rights of all human beings.

Almost every government in the world has given its assent to the concept of human rights giving it a universality that is unprecedented in recorded human history. However, this leaves us with no room for complacency as the degree of suffering in the world is perhaps at a higher level now than at any time in the past. With the enormous increase in human population and the multiplication of the demands placed upon the environment by that population, or sections of that population, the level of violence in the world has registered a massive increase.

The gravity of this fact lies in the hidden dimension of the violence to be found in the world today. It is true that no human society will openly condone the imposition of suffering on other forms of life and openly derive pleasure from it as in the past. Of course, even this statement is debatable as we saw during the war prosecuted by the United Nations against Iraq. The truth is that as the world becomes ever more polarised between a global affluent and privileged minority and a poverty-stricken and powerless majority, new and hidden forms of violence are considered necessary by the former to keep the latter in check. As Mahatma Gandhi said some half a century go, "if true freedom were to come to India, the hovels of the poor and the palaces of the rich will not be able to coexist for even a moment." There is an appearance of freedom and democracy but the substance of it is drained away in unseen and hidden ways. Both subtle and crude forms of violence are the greatest violaters of human rights. Finding a nonviolent response to violence is our greatest challenge.

ALL-ENCOMPASSING VIOLENCE

What are these new forms of violence that impose unjust structures and unjust outcomes on others? We need to go back to the very definition of violence in order to understand what is sometimes not immediately visible to the eye. Any external factor interfering with the normal growth, functioning, and survival of a living organism can be broadly defined as violence. When human society was less sophisticated, we could have confined the meaning of violence to the inflicting of harm by human beings on other human beings in thought, word, or deed. To this type of personal violence, which imposes pain on mind and body we could have added structural forms of violence through social, economic, and political instruments of control. The most important characteristic of both these forms of personal and structural violence for our purposes was the ability to identify the person or group on whom the violence was imposed.

In the present day, however, the victim need not necessarily be an individual human being or a group. The victim of the new violence can be as small as a living cell or microorganism that has its integrity, which is the result of millions and billions of years of evolution, violated by the sophisticated instruments of modern science that probe it without having any comprehensive understanding of the probable outcome. On the other hand, the victim can be as big as the planet itself, including the entire biosphere, atmosphere and stratosphere which humanity is abusing in a manner unprecedented in history. To add to the complexity of the problem, the imposer of the violence and the victim are difficult to identify, and quite often they happen to be both the subject and object of violence.

Those of us who believe in Sarvodaya believe in a concept which is of Gandhian origin, meaning the wellbeing or awakening of all. Ours is a universal thought for the wellbeing of all life where personal and structural violence as well as identifiable and unidentifiable violence are neither condoned nor permitted. Our ideal is to create a human society where the human mind and the social, economic, and political institutions created by human beings and their relationship with Nature in its microscopic and macroscopic dimensions sustain themselves with the least opportunity for self-destruction. This demands a reappraisal of the Sarvodaya and Gandhian approaches to counter violence and to disseminate new thinking, techniques, and technologies.

FEAR PSYCHOSIS

Now I would briefly look at the situation in Sir Lanka as analysed by the Sarvodaya Shramadana Movement to which I belong and give a few examples of the processes we are trying to release to ensure peace within human personalities and human communities as also between human beings and Nature itself.

Sarvodaya has worked in the villages of Sri Lanka for over thirty-four years. At present we work in over 8,000 villages which constitute more than a third of the village communities in the country. Sarvodaya is involved in all aspects of community development under ten broad basic human needs. They are: environment, water, clothing, food, housing, health, energy, communication, education, and cultural and spiritual needs.

Sarvodaya means the awakening of all in every aspect of human life. We believe in six aspects of integrated development: at the levels of the human being, the family, the village and urban community, the national and the world community. These are the spiritual, moral, cultural, social, economic, and political aspects of life. For a world where peace, nonviolence, and justice will prevail, we believe that human beings and society should awaken simultaneously at all these levels.

However, the political and economic mismanagement of our

country since independence has resulted in an appalling degeneration of commonly accepted social norms and values which prevailed for at least the two millennia for which we have recorded history. The inevitable result is that in every profession, from teaching to farming and from religion to judiciary, there is a moral and spiritual decay in the quality of the personalities involved in those activities.

The ensuing frustration and desperation conspire to bring about a fear psychosis in which even homicidal tendencies become a means to survive. I will not say that everybody would take it that far. But certainly a substantial minority in Sri Lanka has already demonstrated a frightening capacity to resort to such actions in order to survive. The young people in the southern parts of the country who attempted twice to overthrow the prevailing system by violence and the militant youth and even children in the north who are still on the battlefield clearly demonstrate this fact. The equally harsh and more repressive instruments of official violence are just as much subjected to this fear psychosis and homicidal mania as their opponents. In the meanwhile, the vast majority of people, whatever their political or racial group, are enveloped in fear and even marginally become subscribers to these evil tendencies. The custodians of values, including the religious personalities, are no less victims of this total social malaise.

RULING COTERIES

In our societies the most powerful establishments for changing the course of society for better or worse in the short-term are the governments. Even though we call ourselves democratic countries, those who run governments are the political leaders and small coteries of their supporters. To varying degrees and perhaps at a much more intense level than those of others, the survival instinct and fear psychosis get control over them.

The Sarvodaya shramadana Movement is not functioning in a vacuum. We work in the reality of this environment. Thousands of our workers, spread across the length and breadth of the country, are a witness to the air bombings, cannon fire, landmine explosions, foot mines, disappearances, burnings on tyres, and unauthorised arrests—all of which constitute nothing but violence and human suffering. They also do witness the apparently carefree and happy-go-lucky affluent lifestyles of a minority who are insensitive to the realities of what is happening in the rest of the country. They zoom about in their air conditioned cars and enjoy sumptuous meals at five-star hotels as if these are normalities in everyone's life.

In this world of contrasts, of poverty and affluence, of fear and sensuality, any practical response with the intention of having an impact has to be manifold and all-embracing. The portfolio of activities should include the awakening of the personalities of unborn children to the creation of a popular mass of consciousness of the people in the country of critical proportions to enable them to realize the grave situation and the way out of it.

While the physical energies and resources of people and the remnants of sanity still prevailing in social structures are utilized to the maximum, the priority for Sarvodaya is creating a critical mass of spiritual consciousness. With extreme caution, the spiritual energies have to be differentiated and harnessed from religious resources, but taking care not to hurt the religious susceptibilities of people. A kind of socially engaged Buddhism, Hinduism, Islam, and Christianity have to be brought to the fore to get individuals, groups, and communities to practise meditation, cultivate respect for life, and radiate loving kindness far and wide.

Material resources have also to be harnessed and directed to bring about a realization of the utter futility of violence and the alternative sustainable social system that can be put into place by nonviolence. Satisfaction of basic, secondary, and tertiary human needs can be initiated by releasing processes through constructive nonviolent action, and participatory ad sustainable village-level socio-economic structures can be created so that democracy evolves from below rather than imposed from the top.

BACKLASH

Sarvodaya has initiated these processes in its three decades of work so that its presence as a nonviolent integrated movement for total change is being felt nationally. The surest indication is that in subtle and devious ways the government itself has launched an all-out attack on the movement and its leaders. Throughout our existence we have on occasions been at the receiving end of governmental displeasure. But in the last three years, this has reached an unprecedented level. I will not be exaggerating if I say that no other organization except one that has embedded itself in the people could have survived the government sponsored campaign of distortion and obstruction.

The first portent of things to come was when, within a week of the swearing in of the new President, I was interrogated by the chief of the National Intelligence Bureau. The weekly educational radio programme we had conducted for several years was suddenly stopped and TV and radio coverage of our activities was completely blacked out. Then using the excuse of the Presidential Commission to investigate NGOs, the police began to question our workers. Foreign funds pledged to us by donor agencies that also assist the government were blocked by the finance ministry.

This was followed by a calumnious campaign against Sarvdaya and myself personally in the largest circulation government-controlled newspaper in which, among other things, we were falsely accused of selling babies abroad for profit. In the middle of these attacks, my family and I began to receive anonymous death threats and we were followed by unidentified men in vehicles. A very large printing machine we had ordered to print low-cost books for the poor was confiscated by the custom authorities. The Central Bank stepped in to restrict our children's savings programme and rural savings and credit programme and ordered us to return our savings deposits. These are some of the highlights. There are a large number of other obstacles that have been put in our path.

INITIAL MEASURES

How are we going to face these new forms of violence which are intended to break our spirit and force us to acquiesce in the injustice that is rampant in our country? From our past experience we have learnt that when there is violence and injustice imposed on us, patiently continuing to do whatever work that can be done helps to diffuse the adversities and the work that was previously being obstructed can be continued. Of course, there is a waste of time and resources on account of the damage that would already have been done.

The injustice and violence have been imposed on us on account of the ignorance regarding the value of the work that we are doing. On the basis of that realization, we regard awareness creation and conscientization through educational programmes as having a very useful role to play. Once the ignorance is dispelled, the erstwhile opponent becomes friendly, subscribes to our ideals, and supports our work. But there are some who cannot be changed this way because they are quite aware of the valuable work that Sarvodaya is doing but still persist in wailfully obstructing our work. If they happen to be administrators working on the instigation of the political authorities and who know very well that they are working against the spirit of the law and justice, then another course of action has to be resorted to, that is, to take resort to courts of law to get justice.

During the present period, Sarvodaya has had to resort to this course of action owing to the continued injustices imposed on us by the abuse of power and vitiation of the law. The difficulty is that there are now an increasing number of laws that are no longer based on the principles of justice, but are drafted and legislated merely to suit the temporary convenience of the government. In a like manner, it is possible that judicial appointments will be made not on the basis of merit and justice but rather on the basis of the consideration to further the unjust purposes of the appointing authority. As a result, the general public is losing faith in the law and in the administration of justice. Still, one has to try it out. Only if we fail to get justice by resorting to legal institutions will the next course of action have to be considered. For a nonviolent revolutionary movement like Sarvodaya, this is nonviolent direct action.

However, unlike during the times of Mahatma Gandhi when he launched his nonviolent satyagraha campaign against the British rule in India, at the present time the nonviolent direct action has to be directed against rulers who are a part of the general population of the country. They have used and misused the democratic processes in both a subtle and crude manner and claim democratic legitimacy for their tyrannical attitude toward their opponents. They believe that their election victories give them the right to define their own rules in their own interests. For instance, they have created and used illegal goon squads to intimidate, kidnap, torture, and kill dissenters even if they were unarmed and nonviolent. Therefore to resort to nonviolent direct action is more difficult today than it was during Gandhi's time.

FINAL OPTION

Under today's circumstances, the votaries of nonviolence and social justice have to depend almost exclusively on the spiritual consciousness they can awaken within themselves. They have to aggregate these energies into a critical mass capable of affecting the mass psyche of the general population. The external manifestations of such a course of spiritual action that is directed to bringing about a change will manifest itself in the form of fearlessness and sacrifice.

The final possibility that is open to Sarvodaya is direct political action. Although Sarvodaya does not believe in power and party politics and has stayed away from it ever since its inception, this very system has caused and is causing untold damage to its work. Now the presser regime has launched an all-out attack to make the movement ineffective and destroy it completely. But people in thousands of Sarvodaya villages want Sarvodaya to exist and succeed. The peoples' strength of the organization has in recent years expanded as a result of the oppression the movement has been subjected to. Therefore it has become both necessary and possible to confront the unjust and violent power and party political system by people's power and replace it by a participatory alternative system of politics. Sarvodaya has decided to take to this kind of political action if all other efforts to bring about sanity and justice do not succeed.

The Goal

Among the objectives of such a political campaign will be:

(i) to introduce nonviolence and justice as the fundamental value systems into the political life of the country.

(ii) to disband the highly concentrated political and economic centres at the top of the hierarchy and re-establish village-level political authorities ensuring protection of people's lives, their properties, life support systems, and the environment,

(iii) to ensure the justice of laws affecting the general population as against the discriminatory legislation that protects he privileges of a few,

(iv) to ensure the freedom and integrity of the judiciary and non-interference with the administration of justice,

(v) to re-establish the dignity and worth of civil servants to function under the law without duress or interference from the political authorities,

(vi) to ensure the freedom of the press and media so that they can play an independent and investigative role befitting a participatory democracy,

(vii) to promote a true open economy in which the private sector, the public corporation sector, and the nongovernmental and cooperative sector are given equal opportunities and incentives for production, marketing, and financial and resource management, and

(viii)to promote the evolution of a democratic political system from below where the ultimate objective of an enlightened Sri Lankan community with diverse cultures but equality before law is achieved.

Under the existing constitutional and political realities in

Sri Lanka, these objectives cannot be achieved without confronting party political politicians and their institutions. However, the objective of the confrontation is not to grab power. It is to ensure the achievement of the objectives sketched out above. Therefore, Sarvodaya has decided to form a political organization and get it registered under the Commissioner of elections so that if the present regime continues, it can be challenged electorally.

I have concentrated on the tragic issues directly affecting human life in Sri Lanka and the immediate sociopolitical issues relating to the need for a nonviolent alternative. This does not mean that we should give less importance to the violence inflicted upon our life support systems by inappropriate applications of science and technology. Violence done to living cells, to human beings, and to the planet as a living organism should also be our constant concern.

Chapter-10

Teaching History in the Framework of a Problem-Based Peace Education

Antonino Drago

Chapter-10

THE MOTIVATIONS: THE EXPERIENCE OF THE ITALIAN GROUP OF NONVIOLENT TEACHERS

MY MOTIVATION FOR the following study was born in a little group of nonviolent teachers that faced basic problems in peace education along fifteen years.

When in 1976 the Italian government discussed for the first time a plan for nuclear power, the group was born by studying the energy problem. By looking for a natural way to link education to such a great problem, the group experienced that a radical change in the teachings of both physics and chemistry is possible, by centering both upon the above basic problems.[1]

The subject-matter of geography also has been reshaped by putting as its crucial problem the following one: "what is the geography of mankind and its environment?" A suggestive answer was a book which took the function of a textbook in many schools.[2]

Further, in 1980 in Italy too arose the peace movement about the problem of the new escalation in the arms race (Cruise missiles). In order to offer an adequate teaching about this problem, the group of nonviolent teachers collected suggestions for a new didactics. A surprising result was that mathematics teaching also may be centered upon a problem, i.e., the problem of understanding arms race in a scientific way by means of graphs, game theory, analytical geometry, algebraic equations, and statistics. As a result, they edited a book on such materials for a suggestive new didactics of mathematics.[3]

Some more experience may be added with reference to several subject-matters. But in this list a very important subject-matter is lacking: history. Many new proposals may look as suggestive,[4] but they do not represent really new solutions for peace education. We have to conclude that in history teaching war is rooted more deeply than in other subject-matters.

History Teaching as Violence Teaching

Really, a moment of reflection on its nature suggests that in traditional education, history teaching results as violence teaching.

There exist two main philosophies about the nature of our society. The first one is called "organistic" which sees society as an organism where any part is harmoniously and hierarchically linked to any other part. In this philosophy, the conflict is meant as an illness to be isolated and to be banished. The second one is called "conflictual" because conflict is considered as an essential component of the social organization and harmony in society is considered merely the target of a voluntary effort.

In the last few decades, many analyses stressed that the traditional approach to peace essentially follows the organistic philosophy. Peace is conceived as negative peace. On the contrary, a notion of positive peace is suggested by a conflictual philosophy, which only may stress the processes for achieving peace as well as the methodologies to be learnt for such an aim.

In particular, confictual philosophy suggests a straightforward way of discovering the innovative content of peace education with respect to the traditional education: one has to ask in what way and to what extent conflicts are taken into account by the particular sector of traditional theory we are investigating. We will follow such an attitude for the case of history teaching.

The traditional teaching of history may be characterized by answering the following question concerning the relationships of the whole set of subject-matters with the conflicts: "by what subject-matters does school teach how pupils could solve conflicts?" As a first approximation, the answer is: "by no one." The standard content of any subject-matter presents neither alternatives nor disputes to be solved by pupils. The most peaceful subject-matter is mathematics: it presents a world where never a conflict is considered; the only conflict occurring in it is a wrong result in calculations; but a new control of the rules to be followed offers the path for gaining peace with himself as well as with the teacher.

Really, in the highschools the philosophy teaching illustrates many conflicts. But there, not persons but ideas only are shocking to one another. As a whole, the cultural world of traditional teaching appears to a pupil as a very attractive world, just because in it conflicts are lacking or at worse they are reduced to merely intellectual conflicts. This kind of education fits an organistic view of reality.

However, as a second approximation, we have to give an opposite answer to the above question. Traditional teaching appears to be highly conflicutal, inasmuch as it presents to pupils a lot of wars. Moreover, it does teach to solve conflicts in a huge way. Indeed, the subject-matter of history teaching essentially says that "wars ever occurred and ever they will occur, no hope to escape from such a destiny of mankind." The subsequent ethical teaching which is addressed to the pupil is the worst once: "Introduce yourself in the cultural world because you see that it is a peaceful world. Yet you must remember that the real world ever presents conflicts and wars, and the only way for solving them is at last the suppression of the opponent. It is just for this reason, if no others, that you must introduce yourself in the privileged world of the culture; indeed culture will give to you a soft way for finding out suitable solutions as well as it will give you a powerful social position which at last will enable you to solve your social conflicts by social power." History teaching ideologizes such an attitude by presenting as exemplary behaviours of those past dominant persons.

In this sense, history teaching constitutes the ideological core of the process of education. It suggests to pupils to reach an organistic community even at the cost of solving conflicts by a "right" violence. As a matter of fact, in the next life of a pupil, education is the most important tool for gaining the highest levels in the social pyramid: thus, to gain culture constitutes an indirect—but highly effective—way for participating in, perpetuating and justifying social power, both inside the society and between nations, namely for justifying the violence of social system.[5]

We must reach to such implicit message of traditional education, otherwise our peace education will collapse into educating the future violent men to a mere fairly.[6]

The Randomness of Wars against the Traditional Methodology of History Teaching

More generally, an analysis of the methodology of history teaching shows that although it has been long studied today, it has to be refound anew. Peace education may offer a new way for such a refinding.

But before changing something we have to know it in details. The traditional teaching of history is well-known. The life of mankind is summarized in the history of some prominent populations; and moreover, dynasties and wars are the main events, because they are meant as the decisive events which everyone of the population of those times shared. In fact, the easy way for justifying such a method is to stress that even when we are remembering our own lives, we organize all events around the decisive or traumatic events in which we may have participated.

As a matter of fact, in our century we cumulated a science of war which gives us some surprising suggestions, largely ignored by history teachers.[7] Among many sophisticated contributions, I select from the mathematics of war a particularly simple study. Quincy Wright first computed the distributions of wars with respect to any relevant parameter (the time interval between two subsequent wars, the number of casualties, etc).[8] It is a shocking fact that any such distribution results to be of the Poissonian kind, i.e., the same distribution holding true for random phenomena. Why the distribution of wars represents nothing of the great values by which people sacrifice themselves? Why the distribution of wars represents no mankind's progress, if not the progress in the number of casualties?

By a more accurate inspection, we discover that wars' distributions are meaningful along a time period greater than 30-50 years (this period is determined essentially by the frequency of wars in the world). Then, the single man lives, years after year, the subjective great ideals—or strong instinctive compulsions—which lead him to fight and to sacrifice himself; while the scientific vision of history along at least a half-century period suggests just what old men emphasized in any times; i.e., wars are irrational in nature. In the present century, our experience of wars constitutes a strong confirmation of such an irrationality. The greatest enemies of the present times (e.g. the USA and the former USSR) were allied in the last war; moreover, the enemies of the last war were allied in the previous one (e.g. Italy and France). We must conclude that in fact the objective, universal knowledge that mankind built, i.e. science, when applied to wars, results in some answers which are at variance with subjective feelings.

Only one conclusion is possible about history teaching and it is the following one: the teaching of secular and millennary history by means of war events amounts to following a zig-zag path with respect to the real history of mankind. In other words, science tells us that the history of wars is not relevant to the real evolution of mankind and hence to the education of new generations.

Beyond the Revolution of the "Annales"

In fact in the last decades, the methodology of history teaching slowly changed under the suggestions of the group of the *Annales,* a well-known historical French review. By following it, a teacher emphasize social life rather than international conflicts. People's life is presented as the basic fact in the history of mankind and is more important to feel what is the true life in the past times at issue than some objective facts say a war, which to people's life gave external constraints only.

The suggestions amount to a reversal of the traditional attitude. Indeed, present-day textbooks on history are inflated by documents on customs of ancient populations, while dynasties and wars stand as the background to the lively daily mutual interactions of the people. The large extension of the set of examined events motivates pupils to study in a new way, i.e., as a research on ever new events for discovering new interesting features of people's past life.

However, such a new methodology is addressed to past times. Since fifty years our history has become dependent on worldwide politics. Today any relevant problem pertains to the world scale. In history textbooks, nuclear war, ecological problems, and North-South relationships are rarely examined. They are at most merely explored by considering them as conflicts subordinate to traditional ones. Unfortunately, all the latter conflicts always allowed destructive solutions, i.e., just the solutions that we are obliged today to banish for ever in order that mankind can survive. By a milennary work mankind enlarged the domain of his self-consciousness; it progressed from that of a little group to that of a people to that of a nation and, since some decades, mankind started to acquire to conscience at the level of the world community. However, even the most advanced textbooks of history seldom deal with that history after 1945, the time when the new self-consciousness arose. We can conclude that they are late with respect to the new historical facts, in particular to just those facts which are decisive for educating conscientious citizens of the world. Today the enlargement of the pupil's horizon is necessity. Not to take into account such a fact would condemn the consciousness of pupils to be blind, like that the consciousness of a dictatorship would desire to impose itself on its subordinate population.

The methodology of "Annales" does not offer clear answers to the present-day conflicts which very often question the mind of a pupil as a consequence of the new world consciousness. It is for this reason that the revolution in history teaching suggested by the "Annales" is unsatisfactory and has to be overcome.

It is necessary to find out a new collective consciousness able to overcome present-day world conflicts. Such a new consciousness has to include the past consciousness—the religious, the classical—liberal, and the Marxist one-as particular cases, i.e., as incomplete consciousness with respect to world conflicts.

Rightly, people today want peace education; only it may

suggest a new history teaching. It stresses not a destructive but a constructive attitude in history and in society. Moreover, it rejects the ordering role wars in the played in traditional methodology. Such a role is played rather by such great problems like peace-asking for constructive, collective solutions.

CONSTRUCTING A HISTORY TEACHING BY FOUNDING IT UPON A MAIN PROBLEM

Problem-based Education vs. Education by Means of Principles

A peace attitude in education puts as first problem the growth of persons rather than intellectual targets. Hence pedagogy is the first problem rather than methodology. Let us inquire into the former discipline.

In the nineteenth century, Western society started an education system by means of the pedagogy of T. Ziller, a fellow of the philosopher Herbart.[9] According to such a pedagogy, a pupil is "an empty sack to be filled up." In order to maximize the lot of knowledge to fill in the sack, one has to compact what has to be learned by the pupil. The more synthetic way to accomplish such a task is to synthesize any subject-matter to a least number of sharp definitions and principles. In such a way, all notions are linked together in a preconceived system and they follow in an objective, definite way from the premises. Of course, such an organization is acquired first of all by the mind of the teacher—the very principle of the learning process. Such a process is accomplished when pupils' minds to achieve such an organization. No inquiry, no invention, no discussion is allowed, if it is not for making the learning process more adequate and quick. In my opinion, such a pedagogy is highly authoritarian in character.

In opposition to such a static pedagogy, a dynamic pedagogy stresses pupil's learning process which is unavoidably problem-based. In order to perform an intelligent work, a teacher has to present to pupils a main problem whose method of solution promises to solve many more problems. In such a way, a pupil dismisses abstract principles but looks for acquiring a general method of solutions. In order for the pupil to be motivated for solving problems, the main problem has to be so general as to involve the teacher, even in the sense that he is not able to offer a unique solution for it. In this way only the learning process is a collective process, where no authoritarian position is allowed and where the field of research includes personal beliefs as well as characteristic features of society.[10]

The Main Problem in Present-day History and its Potential Solution by Peace Education

What is a candidate for representing the main problem of peace education?

Peace—meant as a problem—emphasizes that in the world the arms race menaces mankind by the casualty of a suicidal, collective act. In any case, it condemns mankind to an observe effort which today converts great resources from the satisfaction of the basic needs of populations.

Such a problem is a crucial one in the present-day situation of mankind. Such a problem has no easy solution, neither the teacher may offer an absolutely right solution, even when he is the best nonviolent teacher. Moreover, it receives no easy solution in the intellectual tradition, because in the present time mankind faces a very new threat. Hence we are pushed to ask: "what education for the survival of mankind in such a conflictual world?" Many more problems of the same relevance may be listed (hunger in the world, ecological problems, kind of progress, kind of economics, etc). We can reasonably hope that to find a solution for the first, one can address oneself to solve the other problems.

Here is apparently a possible answer for education: we have to educate pupils for solving international conflicts without destroying mankind, or better, without destruction of the conflicting persons. This will be the real first task of any pupil when he becomes an adult person, i.e., a full member of mankind. This kind of teaching is the real task of peace education when the notion of peace is meant in a positive way and it is applied to world conflicts.

Past religions all contributed to such an aim. Nevertheless, an analysis of our intellectual tradition gives a surprising result, inasmuch as conflicts and their ways of solution have been seldom theorized. Our intellectual tradition appeals at last to the instinctual solution, i.e., the physical destruction of the opponent by depicting him as an irreducible enemy. To start to think of conflicts by means of not destructive solutions constitutes a very few foundation of our whole cultural tradition. The main task of peace educators is that of reshaping our traditional culture as a collective self-consciousness of the greatest conflicts we are faced with the potentialities for solving them.

The New Meaning to be Attributed to History Teaching

An easy objection is the following one: "why you want to look for solutions to greatest problems when even the least ones may be very difficult?" Really, it is just an objection which constrained traditional education to confine itself to only individual and national problems. Under a general setting, one may answer this objection by recalling that the very characteristic of a man is his capability of enlarging his conscience in order to look at his problems from a general viewpoint. In society education essentially represents such an effort of enlargement of consciousness to a world scale. As teachers, we are forced to follow the process of enlargement of consciousness to a world scale. Really—and this is the most appropriate answer—the subjective conscience may differ from a world-scale conscience in the same way that the vision of our own eyes differs from the ideas of our mind. Let us remember that we see the round Earth as flat. As an example of the difference between the two kinds of consciences about historical facts concerning great problems, let us remember that in the above we examined the statistical history of wars and we obtained a surprising result for a subjective conscience. A similar intellectual opposition between subjective conscience and world-scale conscience may be obtained about the other kinds of world conflicts.

As a matter of fact, just such a difference in conscience is the point Gandhi stressed in our century. The Machiavellian policy represents the viewpoint of a restricted conscience. This is the same point which peace education supports for assuring mankind's future, namely a comprehensive viewpoint to find out new solutions—the nondestructive ones—to the greatest problems at a world scale which we see so often solved by destructive means.

According to a problem-based teaching, history teaching now starts from the contemporary time for overseeing the present situation, recognizing a main problem, stating it in a sharp and appealing way, and then just asking past history about both what causes occasioned the present situation and what suggestions past events teach us for overcoming our problems.[11] Hence, there is no abstract study, no appeal to exotic old populations, no imaginative pictures of past times-on the contrary, only the maximum of adequacy to the present life of mankind.

As a second consequence, inasmuch present problems pertain to the world scale, history teaching becomes a worldwide study, no more restricted to a nationalistic or a regional viewpoint. Its main intellectual task is to stress the differences between a subjective conscience and a world-scale conscience. As a result, inasmuch it is able to suggest solutions to our greatest problems, history becomes again a "teacher of life" (*historia magistra vitae*).

As a third consequence, history teaching merges a pupil in the flux of history as it is perceived by the people of our country and becomes a collective task for achieving collective aims. In other words, both problems and solutions will be either collective in nature or they will not be. By this change of attitude, history is no more a deterministic history. It becomes a theater of interacting social forces which at last shape the new directions of development for the populations. History teaching becomes a teaching for doing history, not for contemplating it or, worse, for being submitted to it—like the past history teaching does.

As a fourth consequence, history teaching becomes an inquiry into the past times for solving clear problems-first of all, for discovering the traditional causes of our situation, both the cultural causes and the institutional causes. Accordingly, th ehistorical method of inquiry becomes of the highest relevance in such a new history. Furthermore, in such a way history's study is an open study even at the lower levels of education-not only memory's efforts and a list of caricatura stories, but a creative effort for inquiring past events for how they are linked to today's life.

The Liberations, the Revolutions, the Myths

From the above viewpoint, what historical events become the essential ones for history teaching—the history of the past fifty years, for achieving a better knowledge of the main problems of the present society? What options in past times led to the present situation? What alternatives were possible? What struggles arose about such options? What solutions they received? What among the past solutions is living today? What perspective of development they suggest?

Being as we are under a crucial threat, the main experience to be learnt from history is the experience of the liberation processes. Indeed, we have to take into account that even in the past times mankind solved great collective problems (although without a collective consciousness). We may study them for confronting the present situation as well as for investigating past solutions. By such historical investigations, we give an orientation to the conscience of the pupil for knowing to what collective work he has to contribute. I can list the following as mankind's past problems and the corresponding liberation processes which are relevant to our purposes:

(i) the liberation of the slaves, in the antiquity and in modern times;
(ii) the liberation from colonialism;
(iii) the liberation of the workers;
(iv) the liberation of citizens from an absolutistic State (French revolution);
(v) the women's liberation;
(vi) the liberation from social myths (absolutistic religion, nationalisms, western world's supremacy, scientism,

and progressism, exclusively destructive defence).

I have illustrated such themes of great relevance elsewhere.[12] Here I would confine myself to some remarks.

The above themes mix past liberation movements with present-day ones (e.g. women's liberation). I think this feature to be a very fortunate one for putting the pupil in the middle of a flux in which actually he is living. Moreover, it is a fortunate result that in such a way we can cover the common programme of history teaching, i.e., the long series of events elongating since ancient times till the twentieth century. Hence the suggestion of a radical alternative in history teaching does not lead us to forget our traditional history. On the contrary, it re-organizes it around great themes or great problems. Hence no fear to be not able to teach a minimum number of crucial dates as well s a minimum number of crucial events of past history. A large part of the traditional programme is recuperated.

The Word "Nonviolence" as Expressing a Problem

However, we have to recognize that in the history of western society, such liberation processes—in as much they lacked a collective consciousness—proceeded in a slow, uncertain, and very difficult way. The resulting image of past history is discouraging pupils, unless we add to it the collective actions by which, in Western society, people tried to gain new social conditions by means of a sharp collective consciousness. In this respect I suggest to add two more episodes: (i) Joachim a flower and St. Francis as an alternative to the trend then followed by Western society; and (ii) the Gandhian movement as the best example of people's conquest of a great historical target. The last movement deserves a particular attention because it is most enlightening to the consciousness of the history of our century.

In a previous section, we concluded that the meaning of history is not given by wars which, on the contrary, misled our minds in a tragic way. Actually in our century a man succeeded to obtain without wars what in the past required a huge number of casualties. Gandhi gave an example of a new consciousness of our history. We can look for a new way of solving collective problems by following his main teaching, i.e., "nonviolence." But the price for being introduced to such a new perspective is to be able to make such a word meaningful. Here I will offer a new solution.

Anyone, when faced with an event of violence, feels in his conscience an appeal to negate violence. Hence we must emphasize that in the word "nonviolence", "violence" stresses a negative value, to be meant as "no-lie."

Traditional logic suggests to us to eliminate the double negation. But such an operation results in suggesting words like "life," "peace," "patience," "tameness" and so on—all unsatisfactory words, inasmuch they are static words; i.e., they do not give the idea of a conflict. Instead, in the word "nonviolence," such conflict is represented both by the word violence" and by "non" which negates it. hence the word "nonviolence" as a double negative word is adequate for presenting what here is the most important point, i.e., a problem. The problem is the following one: in what way we may overcome conflicts without doing violence to the opponents.

In other words, "nonviolence" expresses just such a problem—and not an idea, an ideal target, an absolute, a programme for our behavior, a fixed method, a technique and so on—rather, all these meanings attempting to give a positive content to the idea obscure the conflict and so miss the real point.

We may conclude that it is typical of nonviolence to put no abstract principles but hard problems and hence to stimulate anyone for new solutions.[13] Let us remember that even many statements of the most famous pedagogical teachings, i.e, the ten commandments, are falsely meant as absolutistic orders by a supreme authority. If such an interpretation was right, the history of mankind would be full of punishments. On the contrary, the ten commandments represent problems, very often by double negative statements. For example, "thou don't kill" is composed by a negation "don't" and by a negative, repugnant idea "kill." In other words, God did not speak to minor ages but to adult persons that everyday face some problems, and He suggested to follow a highly problematic direction: to base life upon the effort of never to resort to kill someone.

All the above substantiate the initial claim of the present paper, according to which a new history teaching amounts to a whole paradigm shift. Really we discovered that by putting not wars but problems as central notions of history teaching, we can achieve just that new education which peace education is urged to offer to people for acting for mankind's survival. At last, such a new approach to history teaching is able to make clear the notion of nonviolence which synthesizes the best experience of peace education in all times.

Notes and Reences

1. Antonino Drago: "Two Ways to Link Science Teaching to Disarmament Education," in M. Haavelsrud ed., *Approaching Disarmament Education* (Wesbury House, 1980), pp. 71-80.
2. G. Martirani, *Geografia come educazione alla pace e allo sviluppo,* Ed. Dehoniane, Napoli, 1982. See also G. Martirani: "Peace Education as Self-Education," *Gandhi Marg* (1986).
3. Coordinamento Insegnanti Nonviolenti: Matematica della guerra, ed. Gruppo Abele, Torino, 1987.
4. I know the Italian debate. G. Bonetta: "La storia storicista serve sempre meno," *Riforma della Scuola,* n. 2 (1989) 24-31; E. Butturini: "Ricerca sul passato, coscienza di complesita. Per un insegnamento di storia che educhi alla pace", *Note Mazziane,* marzo 1988, 10-15; G. Traniello: "Storia ed educazione alla pace", in AA. VV., Una scuola di pace, LDC, Torino, 1988, 5-11.
5. I developed such ideas in "Pedagogia nonviolenta come educazione al conflitto", *Servire* 33 (1979), pp. 25-37.
6. Such a radical view is expressed in my paper "Education a la paix pour la refonte de l'ecole", *Pourquoi?,* October 1986, pp. 18-22.
7. I remember, for example, the game theory. A prominent text is A. Rapoport, *Strategy and Consciousness* (Harper and Row,

1964). Here I do not refer to science as a whole; instead I appeal to alternative science, in the meaning I illustrated in "What Science for Peace?" *Gandhi Marg, 7* (1986), 733-742, and in a more detailed way in "An Effective Definition of Incommensurability," VIII Int. *Congr. Logic Phil. Meth. of Sci., Moscow,* 1987, vol. 4, pt. I, 159-162 and in C. Cellucci et alii (eds.): *Temi e prospetive della Logica e della Filosofia della Scienza Contemporanea,* (CLUEB, Bologna, 1988, Vol. II, 117-120). An interesting result of such viewpoint is the discovery of a physical theory of defence: "Mecanique et Defense dans la pensee de lazare Cannot". J.P. Charnay (ed.): *Lazare Carnot cu le savant-citoyen,* Presses Universitaires Paris-Sorbonne, 1990, 557-576.

8. In J.R. Newmann: *The World of Mathematics* (Simon and Schuster, 1956), Vol. II, pp. 1254-63.
9. Not so many books on the history of pedagogy tell us such remarkable facts. I know it from D. Lindenberg: *Is'internationale socialiste et l'ecole de classe,* Maspero, 1971.
10. I found such a dichotomy in the case of scientific theories which falsely are meant as organized exclusively in a deductive, axiomatic way. Classical chemistry, L. Carnot's mechanics, S. Carnot thermodynamics, Marx' political economy are examples of such a problematic organization. Antnino Drago, "The Relationship between Chemistry and Mathematics," *Fres. J. Anal. Chem.,* 337 (1990), pp. 220-24. At the origins the deductive way of learning and reasoning has been theorized by Aristotle in *analytica Posteriora.*
11. In Italy such a suggestion has been advanced first by the alternative school of Barbiana: Scuola di Barbiana: *Lettera an una professoressa,* LEF, Florence, 1967. A similar further suggestion is that by A. Dogliotti Marasso: "Insegnamento della storia ed educazione alla pace," *Il foglio,* n. 157 (1988), pp. 4-5.
12. Antonino Drago: "Un nuovo insegnamento della storia," *Quale-vita,* (1989), pp. 8-9.
13. By studies in history of science I recognized that any alternative theory has been based upon a double negative

statement which in this way puts a main problem and stuggests the search for a suitable method for solving it.. See "A new way of reasoning as suggested by some theories of classical physics," submitted to *J. Phil Logic.* In "From Newton to Hegel via Berkeley and L. Carnot," M. Petry (ed.): *Hegel and Newtonianism* (in press), I recognized the origin of such a way of structuring a scientific thoery in Leibniz' philosophy. It is interesting that the whole strategic thinking may be synthosized by the statement: "*It is not true that to fight a war is not a civil work,*" which has been interpreted in several ways by the most prominent strategists. See my "Entropia e difesa," in Antonino Drago, ed., *Una strategia di pace: la difesa popolare nonviolenta,* LDC, Torino (in press).

Chapter-11

Civil Disobedience

Henry David Thoreau

Chapter-11

It is intriguing to think that Thoreau's arrest for not paying his Massachusetts poll tax and his subsequent one, night stay in jail may have caused him to write his most famous essay "Civil Disobedience." However, we know that the reasons for writing the essay (he composed it first as a lecture titled "The Rights and Duties of the Individual in Relation to Government," and later retitled to "Resistance to Civil Government" for publication in the *Aesthetic Papers*. May 1849) go much deeper into the convictions of the man than the influence of an arrest and one night in jail.

Being a peace-loving citizen and an abolitionist, Thoreau refused to support the Mexican War, which in his mind was not only the government's interference with an individual's personal liberty, but was also a war of expansionism which threatened to add new slave states to the Union. He proclaimed, therefore, his one man, nonviolent rebellion against the government by refusing to pay his tax. His protect did not go unnoticed. One story—perhaps apocryphal—relates that Reliph Waldo Emerson went to jail and asked Thoreau, "Henry, why are you here?" The reply was immediate, "Why are you not here?" Many contemporary followers of this type of civil disobedience ask the same question of observers who watch as they fill the jails for a cause of conscience. Thus it is apparent that although Thoreau's protest was a particular one in its reference to the Mexican War and slavery, it is still universal in its meaning and application to other persons, in other places, and at other times in history. The most outstanding example of this is Gandhi, who when asked whether he had read Thoreau, responded with bright eyes and a chuckle, "Why, of course I read Thoreau."

I heartily accept the motto, "That government is best which governs least"; and I should like to see it acted up to more rapidly and systematically. Carried out, it finally amounts to this, which also I believe, "That government is best which governs not at all"; and when men are prepared for it, that will be the kind of government which they will have. Government is at best but an expedient; but most governments are usually, and all governments are sometimes, inexpedient. The objections which have been brought against a standing army, and they are many and weighty, and deserve to prevail, may also at last be brought against a standing government. The standing army is only an arm of the standing government. The government itself, which is only the mode which the people have chosen to execute their will, is equally liable to be abused an perverted before the people can act through it. Witness the present Mexican war, the work of comparatively a few individuals using the standing government as their tool; for, in the outset, the people would not have consented to this measure.

This American government—what is but a tradition, though a recent one, endeavoring to transmit itself unimpaired to posterity, but each instant losing some of its integrity? It has not the vitality and force of a single living man; for a single man can bend it to his will. It is a sort of wooden gun to the people themselves. But it is not the less necessary for this; for the people must have some complicated machinery or other, and hear its din, to satisfy that idea of government which they have. Governments show thus how successfully men can be imposed on, even impose on themselves, for their own advantage. It is excellent, we must all allow. Yet this government never of itself furthered any enterprise, but by the alacrity with which it got out of it way. *It* does not keep the country free. *It* does not settle the West. *It* does not educate. The character inherent in the American people has done all that has been accomplished; and it would have done somewhat more, if the government had not sometimes got in his way. For government is an expedient by which men would fain succeed in letting one another alone; and, as has been said, when it is most expedient, the governed are most let alone by it. Trade and commerce, if they were not made of India—rubber, would never manage to bounce over the obstacles which legislators are continually putting in their way; and, if one were to judge these men wholly by the effects of their actions and not partly by their intentions, they would deserve to be classed and punished with those mischievous persons who put obstructions on the railroads.

But, to speak practically and as a citizen, unlike those who call themselves no—government men, I ask for, not at once no government, but *at once* a better government. Let every man make known what kind of government would command his respect, and that will be one step toward obtaining it.

After all, the practical reason why, when the power is once in the hands of the people, a majority are permitted, and for a long period continue, to rule is not because they are most likely to be in the right, nor because this seems fairest to the minority, but because they are physically the strongest. But a government in which the majority rule in all cases cannot be based on justice, even as far as men understand it. Can there not be a government in which majorities do not virtually decide right and wrong, but conscience? in which majorities decide only those questions to which the rule of expediency is applicable? Must the citizen ever for a moment, or in the least degree, resign his conscience to the legislator? Why has every man a conscience, then? I think that we should be men first, and subjects afterward. It is not desirable to cultivate a respect for the law, so much as for the right. The only obligation which I have a right to assume is to do at any time what I think right. It is truly enough said, that a corporation has no conscience; but a corporation of conscientious men is a corporation *with* a conscience. Law never made men a whit more just; and, by means of their respect for it, even the well—disposed are daily made the agents of injustice. A common and natural result of an undue respect for law is, that you may see a file of soldiers, colonel, captain, corporal, privates, powder—monkeys, and all, marching in admirable order over hill and dale to the wars, against their wills, against their common sense and consciences, which makes it very steep marching indeed, and produces a palpitation of the heart. They have no doubt that it is a damnable business in which they are concerned; they are all peaceably inclined. Now, what are they? Men at all? or small movable forts and magazines, at the service of some unscrupulous man in power? Visit the Navy Yard, and behold a marine, such a man as an American government can make, or such as it can make a man with its black arts—a mere shadow and reminiscence of humanity, a man laid out alive and standing, and already, as one may say, buried under arms with funeral accompaniments, though it may be,

Not a drum was heard, not a funeral note,
As his corpse to the rampart we hurried;
Not a soldier discharged his farewell shot
O'er the grave where our hero we buried.

The mass of men serve the state thus, not as men mainly, but as machines, with their bodies. They are the standing army, and the militia, jailors, constables, posse comitatus, etc. In most cases there is no free exercise whatever of the judgment or of the moral sense; but they put themselves on a level with wood and earth and stones; and wooden men can perhaps be manufactured that will serve the purpose as well. Such command no more respect than men of straw or a lump of dirt. They have the same sort of worth only as horses and dogs. You such as these even are commonly esteemed good citizens. Others——as most legislators, politicians, lawyers, ministers, and office—holders—serve the state chiefly with their heads; and, as they rarely make any moral distinctions, they are as likely to serve the Devil, without *intending* it, as God. A very few, as heroes, patriots, martyrs, reformers in the great sense, and *men*, serve the state with their consciences also, and so necessarily resist it for the most part; and they are commonly treated as enemies by it. A wise man will only be useful as a man, and will not submit to be "clay," and "stop a hole to keep the wind away," but leave that office to his dust at least:

I am too high-born to be propertied,
To be a secondary at control,
Or useful serving-man and instrument
To any sovereign state throughout the world.

He who gives himself entirely to his fellow-men appears to them useless and selfish; but he who gives himself partially to them is pronounced a benefactor and philanthropist.

How does it become a man to behave towards this American government today? I answer, that he cannot without disgrace be associated with it. I cannot for an instant recognize that political organization as *my* government which is the *slave's* government also.

All men recognize the right of revolution; that is, the right to refuse allegiance to, and to resist, the government, when tyranny any or its inefficiency are great and unendurable. But almost all say that such is not the case now. But such was the case, they think, in the Revolution of '75. If one were to tell me that this was a bad government because it taxed certain foreign commodities brought to its ports, it is most probable that I should not make an ado about it, for I can do without them. All machines have their friction; and possibly this does enough good to counterbalance the evil. At any rate, it is a great evil to make a stir about it. But when the friction comes to have its machine, and comppression and robbery are organized, I say, let us not have such a machine any longer. In other words, when a sixth of the population of a nation which has undertaken to be the refuge of liberty are slaves, and a whole country is unjustly overrun and conquered by a foreign army, and subjected to military law, I think that it is not too soon for honest men to rebel and revolutionize. What makes this duty the more urgent is the fact that the country so overrun is not our own, but ours is the invading army...

A drab of state, a cloth-o-silver slut,
To have her train borne up, and her should trail in the
dirt.

Practically speaking, the opponents to a reform in Massachusetts are not a hundred thousand politicians at the South, but a hundred thousand merchants and farmers here, who are more interested in commerce and agriculture than they are in humanity, and are not prepared to do justice to the slave and to Mexico, *cost what it may*. I quarrel not with far-off foes, but with those who, near at home, co-operate with, and do the bidding of, those far away, and without whom the latter would be harmless. We are accustomed to say, that the mass of men are unprepared; but improvement is slow, because the few are not materially wiser or better than the many. It is not so important that many should be as good as you, as that there be some absolute goodness somewhere; for that will leave the whole lump. There are thousands who are *in opinion* opposed to slavery and to the war, who yet in effect do nothing to put an end to them; who, esteeming themselves children of Washington and Franklin, sit down with their hands in their pockets, and say that they know not what to do, and do nothing; who even postpone the question of freedom to the question of free trade, and quietly read the prices-current along with the latest advices from Mexico, after dinner, and, it may be, fall asleep over them both. What is the price-current of an honest man and patriot today? They hesitate, and they regret, and sometimes they petition; but they do nothing in earnest and they with effect. They will wait, well-disposed, for others to remedy the evil, that they may no longer have it to regret. At most, they give only a cheap vote, and a feeble countenance and God-speed, to the right, as it goes by them. There are nine hundred and ninety-nine patrons of virtue to the virtuous man. But it is easier to deal with the real possessor of a thing than with the temporary guardian of it.

All voting is a sort of gaming, like checkers or backgammon, with a slight moral tinge to it, a playing with right and wrong, with moral questions; and betting naturally accompanies it. The character of the voters is not staked. I cast my vote, perchance, as I think right; but I am not vitally concerned that right should prevail. I am willing to leave it to the majority. Its obligation, therefore, never exceeds that of expediency. Even voting *for the right* is *doing* nothing for it. It is only expressing to men feebly your desire that it should prevail. A wise man will not leave the right to the mercy of chance, nor wish it to prevail through the power of the majority. There is but little virtue in the action of masses of men. When the majority shall at length vote for the abolition of slavery, it will be because they are indifferent to slavery, or because there is but little slavery left to be abolished by their vote. *They* will then be the only slaves. Only *his* vote can hasten the abolition of slavery who asserts his own freedom by his vote.

I hear of a convention to be held at Baltimore, or elsewhere, for the selection of a candidate for the Presidency, made up chiefly of editors, and men who are politicians by profession; but I think, what is it to any independent, intelligent, and respectable man what decision they may come to? Shall we not have the advantage of his wisdom and honesty, nevertheless? Can we not count upon some independent votes? Are there not many individuals in the country who do not attend conventions? But no: I find that the respectable man, so called, has immediately drifted from his position, and despairs of his country, when his country has more reason to despair of him. He forthwith adopts one of the candidates thus selected as the only *available* one, thus proving that he is himself *available* for any purposes of the demagogue. His vote is of no more worth than that of any unprincipled foreigner or hireling, native, who may have been bought. O for a man who is a *man,* and, as my neighbor says, has a bone in his back which you cannot pass your hand through! Our statistics are at fault: the population has been returned too large. How many *men* are there to a square thousand miles in this country? Hardly one. Does not America offer any inducement for men to settle here? The American has dwindled into an Odd Fellow—one who may be known by the development of his organ of gregarious business, and a manifest lack of intellect and cheerful self—reliance; whose first and chief concern, on coming into the world, is to see that the Almshouses are in good repair; and, before yet he has lawfully donned the virile garb, to collect a fund for the support of the widows and orphans that may be; who, in short, ventures to live only by the aid of the Mutual Insurance company, which has promised to bury him decently.

It is not a man's duty, as a matter of course, to devote himself to the eradications of any, even the most enormous wrong; he may still properly have other concerns to engage him: but it is his duty, at least, to wash his hands of it, and, if he gives it no thought longer, not to give it practically his support. If I devote myself to other pursuits and contemplations, I must first see, at least, that I do not pursue them sitting upon another man's shoulders. I must get off him first, that he may pursue his contemplations too. See what gross inconsistency is tolerated. I have heard some of my townsmen say, "I should like to have them order me out to help put down an insurrection of the slaves, or to march to Mexico—see if I would go; and yet these very men have each, directly by their allegiance, and so indirectly, at least, by their money, furnished a substitute. The soldier is applauded who refuges to serve in an unjust war by those who do not refuse to sustain the unjust government which makes the war; is applauded by those whose own act and authority he disregards and sets at naught; as if the state were penitent to that degree that it hired one to scourge it while it sinned, but not to that degree that it left off sinning for a moment. Thus, under the name of Order and Civil Government, we are all made at last to pay homage to and support our own meanness. After the first blush of sin comes its indifference; and from immoral it becomes, as it were, *un*moral, and not quite unnecessary to that life which we have made.

The broadest and most prevalent error requires the most disinterested virtue to sustain it. The slight reproach to which the virtue of patriotism is commonly liable, the noble are most likely to incur. Those who, while they disapprove of the character and measurers of a government, yield to it their allegiance and support and undoubtedly its most conscientious supporters, and so frequently the most serious obstacles to reform. Some are petitioning the state to dissolve the Union, to disregard the requisitions of the President. Why do they not dissolve it themselves—the union between themselves and the state—and refuse to pay their quota into its treasury? Do not they stand in the same relation to the state that the state does to the Union. And have not the some reasons prevented the state from resisting the Union which have prevented them from resisting the state?

How can a man be satisfied to entertain an opinion merely, and enjoy it? Is there any enjoyment in it, if his opinion is that he is aggrieved? If you are cheated out of a single dollar by your neighbor, you do not rest satisfied with knowing that you are cheated, or even with petitioning him to pay you your due; but you take effectual steps at once to obtain the full amount, and see that you are never cheated again. Action from principle, the perception and the performance of rights, changes things and relations; it is essentially revolutionary, and does not consist wholly with anything which was. It not only divides states and churches, it divides families; may, it divides the *individual,* separating the diabolical in him from the divine.

Unjust laws exist: shall we be content to obey them, or shall we endeavor to amend them, and obey them until we have succeeded, or shall we transgress them at once? Men generally, under such a government as this, think that they ought to wait until they have persuaded the majority to alter them. They think that, if they should resist, the remedy would be worse that the evil. But it is the fault of the government itself that the remedy is worse than the evil. *It* makes it worse. Why is it not more apt to anticipate and provide for reform? Why does it not cherish its wise minority? Why does it cry and resist before it is hurt? Why does it not encourage its citizens to be on the alert to point out its faults, and *do* better than it would have them? Why does it always crucify Christ, and excommunicate Copernicus and Luther, and pronounce Washington and Franklin rebels?

One would think, that a deliberate and practical denial of its authority was the only offense never contemplated by government; else, why has it not assigned its definite, its suitable and proportionate penalty? If a man who has no property refuses but once to earn nine shillings for the state, he is put in prison for a period unlimited by any law that I know, and determined only by the discretion of those who placed him there; but if he should steal ninety times nine shillings from the state, he is soon permitted to go at large again.

If the injustice is part of the necessary friction of the machine of government, let it go: perchance it will wear smooth—certainly the machines will wear out. If the injustice has a spring, or a pulley, or a rope, or a crank, exclusively for itself, then perhaps you may consider whether the remedy will not be worse than the evil; but if it is of such a nature that it requires you to be the agent of injustice to another, then, I say, break the law. Let your life be a counter friction to stop the machine. What I have to do is to see, at any rate, I do not lend myself to the wrong which I condemn.

As for adopting the ways which the state has provided for remedying the evil, I know not of such ways. They take too much time, and a man's life will be gone. I have other affairs to attend to. I came into this world, not chiefly to make this a good place to live in, but to live in it, be it good or bad. A man has not everything to do, but something; and because he cannot do *everything,* it is not necessary that he should do *something* wrong. It is not my business to be petitioning the Governor or the Legislature any more than it is theirs to petition me; and if they should not hear my petition, what should I do then? But in this case the state has provided no way: its very Constitution is the evil. This may seem to be harsh and stubborn and unconciliatory; but it is to treat with the utmost kindness and consideration the only spirit that can appreciate or deserves it. So is all change for the better, like birth and death, which convulse the body.

I do not hesitate to say, that those who call themselves Abolitionists should at once effectually withdraw their support, both in person and property, from the government of Massachusetts and not wait till they constitute a majority of one, before they suffer the right to prevail through them. I think that it is enough if they have God on their side, without waiting for the other one. Moreover, any man more right than his neighbors constitutes a majority of one already.

I meet this American government, or its representative, the state government, directly, and face to face, once a year—no more—in the person of its tax-gatherer; this is the only mode in which a man situated as I am necessarily meets it; and it then says distinctly, Recognize me; and the simplest, most effectual, and, in the present posture of affairs, the indispensablest mode of treating with it on this head, of expressing your little satisfaction with and love for it, is to deny it then. My civil neighbor, the tax-gatherer, is the very man I have to deal with—for it is, after all, with men and not with parchment that I quarrel—and he has voluntarily chosen to be an agent of the government. How shall he ever know well what he is and does as an officer of the government, or as a man, until he is obliged to consider whether he shall treat me, his neighbor, for whom he has respect, as a neighbor and well-disposed man, or as a maniac and disturber of the peace, and see if he can get over this obstruction to his neighborliness without a ruder and more impetuous thought or speech corresponding with his action. I know this well, that if one thousand, if one hundred, if ten men whom I could name—if ten *honest* men only—any, if *one* HONEST man, in this State of Massachusetts, *ceasing to hold slaves* were actually to withdraw from this copartnership, and be locked up in the country jail therefore, it would be the abolition of slavery in America. For it matters not how small the beginning may seem to be what is once well done for ever. But we love better to talk about it: that we say is our mission. Reform keeps many scores of newspapers in its service, but one man. If my esteemed neighbor, the State's ambassador, who will devote his days to the settlement of the question of human rights in the Council Chamber, instead of being threatened with the prisons of Carolina, were to sit down the prisoner of Massachusetts, that State which is so anxious to foist the sin of slavery upon her sister—though at present she can discover only an act of inhospitality to be the ground of a quarrel with her—the Legislature would not wholly waive the subject the following winter.

Under a government which imprisons any unjustly, the true place for a just man is also a prison. The proper place today, the only place which Massachusetts has provided for her freer and less desponding spirits, is in her prisons, to be put out and locked out of the State by her own act, as they have already put themselves out by their principles. It is there that the fugitive slave, and the Mexican prisoner on parole, and the Indian come to plead the wrongs of his race should find them; on that separate, but more free and honorable ground, where the State places those who are not *with* her, but *against* her—the only house in a slave State in which a free man can abide with honor. If any think that their influence would be lost there, and their voices no longer afflict the ear of the State, that they would not be as an enemy within its walls, they do not know by how much truth is stronger than error, nor how much more eloquently and effectively he can combat injustice who has experienced a little in his own person. Cost your whole vote, not a strip of paper merely, but your whole influence. A minority is powerless while it conforms to the majority; it is not even a minority then; but it is irresistible when its clogs by its whole weight. If the alternative is to keep all just men in prison, or give up war and slavery, the State will not hesitate which to choose. If a thousand men were not to pay their tax—bills this year, that would not be a violent and bloody measure, as it would be to pay them, and enable the State to commit violence and shed innocent blood. This is, in fact the definition of a peaceable revolution, if any such it possible. If the tax-gatherer, or any other public officer, asks me, as one has done, "But what shall I do?" my answer is, "If you really wish to do anything, resign your office." When the subject has refused allegiance, and the officer has resigned his office, then the revolution is accomplished. But even suppose blood should flow. Is there not a sort of blood shed when the conscience is wounded? Through this wound a man's real manhood and immortality, low out, and he bleeds to an everlasting death. I see this blood flowing now.

I have contemplated the imprisonment of the offender, rather than the seizure of his goods—though both will serve the same purpose—because they who assert the purest right, and conseq-uently are most dangerous to a corrupt State, commonly have not spent much time in accumulating property. To such the State renders comparatively small service, and a slight tax is wont to appear exorbitant, particularly if they are obliged to earn it by special labor with their hands. If there were one who lived wholly without the use of money, the State itself would hesitate to demand it of him. But the rich man—not to make any invidious comparison—is always sold to the institution which makes him rich. Absolutely speaking, the more money, the less virtue, for money comes between a man and his objects, and obtains them for him; and it was certainly no great virtue to obtain it. It puts to rest many questions which he would otherwise be taxed to answer; while the only new question which it puts is the hard but superfluous one, how to spend it. Thus his moral ground is taken from under his feet. The opportunities of living are diminished in proportion as what are called the "means" are increased. The best thing a man can do for his culture when he is rich is to endeavor to carry out those schemes which he entertained when he was poor. Christ answered the Herodians according to their condition. "Show me the tribute-money," said he—and one took a penny out of his pocket; if you use money which has the image of Caesar on it and which he had made current and valuable, that is, *if you are men of the State,* and gladly enjoy the advantages of Caesar's government, then pay him back some of his own when he demands it. "Render therefore to Caesar that which is Caesar's, and to God those things which are God's—"leaving them no wiser than before as to which was which; for they did not wish to know....

I have paid no poll-tax for six years. I was put into a jail once on this account, for one night; and, as I stood considering the walls of solid stone, two or three feet thick, the door of wood and iron, a foot thick, and the iron grating which strained the light, I could not help being struck with the foolishness of that institution which treated me as if I were flesh and blood and bones, to be locked up. I wondered that it should have concluded at length that this was the best use it could put me to, and had never thought to avail itself of my services in some way. I saw that, if there was a wall of stone between me and my townsmen, ther ewas a still more difficult one to climb or break through before they could get to be as free as I was. I did not for a moment feel confined, and the walls seemed a great waste of stone and mortar. I felt as if I alone of all my townsmen had paid my tax. They plainly did not know how to treat me, but behaved like persons who are underbred. In every threat and in every compliment there was a blunder; for they thought that my chief desire was to stand the other side of that stone wall. I could not but smile to see how industriously they locked the door on my meditations, which followed them out again without let or hindrance, and *they* were really all that was dangerous. As they could not reach me, they had resolved to punish my body; just as boys, if they cannot come at some person against whom they have a spite, will abuse his dog. I saw that the State was half-witted, that it was timid as a lone woman with her silver spoons, and that it did not know its friends from its foes, and I lost all my remaining respect for it, and pitied it.

Thus the State never intentionally confronts a man's sense, intellectual or moral, but only his body, his senses. It is not armed with superior wit or honesty, but with superior physical strength. I was not born to be forced. I will breathe after my own fashion. Let us see who is the strongest. What force has a multitude? They only can force me who obey a higher law than I. They force me to become like themselves. I do not hear of *men* being *forced* to live this way or that by masses of men. What sort of life were that to live? When I meet a government which says to me, "Your money or your life," why should I be in haste to give it my money? It may be in a great strait, and not know what to do: I cannot help that. It must help itself: do as I do. It is not worth the while to snivel about it. I am not responsible for the successful working of the machinery of society. I am not the son of the engineer. I perceive that, when an acorn and a chestnut fall side by side, the one does not remain inert to make way for the other, but obey their own laws, and spring and grow and flourish as best they can, till one, perchance, overshadow and destroys the other. If a plant cannot live according to its nature, it dies; and so a man . . . .

When I came out of prison—for someone interfered, and paid that tax—I did not perceive that great changes had taken place on the common, such as he observed who went in a youth and emerged a tottering and gray—headed man; and yet a change had to my eyes come over the scene—the town, and State, and country—greater than any that mere time could effect. I saw yet more distinctly the State in which I lived. I saw to what extent the people among whom I lived could be trusted as good neighbors and friends; that their friendship was for summer weather only; that they did not greatly propose to do right; that they were a distinct race from me by their prejudices and superstitions, as the Chinamen and Malays are; that in their sacrifices to humanity they ran no risks, not even to their property; that after all they were not so noble but they treated the thief as he had treated them, and hoped by a certain outward observance and a few prayers, and by walking in a particular straight though useless path from time to time, to save their souls. This may be to judge my neighbors harshly; for I believe that many of them are not aware that they have such an institution as the jail in their village.

It was formerly the custom in our village, when a poor debtor came out of jail, for his acquaintances to salute him, looking through their fingers, which were crossed to represent the grating of a jail window. "How do ye do?" My neighbors did not thus salute me, but first looked at me, and then at one another, as if I had returned from a long journey. I was put into jail as I was going to the shoemaker's to get a shoe which was mended. When I was let out the next morning, I proceeded to finish my errand, and having put on my mended shoe, joined a huckleberry party, who were impatient to put themselves under my conduct; and in half an hour—for the horse was soon tackled—was in the midst of a huckleberry field, on one of our highest hills, two miles off, and then the State was nowhere to be seen....

I have never declined to pay the highway tax, because I am as desirous of being a good neighbor as I am of being a bad subject; and as for supporting schools, I am doing my part to educate my fellow countrymen now. It is for no particular item in the tax-bill that I refuse to pay it. I simply wish to refuse allegiance to the State, to withdraw and stand aloof from it effectually. I do not care to trace the course of my dollar, if I could, till it buys a man or a musket to shoot with—the dollar is innocent—but I am concerned to trace the effects of my allegiance. In fact, I quietly declare war with the State, after my fashion, though I will make what use and get what advantage of her I can, as is usual in such cases.

If others, pay the tax which is demanded of me, from a sympathy with the State, they do but what they have already done in their own case, or rather they abet injustice to a greater extent than the State requires. If they pay the tax from a mistaken interest in the individual taxed, to save his property, or prevent his going to jail, it is because they have not considered wisely how far they let their private feelings interface with the public good.

This then is my position at present. But one cannot be too much on his guard in such a case, lest his action be biased by obstinacy or an undue regard for the opinions of men. Let him see that he does only what belongs to himself and to the hour.

I think sometimes, Why, this people mean well, they are only ignorant; they would do better if they knew how: why give your neighbors this pain to treat you as they are not inclined to? But I think again, This is no reason why I should do as they do, or permit others to suffer much greater pain of a different kind. Again, I sometimes say to myself. When many millions of men, without heat, without ill will, without personal feeling of any kind, demand of you a few shilling only, without the possibility, such is their constitution, of retracting or altering their present demand, and without the possibility, on your side, of appeal to any other millions, why expose yourself to this overwhelming brute force? You do not resist cold and hunger, the winds and the waves, thus obstinately; you quietly submit to a thousand similar necessities. You do not put your head into the fire. But just in proportion as I regard this as not wholly a brute force, but partly a human force, and consider that I have relations to those millions as to so many millions of men, and not of mere brute or inanimate things, I see that appeal is possible, first and instantaneously, from them to the Maker of them, and secondly, from them to themselves. But if I put my head deliberately into the fire, there is no appeal to fire or to the Maker of fire, and I have only myself to blame. If I could convince myself that I have any right to be satisfied with men as they are and to treat them accordingly, and not according, in some respects, to my requisitions and expectations of what they and I ought to be, then, like a good Mussulman and fatalist, I should endeavor to be satisfied with things as they are, and say it is the will of God. And above all, there is this difference between resisting this and a purely brute or natural force, that I can resist this with some effect; but I cannot expect, like Orpheus, to change the nature of the rocks and trees and beasts.

I do not wish to quarrel with any man or nation. I do not wish to split hairs, to make fine distinctions, or set myself up as better than my neighbors. I seek rather, I may say, even an excuse for conforming to the laws of the land. I am but too ready to conform to them. Indeed, I have reason to suspect myself on this head; and each year, as the tax-gatherer comes round, I find myself disposed to review the acts and position of the general and State governments, and the spirits of the people, to discover a pretext for conformity.

> We must affect our country as our parents,
> And if at any time we alienate
> Our love or industry from doing it honor,
> We must respect effects and teach the soul
> Matter of conscience and religion,
> And not desire of rule or benefit.

I believe that the State will soon be able to take all my work of this sort out of my hands, and then I shall be no better a patriot than my fellow-countrymen. Seen from a lower point of view, the Constitution, with all its faults, is very good; the law and the courts are very respectable; even this State and this American government are, in many respects, very admirable, and rare things, to be thankful for, such as a great many have described them; but seen from a point of view a little higher, they are what I have described them; seen from a higher still, and the highest, who shall say what they are or that they are worth looking at or thinking of at all?

However, the government does not concern me much, and I shall bestow the fewest possible thoughts on it. It is not many moments that I live under a government, even in this world. If a man is thought-free, fancy-free, imagination-free, that which is *not* never for a long time appearing *to be* to him, unwise rulers or reformers cannot fatally interrupt him.

I know that most men think differently from myself; but those whose lives are by profession devoted to the study of these or kindred subjects content me as little as any. Statesmen and legislators, standing so completely within the institution, never distinctly and nakedly behold it. They speak of moving society, but have no resting-place without it. They may be men of a certain experience and discrimination, and have no doubt invented ingenious and even useful systems, for which we sincerely thank them; but all their wit and usefulness lie within certain not very wide limits. They are wont to forget that the world is not governed by policy and expediency. Webster never goes behind government, and so cannot speak with authority about it. His words are wisdom to those legislators who contemplate no essential reform in the existing government; but for thinkers, and those who legislate for all time, he never once glances at the subject. I know of those whose serene and wise speculations on this theme would soon reveal the limits of his mind's range and hospitality. Yet, compared with the cheap professions of most reformers, and the still cheaper wisdom and eloquence of politicians in general, his are almost the only sensible and valuable words, and we thank Heaven for him. Comparatively, he is always strong, original, and above, all practical. Still, his quality is not wisdom, but prudence. the lawyer's truth is not Truth, but consistency or a consistent expediency. Truth is always in harmony with herself, and is not concerned chiefly to reveal the justice that may consist with wrong-doing. He well deserves to be called, as he has been called, the Defender of the Constitution. There are really no blows to be given by him but defensive ones. He is not a leader, but a follower. His leaders are the men of '87. "I have never made an effort," he says, "and never propose to make an effort; I have never countenanced an effort, and never mean to countenance an effort, to disturb the arrangement as originally made, by which the various States came into the Union." Still thinking of the sanction which the Constitution gives to slavery, he says, "Because it was a part of the original compact—let it stand." Notwithstanding his special acuteness and ability, he is unable to take a fact out of its merely political relations, and behold it as it lies absolutely to be disposed of by the intellect—what, for instance, it behooves a man to do here in America today with regard to slavery—but ventures, or is driven, to make some such desperate answer as the following while professing to speak absolutely, and as a private man—from which what new and singular code of social duties might be inferred? "The manner," says he, "in which the governments of those States where slavery exists are to regulate it is for their own consideration, under their responsibility to their constituents, to the general laws of propriety, humanity, and justice, and to God. Associations formed elsewhere, springing from a feeling of humanity, or other cause, have nothing whatever to do with it. They have never received any encouragement from me, and they never will."

They who know of no purer sources of truth, who have traced up its stream no higher, stand, and wisely stand, by the Bible and the Constitution, and drink at it there with reverence and humility; but they who behold where it comes trickling into this lake or that pool, gird up their loins once more, and continue their pilgrimage toward its fountain-head.

No man with a genius for legislation has appeared in America. They are rare in the history of the world. There are orators, politicians, and eloquent men, by the thousand; but the speaker has not yet opened his mouth to speak who is capable of settling the much-vexed questions of the day. We love eloquence for its own sake, and not for any truth which it may utter, or any heroism it may inspire. Our legislators have not yet learned the comparative value of free-trade and of freedom, of union, and of rectitude, to a nation. They have no genius or talent for comparatively humble questions of taxation and finance, commerce and manufactures and agriculture. If we were left solely to the wordy wit of legislators in Congress for our guidance, uncorrected by the seasonable experience and the effectual complaints of the people, America would not long retain her rank among the nations. For eighteen hundred years, though perchance I have no right to say it, the New Testament has been written; yet where is the legislator who has wisdom and practical talent enough to avail himself of the light which it sheds on the science of legislation?

The authority of government, even such as I am willing to submit to—for I will cheerfully obey those who know and can do better than I, and in many things even those who neither know nor can do as well—is still an impure one: to be strictly just, it must have the sanction and consent of the governed. It can have no pure right over my person and property but what I concede to it. The progress from an absolute to a limited monarchy, from a limited monarchy to a democracy, is a progress toward a true respect for the individual. even the Chinese philosopher was wise enough to regard the individual as the basis of the empire. Is a democracy, such as we know it, the last improvement possible in government? Is it not possible to take a step further toward recognizing and organizing the rights of man? There will never be a really free and enlightened State until the State comes to recognize the individual as a higher and independent power, from which all its own power and authority and derived, and treats him accordingly. I please myself with imagining a State at last which can afford to be just to all men, and to treat the individual with respect as a neighbor; which even would not think it inconsistent with its own repose if a few were to live aloof from it, not meddling with it, nor embraced by it, who fulfilled all the duties of neighbors and fellow-men. A State which bore this kind of fruit, and suffered it to drop off as fast as it ripened, would prepare the way for a still more perfect and glorious State, which also I have imagined, but not yet anywhere seen.

Chapter-12

The "Politics of Love" In the Cause of Peace

Liane Norman

Chapter-12

LIANE NORMAN IS A PRACTITIONER OF NONVIOLENCE, both as a lactic and as a principle. In the following article, she describes her experience of being arrested for blocking the entrance to Rockwell International, a manufacturer of components for first-strike weapon systems. She protested with other members of the River City Nonviolent Resistance Campaign. Norman describes her experience of arrest and jail and the different reactions of other members of her family. She reflects on the power and the politics of love which were at work when she was kneeling at Rockwell International's door.

By the time we four were arrested we had been on our knees some forty minutes, blocking the major entrance into Rockwell International's corporate headquarters on the fiftieth floor of the U.S. Steel Building in Pittsburgh. Some of Rockwell's employees ostentatiously pretended that we were not there; they walked stiffly past us with a great show of indifference, caught up in conversations or fascinated with the walls opposite. Some, on their way out, came rushing toward elevator doors, only to be brought up short by our obstructive presence. Some were plainly interested or curious, some nonplussed and embarrassed.

It surprised me that was not embarrassed. I had thought I might feel the fool that I no doubt looked to others. But I felt fine, gathered from time to time into a silence that needed no external quiet. It reminded me of Quaker Meeting. I was engrossed by what I have come to call prayer — the seareh for some deep and essential part of myself that I regard as God, the seareh for the same resonating essence in those I felt I must confront.

Michael Cuddy, the twenty-one-year-old graduate student to my left, was nervous. He shivered and whispered that his heartbeat was surely audible. I reached over to hold his hand for a few minutes: he is not much older than my son. To his left knelt young Reverend Tom Taylor, a local Methodist minister, and father of a little boy. To his left knelt Molly Rush, director of the local Thomas Merton Center, a storefront ministry for peace and justice. Molly is a small, middle-aged woman, mother of six children, grandmother of two. I wrote about her in *The Center Magazine* for November/December, 1981, "Companions Against the Storm." I am an English teacher at the University of Pittsburgh, an essayist, and the mother of three teenagers, whose children-to-be are my fondest dream.

What struck me as we knelt there, our knees and thigh muscles screaming bloody murder, was our power at a time and in circumstances in which nearly everyone claims to be powerless. It was clear from reactions to us how broad, deep, and controlling were the expectations that business would go on in this place in the usual way, that people would do what they did day in and day out. We were only four and we were unarmed — in fact, committed to nonviolence as exemplified by individuals like Antigone, Socrates, Jesus, Thorcau, and Dorothy Day, and by movement-builders like Gandhi and Martin Luther King. Nonviolence, as we saw it, was both a tactic and a principle. Our power lay in refusing to do the ordinary thing. For at least forty minutes we were able to disrupt Rockwell's business. Some part of every mind had to be aware that something untoward was happening had no way of knowing whether the shock, perturbation, disgust, irritation, wonder—whatever it was that Rockwell employees felt — lasted beyond the time of our presence, but I guessed that we would trouble many dinnertime conversations that evening. What I felt forcefully was that if just four of us could cause so much disruption, ordinary people could end the nuclear arms race.

"Power," writes Hannah Arendt in *Crises of the Republic,* "corresponds to the human ability not just to act but to act in concert." She notes that "civil disobedients are nothing but the latest form of voluntary association, and...are thus quite in tune with the oldest traditions of the country." In 1982, according to *The Progressive* (August, 1983), about four thousand people all over the country engaged in similar "trespassing, blockading, or in some other way breaking the laws that protect business-as-usual at offices and factories carrying out nuclear weapons policies." (Since then, the number has increased by leaps and bounds.) Arendt quotes Alexis dc Tocqueville, who noted that such associations and actions are "a necessary guarantee against the tyranny of the majority." For, in *The Progressive's* words, "every subsequent step in the arms race (since the first atomic bombing in 1945] has been sanctioned by U.S. law."

We meant to be disruptive, not because disruption pleases us, but because we wanted to break through the psychological and moral numbness that is a precondition for the researeh and development, the lobbying, the planning, the managing, and the production of nuclear weapons — particularly those designed to equip our country with first-strike nuclear capability. Though such work occupies perfectly good and honorable men and women every day and provides them with paychecks every month, it amounts to the preparation for atrocities unrivaled even in our own savage time.

Paul Henry Furfey, in a little treatise entitled *The Respectable Murderers* (1966), writes of the human being's "vast powers of moral self-deception." He catalogues the means of achieving such self-deception: refusing to think about it, rationalizing; false logic, denying "that there is anything [a person] can do"; suppressing "a feeling of guilt by developing some public virtue of a bizarre and superficial sort."

Furfey attributes these mental processes to both individuals and whole communities, which "can stifle conscience and embrace the mores of a paramoral society...The choice between conscience and evil mores is a choice which can be evaded." This evasion, he says, is "the easy solution; and it does bring the temporary satisfaction of avoiding both a break with society and the pain of guilt."

We meant to short-circuit that temporary satisfaction. We meant to increase the conflict between the conscience of Rockwell employees and their consent to the mores that permitted every day's lethal business-as-usual. We intended to disrupt, to inconvenience, to confront.

We knew we would offend and outrage, it is our contention that in order to take ethical responsibility for what one does, one must first of all acknowledge what it is that one does. In his book *The Fate of the Earth* (1982). Jonathan Schell writes: "Our failure to acknowledge the — magnitude and significance of the peril [of nuclear war] is a necessary condition for doing the deed." This deed is "an act that, without quite admitting it to ourselves, we plan in certain circumstances to commit A part of our prayer, as we knelt in the U.S. Steel Building, was for the people whose work we were disrupting, whom we were inconveniencing and confronting, whose moral and emotional conflict we hoped to stimulate. We knew we were asking them to take on themselves the pain of knowing what they did. We wanted to do what we could to open them to the demands of their own consciences, and that would not be easy for them. We therefore had to acknowledge *our* complicity in the work they did, so we also prayed for ourselves. It was, after all, our taxes that paid the corporation for its work. Had we not, as a community of citizens, yielded up our power to government and corporations so consistently — granting them a sort of permanent proxy to act for us except on election day (at which time the-real choices had already been made) — we would not as a community of human beings be face to face with the quite likely end of our kind. Schell writes that in order to prevent this end:

> The-first urgent, immediate step. . .is for each person to make known, visibly and unmistakably [the] desire that the species survive. Extinction, being in its nature outside human experience, is invisible, but we, by rebelling against it, can indirectly make it visible. No one will ever witness extinction, so we must bear witness to it before the fact. And the place for the rebellion to start is in our daily lives. We can each perform a turnabout right where we are — let our daily business drop from our hands for a while, so that we can turn our attention to securing the foundation of all life, out of which our daily business grows and in which it

finds its justification. This disruption of our lives will be a preventive disruption...

We four were trying to "bear witness before the fact" to engage in "preventive disruption" of our own lives as well as of those whose lives we confronted.

For two months, we four and several others had been outside of Rockwell every other Wednesday noon (alternating at Westinghouse Electric headquarters, because Westinghouse, like Rockwell, manufactures comments for first-strike weapons systems). We handed out leaflets designed, executed, and paid for by various religious and secular groups from the Pittsburgh are whose members joined us.

From the beginning, we had announced to the corporations as well as to groups whose participation we solicited, our plans for persistent vigilance and leaflet distribution. We explained that civil disobedience would occur from time to time and that in the spirit of nonviolence, we would do nothing secret, nothing to frighten or terrorize. We named ourselves the River City Nonviolent Resistance Campaign. After a year or so of thought, discussion, and prayer, we had chosen 1983 as a crucial year, since by December, first-strike weapons — Pershing 2 and Cruise missiles — were to be deployed by NATO in Europe.

Rockwell (like Westinghouse) is among the top one hundred military contractors in the United States. Though headquartered in Pittsburgh, its factories are located all around the country — in California, Colorado, Iowa, Texas. Utah, Ohio. Georgia, Alabama, Oklahoma—even Canada. A little less than half of Rockwells profits come from its military contracts with the government. In the year that ended September 30. 1982, Rockwell earned $331.6 million on sales of $74 billion (But the following year, earnings were $389.1 million on sales of $8.1 billion) Robert Anderson, the chairman of the board (whose annual salary is more than a million dollars), wrote in a 1983 report to shareholders:

> The results for the second quarter reflect strong performances by the company's government businesses. . .

> The higher earnings resulted primarily from a $279 million, or forty-four per cent, increase in sales, principally in the B-1 B program...While defense electronics programs continued to be strong, the quarter was adversely affected by depressed commercial markets. The weak economy continued to adversely affect the commercial businesses.

(A year later, Mr. Anderson repeated himself, even though the annual sales to the government were now up to sixty-four per cent from fifty-two per cent.)

Mr. Andersoir did not mention the may not know — that a number of economists sec the weak economy as a *result* of its materialization, since military spending promotes and exacerbates inflation, unemployment, and low productivity.

The B-1 Bomber, to which Mr. Anderson referred, can launch precision-guided missiles, on which Rockwell also works. In addition, Rockwell makes plutonium triggers, for every nuclear weapon manufactured in the United States. Each trigger is a "little" bomb, about the magnitude of the one dropped on Hiroshima, which killed more than one hundred thousand people (and is still killing some people who were affected by radiation). The trigger sets off the larger thermonuclear bomb, which is many times more destructive. With understandable delicacy and restraint, Rockwells 1982 Annual Report refers to these triggering bombs as "certain components for nuclear weapons."

At its annual shareholders' meeting, held in Pittsburgh in February, the corporation boasted of its part in all of the present first-strike weapons systems — though it did not describe them as "first strike," but "defense." Rockwell makes the fourth stage of the MX missile, including the guidance and precision-targeting mechanisms which send the warheads (bombs) to their separate targets.

Rockwell also makes the NAVSTAR satellite, which provides navigational and positioning information necessary for precision targeting and coordination, making missiles into first-strike weapons. Rockwell's 1982 Annual Report says that its Space Shuttle has "demonstrated the sortie mission concept when payloads were carried into space." The shuttle will launch NAVSTAR.

University of Pittsburgh physicist John Parmentola says that the Space Shuttle will transport nuclear fuel into space to provide energy for laser and particle beam weapons systems. Rockwell does researeh and development on these "star wars" weapons, contemplated not for defense against an enemy first strike, but as backup for our own first strike, to destroy such enemy missiles as might survive a first strike. Rockwell also makes part of the Trident II submarine, which Robert Aldridge, a former missile engineer, has called "the ultimate first-strike weapon."

First-strike, or counterforce, strategy is not defensive. It requires weapons of great accuracy and destructiveness to blow up simultaneously an enemy's missiles, airfields, submarine ports, submarines at sea, and command-communication-control centers before the adversary can launch its warheads, and to be able to destroy such retaliatory missiles as might survive our first strike. Mr. Aldridge citys a study undertaken by the Carter Administration to:

* Determine the nuclear strategy that would eliminate the U.S.S.R. as a functioning national entity;
* Investigate promoting separatism by destroying areas in the U.S.S.R which support the present Soviet government;
* Identify the targets which would "paralyze, disrupt, and dismember" the Soviet government by annihilating the ruling group.

Such language, backed up by first-strike weapons, whose capabilities are not needed for defense, suggests a purpose that Mr. Aldridge describes as "sinister."

Ever since the end of World War II, the people of the United States have been systematically taught to hate and fear the Soviet Union as the rationale for the continued buildup of our own nuclear arsenals. The first-strike nature of increasingly sophisticated technology has always been masked by the rhetoric of defense. Counterforce is sometimes represented as the humane alternative to bombing cities. But however "successful" such a counterforce strike were to be in the event—that is, however thoroughly it destroyed enemy military capabilities—it would also kill millions of people, civilians and soldiers indiscriminately; destroy civilian structures - homes, libraries, hospitals, schools, museums, water supplies—poison the environment with radioactive fallout and debris. Furthermore, radioactive fallout would not be restricted to belligerents. Carried by clouds and wind, it would rain on non belligerents and neutrals alike. Now we know that the dust and smoke generated by nuclear explosions might bring on an zoologically disastrous "nuclear winter."

Molly Rush and I had been arrested the previous year when, to protest Rockwell's profitable military contracts, we and three others rose during a shareholders' meeting to chant. The year "before that, Molly had been cut off when she tried to speak: I had been harassed by the chair as I spoke. We had tried hard and consistently to work "within the system." We had spoken to corporate officials; had written letters to public officials and newspapers; had published articles; had spoken to groups, on radio, and on television. I had run for the U.S. Senate as a third-party candidate. Even though I qualified as a legal candidate, the news media would neither cover my campaign nor take my candidacy seriously.

It was increasingly clear to me that war and the preparation for it were *themselves* the system. To work within the system legitimized war.

Hannah Arendt notes that when the legality and the constitutionality of certain governmental acts are brought before the courts, particularly those having to do with state sovereignty, "the Supreme Court has no more power than an international court: both are unable to enforce decisions that would hurt decisively the interests of sovereign states and both know that their authority depends on...not raising issues or making decisions which cannot be enforced." She suggests that "the establishment of civil disobedience among our political institutions might be the best possible remedy for this ultimate failure of judicial review."

The River City Campaign came from our growing recognition that no matter how much we lobbied and protested, the weapons kept right on being developed, often secretly, decided upon in ignorance by elected officials. When close to a million people assembled in New York during the 1982 United Nations Second Special Session on Disarmament, the President and the Secretary of Defense proclaimed that they would not be influenced by this outpouring of public sentiment, though democracy is premised on the ability the people to influence their public servants by petitioning for the redress of grievances. Those of us who have demonstrated and organized are routinely called "activists," the inference being that inactivists — those who do not so exercise their citizenship — are normal.

The Friends Committee on National Legislation, studying the financial contributions by military-manufacturing corporations, noted that Rockwell was among those that contributed heavily, just before elections, to "members of the House and Senate Committees who made the crucial decisions on military spending." Gordon Adams, in *The Politics of Defense Contracting: The Iron Triangle* (1981), documents that Rockwell spent more than seven million dollars to maintain Washington offices in order to lobby Congress. I angered Chairman Anderson when I pointed this out at the 1983 shareholders' meeting. He insisted that Rockwell does nothing illegal in this respect. Indeed, what Rockwell does is perfectly legal, just as it was perfectly legal for a German company to manufacture the gas that was used to kill Jews in Nazi Germany. Rockwell simply carries out government orders.

So while we had worked "within the system," and would no doubt continue to write and visit our congressional representatives, we believed, with Gandhi, that "civil disobedience is the inherent right of a citizen...Civil disobedience...becomes a sacred duty when the state has become lawless, or, which is the same thing, corrupt...It is a birthright that cannot be surrendered without surrender of one's self-respect."

The state and corporations like Rockwell and Westinghouse, though protected by domestic statute, are lawless in promulgating policies and manufacturing weapons which violate international and fundamental law. International law is based on the idea that there are some acts which are impermissible among even sovereign states. As Hugo Grotius, the seventeenth-century founder of international law, put it, "Things which are manifestly iniquitous are not to be done." Such law is not much thought of in public discourse today. Grotius noted that even "in our day, as in former times, there is no lack of men who view this branch of law with contempt as having no reality outside of an empty name. . . that in the case of a king or imperial city nothing is unjust which is expedient," *(The Law of War and Peace,* 1646)

International law is derived in part from the theory of a just war, which tried to distinguish legitimate from illegitimate fights and to impose limits on the mans of conducting them. After World War II and the Nazi destruction of civil society, the Nuremberg tribunal - in which the United States took the lead — established that individuals have responsibilities which supersede their obedience to the state. In fact, it was held at Nuremberg that "superior orders" do not excuse acts that violate certain norms of international and human behavior. Our own Constitution recognizes that international agreements "shall be the supreme law of the land." The Supreme Court, however much it defers to state sovereignty in matters of war and peace, has repeatedly held that customary international law has the same status as treaty law and is thus binding in the United States.

International law has been a long time in the formulating. The definition of war crimes at Nuremberg was based on principles developed, updated, and reaffirmed from the time of the Hague Conventions of 1899 and 1907 to the present. These principles are: that the right to injure an enemy is not unlimited: that the crucial distinction between civilians and combatants and between neutrals and belligerents must be maintained; that weapons are prohibited if they contaminate or poison the environment, destroy hospitals, schools, or food supplies, or inflict unnecessary suffering. The Hague Convention of 1922 says;

"Where a military objective is so situated that it cannci be bombarded without the indiscriminate bombardment of the civilian population, it cannot be bombarded at all. Which is to say that international law recognizes that winning isn't everything.

Because state sovereignty is regarded by the judicial system as the "bottom line," and because profits are regared by the economic system as "the bottom line," it is difficult to renumber Grotius' observation that the root of all law is the maintenance of the social order. The social order *seems* to rest on the bottom of obedience to law and the of profits. Therefore, corporate and governmental planners can prepare weapons of first-strike accuracy by Nuremberg standards a crime against the peace and enormous megatonnage (by Nuremberg standards a crime against humanity). The say these weapons will defend us, which is not true. But even if it were true, the right to injure an enemy is not unlimited. Civilians in international legal terms, be brushed aside as "soft-targets nor can their deaths be legitimized by referring to them as "collateral damage." The environment cannot, according the these standards, be irradiated for generations, nor can the random destruction of civilian structures, food. and water be tolerated.

Furthermore, Pennsylvania law says that a citizen may be justified in "conduct which the actor believes to be necessary to avoid a harm or evil to himself or to another...if the harm or evil sought to be avoided is greater than that sought to be prevented by the law defining the offense charged." As we saw it on that Maundy Thursday, 1983, to trespass and to obstruct passage at Rockwell headquarters in an attempt to interfere with the business transacted therein was the fulfillment of just such obligations as Pennsylvania and international law spell out. Pennsylvania statute justifies otherwise unlawful conduct "when it is required or authorized by...the judgment or order of a competent court or tribunal; the law governing the armed services or the lawful conduct of war."

Feeling ourselves bound by the judgments rendered at Nuremberg and seeing atrocities in the making beyond what

Hitler imagined, we also felt bound by another part of Pennsylvania criminal statute, which imposes a further public duty: "A person who knowingly or recklessly fails to take reasonable measures to present or mitigate a catastrophe, when he can do so without substantial risk to himself, commits a misdemeanor of the second degree if: (1) he knows that he is under...[a] legal duty to take such measures; or (2) he did or assented to the act causing or threatening the catastrophe' In other words, since we knew what we knew about both international law and the state of first-strike weapons preparation, we had a positive duty to act in accordance with that knowledge. Had we been ignorant that duty would not have existed. Furthermore, as long as Rockwell employees were ignorant they could ignore their duty. By acting on our knowledge, we hoped to erode their ignorance and thus impose on them a legal duty.

We were, of course, well aware that Rockwell did not see the same necessities we saw. We tried to engage in direct communication. We wrote to Rockwells chairman, Robert Anderson, asking that he meet with us. Instead, William Swanson, the vice-president and secretary of the corporation, answered our letter. "Rockwell International is familiar with the view of the group composing the 'River City Campaign' and I am sure that you are quite aware of the position the corporation has consistently taken regarding its participation in programs supporting national defense and security..." he wrote. "You should also be well aware that our differences of opinion are not about the desirability of peace, but about the best means of achieving it. In view of this, we believe no useful purpose would be served by a meeting."

We believed he was sincere. But we thought Rockwell had a conflict of interest, profits being what they are. And so we answered his letter, which I quote entire to show the kind of communication we hoped to achieve.

Dear William Swanson:

We were sorry to read, in your response to our request

for a meeting with Robert Andcrson, chairman of the board of Rockwell, that "no useful purpose would be served" by such a meeting. We believe that our capacity to communicate is a sacred gift, the means of human community, whereby we members of a common species strengthen what we share and reconcile our differences.

We will be in the chapel at Smithfield United Churchy Thursday, Mareh 31, at 2:00 p.m. to celebrate communion. We are people of many faiths. By sharing this communion supper, we hope to revitalize its meaning for our time. We invite you, Mr. Andcrson, and your colleagues to join us.

Mareh 31 is Maundy Thursday of the Christian Holy Week, falling between Passover and Easter. On Passover, Jews celebrate the reprieve given them by the Angel of Death. On Easter, Christians celebrate the triumph of the Prince of Peace or the principalities and powers and the death they inflicted as the ultimate exercise of their power. These celebrations come in the spring of the year, when the earth comes back to life after the apparent death of winter Communion of Maundy Thursday recreates a meal, caten in an ordinary upstairs room, a meal at which all were welcome, regardless of status, income, or work. The host of that meal, for whom it was the last supper, explained to those who joined him that henceforth they should understand bread and wine as symbols of shared vulnerability. Those who partook acknowledged that while they too could be killed, the) need not break faith with God, they need not hate enemies, they need not forget the poorest and weakest of their fellows.

In this time of nuclear weapons, each supper may be our last. Our common vulnerability—which you share with us, being but flesh and blood—mandates that we rediscover communion, community, communication. For many centuries we have felt our separateness more keenly than our likeness. Catholics, Protestants. Jews, Moslems, Hindus, Buddhists, atheists, capitalists, and Communists have claimed exclusive access to the Truth. Each has found tribal communities, excommunicated others, communicated and celebrated communion is sectarian fashion. But weapons capable of destroying soldiers, innocents and their environment i; indiscriminately, which cannot protect and defend but only obliterate, bring us together to make community with you. We bear some of the responsibility for the evil of our time and we hold your lives as precious as our own. We are all creatures of the Great Spirit, which some of us name God, some Jehovah, some Allah, some Brahma, and some do not name at all. No matter how we see the world, we are a community in peril. We have the chance to break bread and drink wine together in an act of reconciliation that turns no one away.

We had at first thought we would bring the elements of communion to you and your colleagues if you were unable to join us. But reflection suggested that to do so might contain an element of coercion. And so, while you are welcome to join us, we will not thrust our worship on you. Instead, several of us will come to meet with you after our communion. We will come in the spirit of community and reconciliation and hope you will welcome us in the same spirit.

Shalom

So it was that on Mareh 31, 1983—Maundy Thursday of the Christian Holy Week—following our communion service, attended by forty-or-so people, those of us who were going into the U.S. Steel Building and (we hoped) up to the fiftieth floor, hugged everyone in the group, received a multitude of good wishes, and set out briskly in the nippy air, followed by our friends who carried fliers with our letter on one side and Mr. Swanson's on the other. We went up Strawberry Lane to the U.S. Steel Building. We were not stopped at the front door or inside. Instead, there were security people all along our route, their walkie-talkies buzzing and snapping. We were not stopped at the elevators.

At the fiftieth floor, we were met by a man who asked our business. We said we had come meet with Mr. Anderson. He nodded at a phone that hung by the glass door and said we should announce ourselves. I picked up the phone and asked the receptionist, whom I could see answer me, if we might see Mr. Anderson. No, she said, he was out of the country. Well, I said, might we meet with Mr. Swanson. No, she said, he's busy.

I hung up the phone. We glanced at one another and knelt close to the glass door. 1 felt calm, cool, utterly clear about why I was to meditate on corporate employees there myself, our endangered species, among whom were our own children—ten among us, and two grandchildren. By being there, 1 wanted to take responsibility for weapons and policies which to assent to I take to be profoundly criminal.

Mr. John Angell, the head of the building's security, is a handsome man with a head of luxurious, well-tended white hair. Over the years, we have come to like and respect him. I think he feels the same way about us. He appeared, went to Molly, told her that we were trespassing and asked us to leave. Molly, speaking for all of us, said we could not. She told him she was sorry to hear his mother-in-law had died the day before, that she was sorry he had to be at work. He spoke with genuine distress. "I'm sorry, Molly," he said. "You know what I have to do." "I know," she said, smiling.

He called the city police. Forty minutes after we knelt down, we were arrested. I felt a light touch on my arm and a man's voice said. "Will you come with me?" It was something of a struggle to stand up. My knees and the muscles of my legs ached fiercely. I think I steadied myself on the door, but it may be that he helped me. When I turned. I saw it was one of the several policemen who had testified against me in court after I had sung in the shareholders, meeting the year before. I smiled. "Oh, hello," I said, and thrust my hand out to shake his. After a startled pause, he shook my hand heartily.

As we were taken down in the elevator to the paddy wagon in the basement, we were treated courteously. Why, one of the policemen asked, do you *do* this? There was neither outrage nor hostility in his question, only puzzlement. We explained. One of them shook his head and said it wouldn't do any good. Over and over we encountered this hopelessness. You—we—are powerless. Objecting to nuclear weapons is useless. There was deep despair, resignation to an arms race which must inevitably lead to nuclear accidents or deliberate exchanges, and which could destroy at least civilization if not life itself.

When we were driven up and out of the building, those who had come with us to the U.S. Steel Building were gathered on the sidewalk, waiting. We had a good look at fond, concerned faces as we drove off.

"We don't need handcuffs for you," one of the policemen said as we got out at the Public Safety Building. We nodded and followed them into the holding-cell area, where our belongings were gone over and confiscated, and then we were locked into a filthy and uncomfortable cell, Molly and I on the women's side, Tom and Michael on the men's side. It was about 3:30 p.m.

We were not permitted telephone calls, water, or food. Molly and I were in a cell whose walls were covered in graffiti written it. finger-nail polish, excrement, felt marking pen. There was a dirty toilet and a dirtier sink. The bed was metal with a sharp edge that cut into our legs when we stretched them out.

We could hear the cursing and screaming of several other women, though one in the next cell grew gentle with an old woman who was distraught and weeping. We could not see our fellow inmates, but there was some shouted conversation from cell to cell. That evening, several pretty, young prostitutes were put in our cell. They seemed to have little on their minds and they smoked nonstop. The cell area was ugly, hot, and airless. Late in the evening, a screaming, thrashing woman was brought into the area. It took a number of policemen to subdue and book her. She screamed for several hours without stopping.

We were instructed to fill out bail bond forms, which provide information indicating whether an arrested person is likely to show up for trial. We put down some information—that we owned our homes, had families and jobs in town—but when the bail bondswoman bullied and blustered without provocation, we decided not to provide more information. It seemed to us that a part of the nonviolence we lived by was to resist the sort of bullying going on We were threatened if we did not give the information, we would end up in jail. Well we said we preferred not to give any more information than we had.

During the evening, we were taken separately for photographs and fingerprinting. About 9:00 p.m, we were taken to another cell outside the magistrate court where 1 went first for arraignment. The magistrate, a small woman with a giant coif of orange hair and eight enormous turquoise rings on her little fingers, was angry because I would not give all the bail information. "She has to abide by the rules," she told my attorney, Paul Boas, a young man who had come to this late court with his tired and fretful infant daughter.

Paul, who had volunteered his legal services, explained that I was a good bail risk: that 1 had always (once) appeared for trial, and that I was not only employed, but a *professor* at the university. The magistrate summoned him to a private conference, and I was left with the weeping baby as they conferred in the hall outside. Later Paul told me that he had insisted on my academic rank in order to impress her with my solid-citizen qualities. She, however, said solemnly that "the enemy is at the gaes, Mr. Boas." When he inquired, puzzled, what she meant, she reminded him that in high school, she had heard that the Communists meant to "nore from within."

After this curious little conference, which Tom and Michael could hear from their holding cell, the magistrate the Paul returned and the magistrate said that if I would not abide by rules and regulation, she would not release me on my own recognizance. She set a two-thousand-dollar straight bail, which meant the entire sum had to be paid rather than the usual ten per cent. Since I had no intention of paying any of it, she sent me to jail. Molly was back not long afterward, after a similar hearing. Michael, having provided information the bail bondsman wanted, was released; and Tom, having been told falsely that we had given all the information, similarly filled out the forms and was released.

After a long hot, miserable three or four more hours in the city jail, the van came to take us to the county jail. We were handcuffed to another woman and put into a paddy wagon with three young handcuffed men. Inside the jail, we had to give all sorts of information all over again and to have more pictures taken. A "psychological counsellor" interviewed us to see if we were suicidal.

By this time, I was aching with fatigue and wanted a bed—any bed—with a passion. But there were more questions asked by a slovenly police matron, who moved as if in show motion. She went through our pckebooks as invasively as possible, ripped apart several sanitary napkins and Tampax in mine, before she locked our possession up for the duration. We were told to strip and were inspected, naked, by a policewoman who compared what bruises and sacrs we brought in with us in the event that we tried to charge the jail with injurious treatment.

We were given uniforms. Mine was hot, scratchy wool pants, too tight and without a zipper, and a cottton shirt on which FEMALE was stencilled. At last we were given a sheet, a thin blanket, a towel, a dormitory bed, and the promise of a toothbrush the next day. It must have been nearly 2:00 a.m. when I crawled under my sheet, but the woman on the bed next to mine rose on her elbow, whispered "hello," and handed me a pocket edition of the New Testament. I slept soundly.

Molly Rush and I were in the Allegheny County Jail for four days, over Easter weekend. After the first night, we were moved out of the dormitory, which had windows and some space, into a tiny shared cell. We had bunk beds, a stainless steel table and attached stool, a stainless steel toilet, and a sink unit. Only one of us could dress or undress at a time for want of floor space. We had no window. Our door was a sliding metal grate, which was flung open with a crash at 7:00 a.m. along with shouts of "Breakfast, ladies. Breakfast, girls." Breakfast, as all meals, was hurried and noisy.

We each had an assigned "detail" for the day. Mine was sweeping the front office. We were "free" for the rest of the day. There was a library, an indiscriminate and unsorted dump of books, from several attics, it appeared, the range was from trashy romance to good literature. I found enough to keep me amused.

Our bars were slammed shut after lunch for an hour and again in the evening. At night we could choose either to watch television or a movie in the smoky library room or be locked up. During the day, we could shower when we wisher but because we had missed the weekly canteen (on Thursday, the day of our arrest), we could not get shampoo. The jail was hot and we felt greasy, but we washed our hair with Dial soap that was in the small toiletries kit we had been given.

On the first night, we were required to have blood drawn by a sleazy, evidently drunk nurse and ordered to have a Pap smear, which we were allowed to do ourselves. On Easter Sunday we were urged to attend church. The sermon turned out to be a description of all the feasts people on the outside might consume on Easter: our own dinner was heavy and tasteless.

Though clean, the jail was noisy, ugly and stifling. There was much shouting, cursing, vulgarity. Food was plentiful but bad, except the freshly baked bread at noon on Monday. Some matrons were friendly, some were hostile. Visits were unsatisfactory. We were permitted three a week. The visitor sat on one side of scratched and blurry glass, prisoner on the other, conversing through a telephone receiver.

On Easter Sunday, my husband, who had been kept waiting and had endured the insults of inefficient bureaucracy, seemed withdrawn and angry. He could not understand why I had refused to provide bail information. It seemed, he told me later, that I preferred being in tail to being with him.

I tried to share with him the exhilaration I felt, despite the oppressiveness of jail. One source of my feeling was the sense of internal wholeness because of having acted on my belief. Another was the deeper friendship with Molly as we planned new tactics and shared our thoughts and lives. Finally, there were the women we met. However crude and foul-mouthed some of them were, there was also a kindness and consideration among them that moved me. One woman, sitting across from me at the unsavory dinner on Easter eve, had begun to cry. During the meal, six or seven women came to sit quietly by her, offering silent sympathy. She came to our cell later to tell us about herself a horrendou story of abuse and poverty—and to ask about us.

The stories were overwhelming. Woman after woman, brought up in poverty without hope, battered, hooked on drugs, hundred with children, unable to find work, he done what she could to survive. There were more black women than white, more young women than old, more common sense than stupidity, more gentleness than harshness. Given the setting, there was, it seemed to me, great generosity.

I cannot easily explain why all of this moved me so deeply. I felt a sense of solidarity that was at once spiritual and human. I felt I would not ever be quite the same again.

May be that was what made my husband lonely, scared, and uneasy. He noted later that for years, men had left their women to go off to war and now he knew how all those women had felt. What were men to do, he wondered, when women took the lead? He approved in his head of what I was doing, but it caused great turbulence of heart and spirit.

Finally, late on Monday, we were told to put our street clothes on and clean our cell. We had been released. We heard from Molly's husband that our lawyers pleas to release us on our own recognizance had been in vain until the district attorney had chimed in that we needed to be out so that Molly could speak at a rally scheduled for two days later, when President Ronald Reagan was due to be in town. I was able to make it to my evening class at the university.

We have been charged with defiant trespass and we await trial (scheduled for early February, 1984). Reactions, however, have not awaited our conviction. (We will not deny that we trespassed at Rock-well and refused to leave when asked. We will, however, plead innocent before a jury and argue that we were legally justified in thus defiantly trespassing.)*

For some peace movement people, going to jail is a sort of rite of passage, and support and approval are automatic. Others, marginal to the peace movement, have seemed to find themselves drawn closer to it as a result of considering why some of us have been impelled to civil disobedience.

Children have seemed fascinated: What is it like in jail? they ask. Their upper-middle-class parents have been embarrassed: How do you greet a friend just released from jail? One said to me. "I haven't seen you since your recent escapade." Some have reacted with terror, as if chaos were about to break loose, others with deep hostility.

My children have been supportive. My son sent a letter addressed to "Mohandas Norman." One daughter thought she might take part in the next such "provocation." Another daughter wrote from her school that she loved her family, even though it was "bizarre."

My husband suffered. There was now « new element in our marriage. In the first place, it seemed fairly clear that the controversy I had stirred up over the years had much to do with my being denied tenure: he could imagine me being unemployable. (Since that denial of tenure, a special review committee at the university judged that the tenure committee had acted unfairly and that I should be given a new hearing outside my department) In the second place, he thought I felt newly obligated to some higher power—conscience—that displaced him. I He could not, he thought, count of me either to be co-provider or to behave in recognizable, moderate, or reasonable ways. He has, however, made a great and gratifying effort to understand, and I have tried to share my thoughts and feelings more fully with him.

Some of my relatives were furious. They thought I had acted

[Editor's note: on the eve of the trial, the District Attorney's office dropped the charges against Ms. Norman and her fellow defendants. The latter surmise that the charges were dropped in compliance with the wishes of Rockwell-International whose annual shareholders' meeting would have coincided with the conn trial.]

out of neurotic compulsion to deny authority, to be conspicuous, to martyr myself. I should work within the system; I should stick to writing; I should not turn people off by such antics; I should remember the Russians, who would take over the world. They brought these matters up, not with me, but with my husband who, despite his reservations, defended me gamely. If my minor act of civil disobedience has been liberating for me dispersing the despair and discouragement I have often felt—it h been worrisome for some of those who know me and love me.

I cannot entirely understand these worries, though I think they have something to do with the recognition of the power that I felt kneeling there at Rockwell's doors It is as if this power, once glimpsed, terrifies because it compels and thus threatens real disruptions in many daily lives. If one person can use that power, others can, too; and it scares many people to realize that they can act.

But if I cannot entirely underhand the upset I have caused, I think I understand my sense of liberation I used to define my responsibility in political terms. That is, I urged others to act through lobbying and voting. I measured the success or of my acts in terms of objectives achieved or not achieved by others. I acted as a sort of minimal remote controller. If my agitation had some tiny part in President Jimmy Carter's cancellation of the B-1 bomber (a cancellation which Rockwell made sure was impermanent), I had succeeded. I do not discount such successes and victories.

But increasingly I have begun to define achievement in terms of trust and love fulfilled. I am not sure we can prevent nuclear war. I am not sure we can stop and then reverse the arms race. But I am sure I can act in concert with the divine part of me, and I am sure I can perceive and speak to that same divinity in others. Hannah Arent's idea of power—she is speaking of political power—is people acting in concert. I believe in that kind of power, but, deeper still, I believe that the association must be between people and their divine part.

The problem for many people, in consideration of such small

acts as the one I have described, is that the civil disobedient will get into trouble. My response is that we are already in trouble, in, as my youngest daughter would put it, "a big, significant way." Living at the brink of planetary cremation is living in trouble.

Jonathan Schell thinks that today "the task is nothing less than to reinvent politics: to reinvent the world." He compares the "realistic" school of political thinking" with the "idealistic" school," noting that the difference between them "lies in different judgments regarding human nature."

Mr. Schell, like many women, has been accused of hysteria and of the same "idealism" which he sees as a practical necessity in our times.

> Historically, a belief in the necessity of violence has been the hallmark of the credo of the "realist." However, if one consistently and thoroughly applies the law of fear in nuclear times one is driven not to rely on violence but to banish it altogether. This comes about as the result not of any idealistic assumption but of a rigorous application to our times of the strictly "military" logic of traditional war. For today the only way to achieve genuine national defense for any nation is for all nations to give up violence altogether.

Chapter-13

THE END OF THE COLD WAR: IMPLICATIONS FOR NEUTRALITY AND NON-ALIGNMENT

RAMON LOPEZ-REYES

Chapter-13

IF ANY ONE event symbolizes the end of the Cold War, then the credit should be given to the destruction of the Berlin Wall. In a similar manner, the forming of the Bastille symbolized the beginning of the French Revolution. But the documentation of the end of the Cold War for all practical purposes occurred a few weeks after the Wall's destruction at the Malta Summit of 1989. It was a point in history when the two conflicting Super Powers of the time declared to a global audience that their conflict had ended to be replaced by a spirit of cooperation. It is the intent of this paper to examine the implications of the end of the Cold War on the peace strategies of the neutral, non-aligned states and to introduce a peace initiative for these states in the Post-Cold War era.

END OF THE COLD WAR: IMPLICATIONS

To assess the implications of the end of the Cold War on the practice of neutrality and nonalignment, the following themes are examined: (i) the demise of the Super-Power balance; (ii) increase in diabolism; (iii) end of neutrality and non-alignment; (iv) "day" of Europe; (v) "dawn" of an Eurasian era; (vi) practice of nonviolence; and (vii) spirit of "cooperation, not conflict."

The Demise of the Super-Power Balance

Historically, International politics proceeds from the principle that national interests dominate and that alliances and balance of power stabilize international relations. Power politics is a "top-down" approach to peace (see *Chart* I), in contract to a neutralist or "in-out" approach, non-aligned or "middle-out" approach globalist or "all in One"

Chart 1

APPROACHES TO PEACE

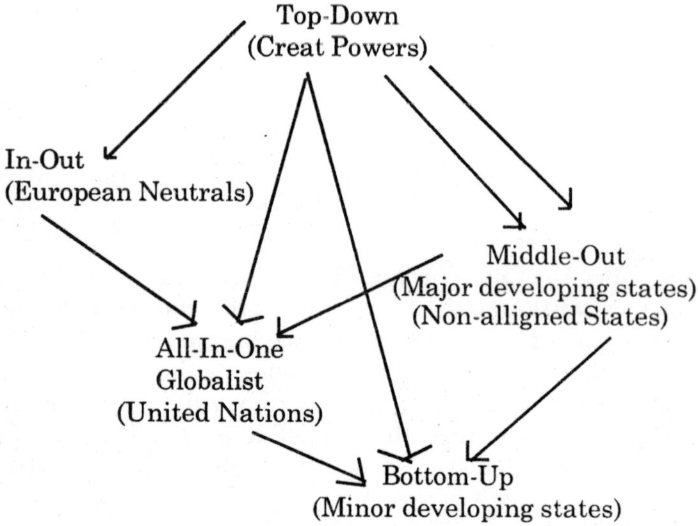

Top-Down.	Supremacy of power politics
In-Out.	Avoid and mediate
Middle-Out.	Gain proper political leverage
Bottom-Up	Avoid and cooperate
All-in One	Join for common security and prosperity

Soviet internal reform and the East European revolution precipitated the demise of the Super-Power balance. This, in turn, destroyed the stabilizing fabric of the "top-down" approach and, theoretically, created an unstable power vacuum. From another point of view, the demise of the Super-Power balance reduced the great fear of nuclear war. And from a third point of view, it unleashed repressed conflicts (which already have surfaced in East Europe and in the former Soviet Union itself). The danger is real and can even lead to a war between ethnic groups as happened in Yugoslavia. These repressed conflicts sooner or later had to be addressed and it is hoped that this working-through of ethnic differences in the former Soviet Union will not recreate the abomination of totalitarian rule and a return to Cold-War rhetoric.

The West does not seem apprehensive about a power vacuum nor have unstable tensions emerged. Uncertainty, however, exists in appraising the reunification of former East Germany with West Germany and prompts a cautious "wait-and-see" attitude in much of Europe. Other disturbing developments have emerged with the end of "Pax Sovietica" not only in the Balkans and Poland, where once against it needs to find its political standing between Germany and Russia, but also in the Near East with the re-surfacing of the Damascus-Baghdad rivalry.

Power or "top-down" politics proposes that force is necessary to ensure peace and that balance will emerge to preclude oppression by a dominant political actor which in the post-Cold War era is the United States. Conceptually, a united Europe (after detaching itself from United States influence) may provide the balance but perhaps economically rather than military, or military the balance may come from a Chinese-Japanese alliance. Balance may also materialize from a globalise challenge, that is, by United Nations restraint on US policy. A globalist balance already is is in evidence as reflected in United Nations efforts to resolve the Cambodian conflict and in the Gulf crisis, where the emphasis is on United Nations authority rather than on US unilateral action.

The end of the Cold War unsettled the known but dangerous world of Super-Power balance. While European states welcome this development, the developing world may perceive circumstances quite differently.

Increased Diabolism

Diabolism, generally considered Utopian in practice and springing from the psychological projection of humanity's oneness, has gained respectability with the end of the Cold War, even among the major powers. The cause for this change may rest not on the theoretical formulation of humanity's oneness but on the economic interdependence of nations, on the ecological unity of the planet, and on the reduction of Super-Power manipulation of the United Nations. Moreover, the nightmare of humanity's creation, nuclear war, has set in train the need to resolve international conflicts nonviolently and to enhance a political atmosphere of cooperation.

The United Nations is the most recent political projection of this human oneness. It was created by the vision and caution of World War II victors. Its ineffectiveness soon became evident when the Cold War saturated UN operations. In short, the Cold War crippled the United Nations. But in the "gap" created between the Super Powers, developing nations, mostly emerging from colonial status, turned to the United Nations both to support it and to be supported by it. The Non-aligned Movement tilted the United Nations away from its founders' grip. Some non-aligned states, however, also attempted to exploit the UN for their own respective interests. Perhaps the only "true" or non-exploitative friends of the UN are the Western neutrals and the minor non-aligned states.

Constitutionally, the sovereign interests of the permanent members of the Security Council restrict United Nations operations. There is no reason to believe that one of the five permanent members will not be, at a later date, in a major conflict with another permanent member. China's cooperation in Cambodia and in the Gulf, while highly praised, was not expected and still is subject to change. Will future Western (to include Russian) initiatives outside of Europe always obtain Chinese support? This is questionable. It follows that the diabolism advanced by the United Nations will need friends who are committed to a globalist approach and nonviolent politics and who will refrain from exploiting the UN for national interests.

End of Neutrality and Non-alignment

Diabolism itself refutes the practice of neutrality. The only "true" neutral is a state outside the global structure. Switzerland, therefore, is the only strict neutral because it has refused to join the United Nations. Members of the United Nations are obliged to support its resolutions; for example, the embargo imposed on Iraq during the Gulf crisis. Diabolism also refutes non-alignment. But this contradiction is mooted by an "active" anti-colonial component implicit in the Non-aligned Movement. Non-aligned states may express reservations consistent with this active anti-colonial factor and fail to comply with United Nations resolutions (when such resolutions are perceived as imperialistic or neo-colonial). Great powers also express reservations when UN resolutions impinge on sovereignty. This is not possible, however, for neutral states that lack an "active" component. Their only real option for non-compliance is withdrawal from the United Nations.

The end of the Cold War removed the primary rationale that propped the Non-aligned Movement. There no longer exists a "neither East nor West" scenario. The other feature of the Non-aligned Movement, its "active" anti-colonial component, is less viable in the 1990s than it was during the 1960s and the 1970s. In short, the Non-aligned Movement survives without a viable justification and, accordingly, is ripe for revision or expiration. (A north-south conflict axis exists which might give rise to a new movement to replace the Non-aligned Movement, but the former flows from economics while the latter is primarily political.)

If the end of the Cold War signals the end of neutrality and non-alignment, as hitherto understood, how will their practice evolve in the post-Cold War era? To answer this question, it may first be necessary to examine what is materializing with the end of the Cold War. Clearly, the "Day" of Europe has emerged; less clear is the "Dawn" of an Eurasian era.

The "Day" of Europe

The Malta Summit of 1989, besides documenting the end of the Cold War, also records the end of a two-hundred-year period of European history that commenced with the violent French Revolution and ended with the nonviolent East European

Revolution. During these two hundred years, areh enemies England and France, and France and Germany, to a large degree, merged political interests. There is a good possibility that arehenemies Germany and Russia may do likewise is political behaviour or cooperation among areh enemies borders on the miraculous, except when notice is taken that the miraculous rests on the horror bred by the wars which these four nations instigated. The fast two hundred years of European history actually borders on a nightmare. Acknowledgement that their wars during the past two centuries were in reality a nightmare should inspire greater cooperation among the four nations.

The joining of interests among European areh enemies ends the European revolutionary era and introduces the "Day of Europe." There is a great expectation of a general era of European prosperity. The emerging European Community, European Parliament, and Conference on Security and Cooperation in Europe provide the framework for the establishment of an integrated Europe. For Europeans, it is a time to be European.

A united Germany will play a central role in the "Day of Europe," with nations from Scandinavia, British Isles, Iberia, Mediterranean, Balkans and Soviet Federation of Republics turning towards Central Europe. The "Day of Europe" has the potential to create a "Pax Europe" which will not only meet the aspirations of European states but would also spread its peace and prosperity to other parts of the globe.

This is not a time for Europeans to be non-European. It is a time to consolidate the gains wrought from the agony of the two hundred-year nightmare. It is a time for neutral European states to participate in this triumph of nonviolent peace and contribute to its solidification. Malta, no different from Finland, belongs in this "Day of Europe" both to benefit economically and to deepen Europe's commitment to a political practice of nonviolent means.

In spite of the hope and great expectations which the Day of Europe an ominous shadow still lurks over Europe. The dismemberment of Yugoslavia has occurred and civil war has ensued from unrest in several of the Soviet Republics. Also "revanchism" may raise its unsettling demands in East Europe.

Dawn of a Eurasian Era

The Iron Curtain riveted global attention on Europe. The dismantling of Curtain, conversely, loosened this intense focus facilitating a more expansive political perspective of areas bordering Europe. Regardless of how mighty Europe looms politically, economically, and militarily, at the geo-political level, it is only a peninsula of the Eurasian mass. More precisely, Europe, geo-politically, is one of the Eurasian quadrants. The closing of Europe's revolutionary era "ends" European history and begin Eurasian history. Europe can now observe itself in the context of the larger Eurasian perspective which perhaps is a more accurate basis for understanding itself. Much of what is called European can only be grasped by discerning the impact which the other Eurasian quadrants have had on Europe. A geo-political analysis of Eurasia, as Inhart II shows, reveals four distinct regions or quadrants:

Northwest—Europe based on a Christian culture;
(Southwest— North Africa*/Middle East based on an Islamic culture;
Northeast—China/Japan based on a Tao-Buddhist culture; and
South east, South Asia based on a Hindu-Buddhist culture.

(the southern territories of the Mediterranean while technically not part of Eurasia, historically and culturally belong more to Eurasia than to Africa)

Chart II

THE POST-COLD WAR WORLD

European Revolutionary Era			1789-1989	
Day of Europe			1990	
Dawn of Eurasian Era			1990	
(Christian)			(Tao-Buddhist)	
UK	Germany	Russia	China	Japan
		Turkistan		

Afghanistan Kashmir?
Morocco Iraq/Iran·Pakistan India? Indo-China
(Islamic) (Hindu-Buddhist)

Eurasian Conflict Zones	Zone of Peace States Network (key state)	(potential state)
Baltic	Finland	(Sweden)
Central Europe	Czechoslovakia/Austria	(Albania)
Balkans		
Mediterranean	Malta	(Lebanon)
Islamic Gulf		(Qatar)/ (Kuwait) (Afghanistan)
Central Asia		
Himalayas	Nepal	
Bengal		(Burma)/(Sri Lanka) (Cambodia)
Southeast Asia	Malaysia	
Northeast Asia	Mongolia	

Zone-of-Peace-Process:Convent conflict zones into zones of peace

Zone-of-Peace States Domestic social justice and human rights; and Internt practice of nonviolent politics.

The European quadrant has had a long history of inter-quadrant conflict with the Islamic quadrant (best seen today in the Kuwait Crisis), Chinese/Japanese quadrant (Mongol invasions, colonial intervention in China, and World War II), and South Asian quadrant (during the colonial era). The Islamic quadrant, besides its conflicts with the European quadrant, vied long against the South Asian quadrant (most visible today in the Kashmir conflict), and formerly, with the Chinese quadrant (Mongol and Turk invasions and Islam penetration of Central Asia). The southeast quadrant in addition to its confrontation with the Southwest quadrant and its anti-colonial struggle with the Northwest quadrant, generally confined its area of contention with the Northeast quadrant to the Indo-China region (witnessed today in Cambodia where India supports the Vietnamese backed government and China supports the Khmer Rouge insurgents), until the 1960s when the Himalayas also became a stage for inter-quadrant conflict.

The analysis of quadrant conflict does not discard intra-quadrant conflicts. Clearly each quadrant has major inner struggles. In the Islamic quadrant, the Iraq-Iran conflict is one struggle while Iraq-Syria is another. The Southeast quadrant does not reflect major intra-quadrant conflict, although India is a large country in the area. The Northeast quadrant experiences intra-quadrant tension most noticeably in the Korean peninsula. (It also should be kept in mind that during the past one hundred years Japan fought several major wars with China, and both China and Japan expressed political designs on Mongolia.)

What quadrant analysis provides is a perspective of Eurasia as a whole and frees the analysis from a Eurocentric preoccupation. (This paper, due to its limited scope, does not address areas outside of Eurasia. To consider Africa and the Americas besides Eurasia, expands the discourse to a global perspective. While there is an increase in diabolism, the next major spiral of conflict-integration most likely will occur in Eurasia which then may lead to a subsequent spiral of conflict-integration at the global level. As an aside, integration does not necessarily mean the end of political, cultural, or economic diversity).

If Europe is slowly moving towards increased integration, there is reason to believe that similar integrating tendencies exist in the other three quadrants. The ability to assess such dynamics may assist in reducing, if not preventing, confrontation and in promoting cooperation. But if quadrant integration among the other three quadrants follows the path of the European quadrant, history may well record another "two-hundred-year nightmare."' And still more frightening, will quadrants, once integrated, enter into horrible inter-quadrant conflicts on a way towards Eurasian integration?

Prior to the nonviolent East European Revolution, the answer to the preceding question might have been an unqualified "yes". But now, at least in Europe, nonviolence competes with power politics on the political stage. There is great expectation that the final steps towards "full" European integration will occur nonviolently. Hopefully, this recent nonviolent European behaviour will spill over on to the experience and practice of the other three Eurasian quadrants.

Practice of Nonviolence

The end of the Cold War and the demise of Super-Power balance and the concomitant rise in diabolism highlight the "power" of nonviolence and cooperation. To stress what already has been mentioned, if the integration of the other three quadrants and of Eurasia itself follows the past two hundred years of European history, then woe to humanity. This pending agony makes a good case to "run" with the nonviolent politics of the East European Revolution. The economic interdependence of nations and the ecological unity of the globe further provide cogent reasons for practising nonviolent politics.

The history of the Cold War sent mixed signals. While highly volatile, the Cold War also provided time, at least in Europe; time to work out conflicts nonviolently; time to mature; time to trust each other. Regretfully, the Cold War erupted into "hot" war in the periphery of Super-Power vital interests. These wars in the so-called periphery, however, did not cease with the demise of Super-Power rivalry. Rather, conflicts ranging from Cambodia, Kashmir, Afghanistan, the "Islamic" Gulf to Palestine indicate a separate reality of intra- and inter-quadrant conflicts outside the purview of Super-Power confrontation. This reality creates an urgent appeal to establish a practice of nonviolence and cooperation in those zones of conflict. The question, "how can the practice of nonviolence which ended the Cold War, and cooperation which guides European integration, creep into what seems a Eurasian cauldron of conflicts" needs to be answered.

Spirit of Cooperation, Not Conflict

The Helsinki Accord, which set in motion a mechanism to reduce armed forces in Europe and to develop confidence-building measures, loomed in the background of the nonviolent East

European Revolution. The "trust" that was missing between East and West Europe began to emerge in the mid-1980s. President Gorbachev "trusted" that the United States would not attack the Soviet Union as it attempted internal reforms. His behaviour risked much in view of prior Western intervention in the Communist revolution and of subsequent German invasion.

The Helsinki Final Act established the Conference on Security and Cooperation in Europe (CSCE) process which interjected a doctrine of common security. This doctrine stressed a spirit of "cooperation, not conflict." The emergence of this CSCE process paralleled the West European mareh towards a European Community. With the end of the Cold War, the "habit" of conflict among European states gave way to a I process of security and cooperation.

This European quadrant integration undoubtedly will keep most European governments fixed to the prevailing Eurocentricity and cause them not to perceive (perhaps even resist) that an Eurasian dawn has risen. But commitment to the CSCE process may also cause its extension to the other three quadrants. This may already be occurring. On Malta's insistence, CSCE members accept, if only perfunctorily, the notion that Europe's security depends on peace in the Mediterranean region. Extending this premise further, the security of Europe and the Mediterranean depends on peace in the other three quadrants. A good case exists to export the CSCE process.

REAVISING NEUTRALITY AND NON-ALIGNMENT

"Continuing cooperation among the permanent members of the UN Security Council would preclude any need for a new international movement to replace the abrogated Non-aligned Movement or to redefine the practice of neutrality. It is the fragile nature of this cooperation, however, which indicates a need to update neutrality and non-alignment, or a new international movement to advance the United Nations' nonviolent practice in the event that the UN again becomes crippled.

The decline of the Non-aligned Movement itself does not suggest a need for a new movement. But the concerns which gave rise to the Non-aligned Movement in the first instance may still be pressing. The question is not necessarily whether a new movement will arise, but how the aspirations of the developing states not to be embroiled in armed struggles will express themselves in the post-Cold War era. The question of neutrality faces a similar challenge, namely how will the need that fashioned a practice of neutrality reveal itself?

Regardless of changes in international relations, it is doubtful that ; major developed states will abandon power politics outside the European quadrant. It can be hoped, however, that existing circumstances will cause great powers to act with restraint in their employment of a "top-down" approach. It is also doubtful that major developing states, in view of intra-quadrant tensions, will reduce their I commitment to armed strength and "trust" that the CSCE process of cooperation will readily transfer to the other Eurasian quadrants. Thus it falls on European neutrals and minor or "bottom-up" states to revise neutrality and non-alignment. The central role of nonviolence in the East European revolution suggests that any revision of neutrality and non-alignment should include a practice of nonviolence.

Any new movement will need a core or connecting thread to join its numbers. Neutral states shared no such thread. In the post-Cold War era nonviolence could well be the core thread for a new movement that replaces the Non-aligned Movement. Without this core practice of nonviolence, revision of neutrality and non-alignment may fail the needs of the post-Cold War era where intra- and inter-quadrant conflicts are prevalent. A movement based on a core practice of nonviolence institutionalizes nonviolence and sustains it in a prolonged contest with power politics. The validity of any revised practice of neutrality and non-alignment, therefore, should be guaged on how effectively it thwarts conflict. If nonviolence gains little institutional adherence, the promise of peace which the Cold War interjected into international relations, might well slip back into a bleakness of war without hope of peace. The post-Cold War era indicates that violent means are obsolete but the "habit" resists the message.

The CSCE process generates an appreciation for how nonviolence can operate with the violent means of "realpolitik." The "right" mix is found in power politics producing balance, and nonviolent means producing grounds for cooperation. In a simplistic way of analysis, this is what happened in Europe: the Super Powers maintained a balance, while the CSCE process introduced grounds for trust and cooperation. Regarding the Gulf crisis, the right mix is the combination of power politics achieving military balance and adequate defence of Saudi Arabia, and nonviolent politics which could find a viable solution to Iraqi occupation of Kuwait. In order to operate in this interaction, nonviolence needs institutional sponsorship, particularly to sustain its moral foundation. Otherwise institutionalized violence may produce not only the balance but also the solution without any concern for ethical issues.

Infusion of Moral Responsibility

Human rights is an issue which should apply to any revision of neutrality and non-alignment. A domestic practice of social justice and human rights reinforces the practice of nonviolence. The Non-aligned Movement did not concern itself with how its members treated their respective population. To a largo degree, the political behaviours of the Non-aligned Movement were politically expedient measures with morality cloaked in rhetoric. President Havel of Czechoslovakia, however, voiced succinctly the need for morality in the post-Cold War era:

> My programme as President is therefore based on the principle of infusing spirituality, moral responsibility, humanity and humility into politics and, thus, insisting on there being something higher than we humans, that our deeds shall not disappearars into the dark holes of our times.

The moral issue is an indispensable factor and complements the price of nonviolence. The infusion of morality is not to create a seat of judgement, but a political practice. For example support for the United Nations would not be based on how a resolution fulfils national interests but on a true commitment to further its principles, even advocating a "UN first and national interest second" principle. Clearly, in the existing international system only minor states would express such an advocacy.

Minor states that espouse social justice internally and rely on the United Nations for their ultimate security are in a position to infuse moral responsibility in politics better, perhaps, than larger states that depend on their own resources for security. Any new movement (most probably consisting of minor states), which updates the practice of neutrality and non-alignment in the post-Cold War era, should incorporate President Havel's principle of infusing morality into politics.

"For" Rather than "Against" and "Avoid"

A neutral or nonaligned state has no behave morally in fact, neutral states have been accused throughout history of profiting from the misery of warring states. Neutral states practise an "in-out" approach to peace. "In," in that they seek self-gain, and "out," in that they serve to mediate conflict objectively. Nonaligned states share with neutral states the characteristic of "avoidance." Neutral states avoid being caught up in conflict between states. Non-aligned states avoid being caught up in Super-Power peripheral conflicts. In addition, nonaligned states display an "against" attitude regarding Western politics which are perceived, correctly or incorrectly, to be imperialistic or neo-colonial.

In contrast, non-violence and moral responsibility suggest a "for" psychology. It requires states to practise, that is, doing rather than rhetorically posturing nonviolence and moral responsibility. And it is this practice that has impact and sets forth ,1 model for international behaviour.

Neutral and nonaligned states nominally are "for" peace. But if nonviolence and moral responsibility are absent, this "for" peace indicates political expediency. Being "for" peace, as Gandhi's life revelas, demands strong commitment, courageous convictions and right practise. Sustained peace is the result of a "for" psychology and is not likely to be achieved by "against" and "avoid" behaviours or by a backed-into-peace psychology.

"For" peace is also "for" humanity. This latter "for" turns the analysis back to globolism. Globalism, however, poses a grave danger when its ideology betrays humanity's peaceful aspirations. Much too often fanaticism overtakes globalist ideologies and morality is subverted into narrowness dressed in repressive righteousness.

At the same time, an emphasis on the practice of nonviolence and moral responsibility acts as a safeguard that diabolism will not constrict but free political intercourse. Humanity may not be ready yet for a global society and for a good reason. The dominance of power politics, however, insures that diabolism will not dominate international politics, at least, well into the future. But for smaller states, diabolism counters power politics manipulation and provides a constructive goal for the future. In spite of its dangers, diabolism gives neutrality and non-alignment a new and urgent purpose: to place humanity's nonviolent aspirations in competition with the power politics of larger states. For the time being, the small or "bottom-up" states remain the main proponents "for" both nonviolence and diabolism.

THE "ZONE-OF-PEACE" CONCEPT

The Non-aligned Movement, in part, traces itself back to Gandhi through Nehru who was India's first prime minister, a close associate of Gandhi, and the prime arehitect of the Nonaligned Movement. In the mid-1940s, Nehru spoke of an "area of peace" where the peaceful aspirations of newly formed nations would create just societies free from involvement in great-power struggles. Later, the "area of peace" concept gave rise to a "zone of peace" concept which the Nonaligned Movement constricted to mean the absence of Super-Power armed forces in the zone. In short, the "zone of peace" concept became a politically expedient ploy of the Nonaligned Movement. But outside of the political field and in a strict Gandhian sense, zone of peace is above all personal, that is, to evolve individually as a zone of peace and subsequently, to project this inner peace outwardly in the political sphere.

Zone-of-Peace Practice, Principles, and States

If an updating of non-alignment and neutrality were to occur and based on the issues discussed in the preceding section (nonviolence, moral responsibility, and diabolism), what, form would such a revision take? In the first place, this network would be Gandhian in outlook. Perhaps the post-Cold War era may provide the opportunity for Gandhian politics to emerge from its rarefied seclusion and enter into the political mainstream.

Sri Lanka advanced the first major zone of peace proposal by the Nonaligned Movement. In December 1971 a United Nations General Assembly resolution declared the Indian Ocean a zone of peace and directed the Super Powers to withdraw their armed forces from the zone. Other efforts to establish zones of peace include: Malaysia's proposal of 1971 to establish a Southeast Asia zone of peace; King of Nepal's proposal to convert his country into a zone of peace, and the United Nations First Special Session on Disarmament (1978) proposed a programme of action to establish zones of peace.

In a Gandhian framework, the zone of peace practice is not a politically expedient act to remove the military presence of the Super Powers, build viable political practice of responsibility grounded on humanity's commonality. A Gandhian-based zone-of-peace practice includes an internal component which stresses social justice and human rights, and an international component of nonviolent politics. The combination of internal and international components form the basis for ZONE OF PEACE PRINCIPLES which can direct the establishment of zones of peace. A draft of these principles is submitted below:

Spirit of cooperation, not conflict

Nonviolent conflict resolution

Maintaining continuing and open process to promote internal social justice and human rights.*

Nuclear weapons-free zones

Removal of non-zonal armed forces

(*Excluded is the nonaligned concept of "peaceful co-existence").

The Helsinki Accord has interjected into international politics the primacy of human rights/social justice over co-existence. This does not mean a "crusade" to rectify injustice but a continuing process which in Gandhian politics is a process of nonviolence (ahimsa) and truth (satyagraha). In addition, the CSCE process promotes cooperation rather than co-existence.

Whether there will be a new movement which will replace the Nonaligned Movement at this time is a matter of conjecture. However, a new category of political practice may emerge and replace the category of neutral and nonaligned states, namely zone-of-peace states. A zone-of peace state is one that practises internally, social justice and human rights and internationally, nonviolent politics. In brief, a zone-of-peace state is one that adheres to or aspires to follow zone-of-peace (ZOP) state principles. These include:

Security: A practice of nonviolent defence (or in some instances, non-offensive defence) that includes a nuclear-weapons-free-zone practice.

Internal: Practice-of social justice and human rights.

International: Spirit of cooperation, not conflict; nonviolent conflict resolution; no military alliances; no arms trade (or in some instances, no arms trade in offensive weapons); support for self-determination of peoples; and human rights.

Global: Practice of submitting inter-nation disputes to the International Court of Justice; participating in United Nations peacekeeping and peacemaking activities.; support for United Nations management of global common heritage (such as space, seas, and polar regions!; furthering United Nations involvement in economic development and ecological security; and supporting United Nations administration of territories when it serves to further world peace.

For the sake of clarity, ZOP State Principles, which refer to the individual states, are distinct from Zone-of-Peace Principles which refer to the establishment of a multinational zone of peace. It is not expelled that all states participating in a zone of peace will be Zone of Peace States. States committed to military alliances and offensive arms, will undoubtedly participate in zones of peace, and it is unlikely that all of these states will abandon their commitment to military alliances and offensive arms. (It can be expected, however, that the , non-Zone of Peace States participating in a zone of peace will adhere to Zone of Peace Principles, and that the zone of peace process will increase the number of states practising ZOP States Principles.)

In an interesting development, the Dalai Lama has called for the establishment of a zone of peace (zone of "ahimsa" or nonviolence) in Tibet. Whether China maintains sovereignly over Tibet is of secondary importance. Primary for the territory of Tibet and its people is a zone-of-peace practice (guided by nonviolence). In this sense, a zone of peace can exist within a sovereign territory that is not a zone of peace. Taking this analogy further, the zone-of-peace concept can apply to the individual, family, and community levels as well as to the autonomous territory, sovereign state, and geographic zone levels. But at any level, the zone of peace can be blatant rhetoric or it can be an authentic practice.

The Dalai Lima's proposal that a non-sovereign territory can become a zone of peace offers a novel approach to territories experiencing major crises. Demilitarized zones and the World War I Mandate System were earlier attempts to defuse conflict in non-sovereign territories. After World War II, the United Nations established a Trusteeship System to administer non-sovereign territories and, thereby, preclude conflict in them. Sovereign states committed to power politics, however, were chosen to administer these trust territories.

The UN Charter permits the Organization itself to administer a trust territory. This has not yet occurred, although in the late 1940s it was proposed that Somalia become a trusteeship under direct UN administration. Also, the United Nations administered West New Guinea for a brief period as a transition between Holland's colonial rule and Indonesian incorporation. Is the international world ready to experiment with establishing zones, of peace through the trusteeship system by placing trust territories under direct UN administration? Likely non-sovereign territories to become zone of peace trusteeship are Palestine and perhaps the Baltic states. The objective here, as it been for UN trusteeship, is independence.

The experiment with "zone of-peace trusteeship" could also include sovereign states that experience connect, if such states were to place their territory in trusteeship status (at least temporarily) with the UN itself, the administering authority.

In this category likely candidates are Cambodia, the Lebanon, and perhaps Afghanistan and Burma (now Myanmar). While the topic of zone of peace trusteeships goes beyond the scope of this paper, the promise contained in this zone of-peace trusteeship mechanism merits a cursory attention.

Zone-of-Peace Process and Network

Within the Conference of Security and Cooperation in Europe, a cluster of states, referred to as "N&N" (neutral and nonaligned) states, joined in a loose network for the purpose of reducing Super-Power conflict and to articulate the role which neutrality and non-alignment performs in the peace process the joining, for example, of European neutral with nonaligned (Albania, Cyprus, and Yugoslavia) states. (The "N&N" states, however, have not seriously required of themselves compliance with the domestic practices of social justice and human rights). In the post-Cold War era, an "N&N" linkage lacks a purposeful focus. In contrast, a "zone-of-peace process", that is, furthering a zone-of-peace practice, contains a twofold mission: development of zone-of- peace states and establishment of zones of peace. A movement or network of zone-of-peace states (composed initially, for example, of Finland, Czechoslovakia, Malta, perhaps Qatar or Maldives, Nepal, Malaysia and Mongolia) would have for its agenda, first, assisting other states in the practice of ZOP state principles and, second, to implement the-United Nations programme of action to establish zones of peace.

A zone of peace is an "area" of peace where cooperation rather than conflict governs the interaction between states. Besides zone of-peace states, any zone of peace undoubtedly will include middle and great power states that belong to military alliances and trade in arms. It to not expected that all states will adopt ZOP state principles, but what can be expected is that all nations in the zone of peace will adhere to me lesser zone of peace principles, and minimize the causes for conflict and maximize the reasons for cooperation. And it is this maximizing and minimizing dynamic that lies beneath the security and cooperation of the CSCE process. Although zone-of-peace states can perform a critical role in the process of establishing zones of peace, their influence is also limited. In the context of a Medirranean zone of peace process, Malta might have little influence in resolving the Palestine crisis. Malta, however, can assist Albania to experiment with a practice of zone-of-peace principles. Malta can similarly assist the Lebanon (once Syrian troops are withdrawn) and Cyprus (once Turkish troops are withdrawn). Albania, Cyprus, and Lebanon all experience internal turmoil, the solution of which is important to any development of a Mediterranean Zone of Peace. As part of the process, Malta can establish itself as a mediating site to address the lesser tensions in the zone.

Clearly, few states now practise the above-mentioned zone-of-peace principles but other states aspire to do so. Such may be the case with Czechoslovakia as it disengages itself from an oppressive communist form of government. The same may be said for Mongolia and Nepal, now that both nations have turned towards more democratic forms of government. Finland and Malta, to a large degree, already exhibit a practice of ZOP state principles, whereas Sweden, because of its arms trade, does not fully "live" up to these principles. As such, Finland and Malta are in a position to exert initial leadership in the formation of a zone-of-peace network. Zone of peace states, if linked for the purpose of furthering ZOP state principles, in actuality, constitute an international network.

The establishment of a "zone-of-peace network" outlines a structure by which states committed to nonviolent politics can join in concerted efforts to address particular international crises. A loosely formed "zone-of-peace network" subsequently may grow into an international movement but only if the zone-of-peace practice finds its niche in the post-Cold War era.

Similar to the Non-aligned Movement, the potential Zone of Peace Movement espouses the goals of the United Nations but perhaps in a more cogent manner. Both the United Nations and nascent Zone of Peace Movement acknowledge the imperative of nonviolence. They activate the "power" of nonviolence. In the Cold War era of two Super Powers and a Third (or Nonaligned) World, the linkage of a zone of peace network with the United Nations would have represented a "Fourth World."

Interaction with the Security and Cooperation Process

An alternative designation for a zone-of-peace process could well be a "security and cooperation" practice. What a zone of peace proposes to accomplish is not dissimilar from what the CSCE process proposes. A major difference, however, is that the CSCE process includes major powers that were committed to military alliances, use violent means (when deemed necessary) and possess a Eurocentric focus. A zone-of-peace process, by contrast, links minor states that are committed to nonviolence and reject military alliances and are global in scope.

For the sake of differentiation, it may be said that the zone-of-peace practice augments the CSCE process, in that the former extends the latter process beyond Europe. A zone-of-peace process transforms! itself into a security and cooperation process as it surfaces in the other three Eurasian quadrants and between quadrants. A zone-of-peace practice is not solely the exclusion of great powers from a region,! Rather, it is the cooperation of all states in the zone to achieve security through a practice of nonviolence. The role of zone-of-peace states in a zone of peace is to advance a practice of nonviolence and champion the infusion of morality into politics.

Exclusion of the United States armed forces from a Zone of Peace is a legitimate goal, but this exclusion does not in itself, create a zone of peace. The presence of non-regional forces is often the result of instability in the region. It may be true that outside forces maintain the instability but such is not always the case. Therefore, the primary objective would be the resolution of regional instabilities and, subsequently, the removal of non-regional forces.

It must be kept in mind that the current success of the CSCE process came after the nightmare of two hundred years of conflict among Great Britain, France, Germany, and Russia. It would be a grave mistake if the promise of peace in Europe promoted by the CSCE process were to gloss over the realities of the past two hundred years and evade the: realities of Eurasian conflicts. As stated before, there can be no real peace in Europe unless intra-Eurasian conflicts are addressed as a whole.

The hope found in Europe with the end of the Cold War perhaps is not shared by the developing world. In fact, there is reason to believe that if the developing world was apprehensive of Super-Power abuse, it can be expected that the European Community, which joins the great imperial powers of Great Britain, Prance, and Germany (perhaps to be joined by Russia, will create a similar, if not greater, apprehension among developing states. A "Pax Europca," while welcomed in Europe, may be a nightmare for the rest of the globe. Can "Pax Europe be trusted?

The best candidates to advance trust in the developing world are states that are first of all European and participate in the CSCE, process and, second, also zone-of-peace states. These small states are "trusted" perhaps because of their weakness and perhaps, because of their nonviolent practice of politics. Accordingly, European zone-of-peace states, such as Finland and Malta, may be influential in spreading adherence to the CSCE process in the other Eurasian quadrants.

The failure on the part of the European Community to appreciate the developing world's apprehension may well harden the confrontation that eventually will give rise to a "South" Super Power, China for example, or attract an insular non-European "North" power, such as Japan, to with the South in order to balance the threat from the European North.

Small states play minor roles when great powers occupy the

centre-stage, but can execute major roles when their strengths have an appropriate forum for expression. The linkage of European and Asian zone-of-peace states in support of the United Nations objectives constitute a new international force, if not a movement, where smallness, although lacking the proverbial "divisions," nonetheless, can render a major contribution to the furtherance of world peace.

The CSCE process and zone-of-peace process share similar dynamics but are distinct processes. The former serves the world best by fashioning a "Pax Europea" that is not a threat to the developing world. The latter serves the world best by furthering security and cooperation beyond the European quadrant with the ultimate goal of 'Tax Mundi." If zone-of-peace states, in the first place, understood the critical role that they can perform in realizing this "Pax Mundi," and second, wished to update their legacy of neutrality and non-alignment, they could forge a movement and mobilize a peace initiative to establish zones of peace and extend the CSCE process beyond Europe.

A ZONE-OF-PEACE INITIATIVE

International movements surface because a specific need exists that is sensed by political leaders or charismatic individuals who subsequently gain support for their interpretation of the need. That is what occurred with the Nonaligned Movement when Nehru, Tito, and Nasser sensed the need for an international arrangement to confront Super-Power domination. In the post-Cold War era there is a need to redifine: neutrality and non-alignment, and perhaps, also a need to replace the Nonaligned Movement by a new international movement. What initiative would be appropriate to address these post-Cold War needs?

Eurasian Linchpin

The updating of neutrality and non-alignment or the fashioning of a zone-of-peace movement may profit if such examination is conducted in the context of the emerging dawn of a Eurasian era. However, there is little understanding of Eurasia as a political unit. Outside of the former Soviet Union, no country reflects a Eurasian concern and it is even doubtful that the former Soviet Union even possessed a true Eurasian identity or was free of a Eurocentric bias. It is further doubtful that the international community appreciates that the "dawn" of a Eurasian era has surfaced. For the most part, nations are governed by forces and affairs operating in their respective geopolitical quadrants. Only a few straddle successfully two quadrants. Malta interacts with both the European and Islamic quadrants; Nepal between the southeast and northeast quadrants, to a lesser degree Mongolia interacts between an extended European (Soviet) quadrant and China; and Afghanistan between extended European (Soviet) and Islamic quadrants. In its more; peaceful days, Lebanon adequately identified itself with the European and Islamic quadrants.

Given this lack of appreciation for the dawn of a Eurasian era, there is a pressing need for a linchpin nation to join European and Asian zone-of-peace states in the context of a Eurasian perspective. Malta, as a neutral state, a member of the Non-aligned movement and a CSCE participant already may be playing this linchpin role. Within the Conference on Security and Cooperation in Europe, Malta was instrumental in adding a Mediterranean chapter to the CSCE process. In short, Malta may be the best situated nation to assume the Eurasian linchpin assignment and extend the CSCE process beyond Europe and join it with the UN programme of action to establish zones of peace.

In the context of Eurasia, the linchpin should perform a mediating role for the United Nations similar to that fulfilled by Austria in Europe. Moreover, the linchpin state becomes a leading actor in fashioning a network among European and Asian zone-of peace states, and in utilizing this network both to assist other states to adopt ZOP state principles, and to further the United Nations programme of action to establish zones of peace. But to accomplish these tasks, the linchpin state requires appropriate means. The question is whether any one state, Malta for example, will accept the linchpin challenge and whether it will seek the appropriate means to realize this endeavour.

Zone-of-Peace Center

Movements, as a rule, do not emerge from institutions or loosely formed networks of states ûnless a truly dynamic force exists in the background As a rule, an institution evolves from a general or specific need. If cultivated appropriately over a period of time, an institution can be in a position to support a movement that desires tò respond to the need in a more direct manner. It may be said that the United Nations, when established, contained the projection of a need which the then existing international system could not meet directly. Today forty-seven years later, the United Nations itself may be ready to act directly upon that need.

If movements do not grow generally from an institution, they also issuer without an organic institution to sustain and refine the "reality" of the precipitating need. The Nonaligned Movement lacked a "think tank" to expand and define its ideology and practice. Such perhaps was the case, because much of nonaligned politics were politically expedient and "against" Super Powers concomitant European colonial exploitation. A zone-of-peacc network, in contrast, would be less politically expedient and more "for" peace.

A "think tank" or a Center to promote a zone-of-peace pracuce and, at the same time, advance the CSCE process beyind Europe, represents an appropriate vehicle through which a linchpin state can carry out its responsibilities. At its Paris Summit, CSCE selected Vienna to host a Conflict Prevention Center to guide the CSCE process. Valletta, Malta, in comparison, would be an appropriate site to establish a similar Center if the CSCE desired to extend its process beyond Europe. As it moves beyond Europe (initially into the Mediterranean), the CSCE process merges with the United Nations' programme of action to establish zones of peace. A Center in Malta, in short, joins CSCE and United Nations interests suggesting co-sponsorship of the Center. This Center, therefore, becomes the locus for a peace initiative.

A detailed outline of a Zone-of-Peace Center is beyond the scope of this paper. However a brief sketch might be useful to introduce the idea of a Center or "think tank" which advances both the zone-of-peace process and the CSCE process beyond Europe. To being with, it is necessary to identify areas where zones of peace should be established. A cursory survey of Euraisan conflicts identifies then tension zones. The Center's operational task is to assist in the conversion of these tension zones into zones of peace.

Tension Zones:	Baltic Central Asia
Central Europe	Himalayas
Balkans	Bengal Bay
Mediterraneam	Southeast Asia
"Islamic" Gulf	Northeast Asia

The proposed Zone-of-Peace Center should establish seminar groups for each zone and each seminar group for each zone and each seminar group should have represetnatives from each nation within the zone. Seminars or study groups should develop policy recommendations that provide governments with procedures that encourage cooperation and creation of zones of peace. When fully operational, all ten study groups would operate concurrently and share visions, problems, and policy recommendations. It is not expected that all study groups will be formed at the same time. Initially, the Mediterranean zone-of-peace study group will be formed and then the other zone-of-peace study groups in their respective zone. At the same time, a separate zone-of-peace study group would address zone-of-peace conceptual formulations an dassss polically expedient and moral considerations. This conceptual study group would also share its deliberations with the other zone-specific study groups. Members of each study group would work independently but periodically meet collectively. Also, governments within their respective zones would convene meetings to discuss policy recommendations.

Because of their vulnerability and motivation to avoid conflict, it is expected that zone-of-peace states (those adhering to ZOP State Principles) will take leadership roles in establishing zones of peace in ZOP State Principles. The Zone of Peace Center would hold periodic meetings for this network of Zone of Peace States to assess the state-of-the-art in respect of a zone of peace practice.

In addition to its role in promoting zones of peace and bringing together zone-of-peace states, the Center would operate as a clearing house to disseminate information on the zone-of-peace process. In brief, the Center should become an international focal point to coalesce interest sin a zone of peace practice.

The success of the Center, however, may rest on how it nurtures and projects a practice of nonviolence or "ahimsa." The organization of a Center in itself is no guarantee to offering meaning full and successful programmes. There are already numerous "peace centers." The proposed Center would have its unique or selling point, namely the addressing of various conflict zones in a comprehensive and simultaneous manner for the purpose of converting them into zones of peace, and the formation of a network to foster a Zone-of-Peace Movement. But without an authentic spirit, at the personal level, of nonviolence within the Center itself, the strategy of the proposed Center will be no more meaningful or successful than any of the other peace centers. Therefore, the proposed Zone of Peace Center should province programmes to deepen a practice of nonviolence so that its spirit can pervade the Center's activities and deliberations.

In closing a Zone of Peace Center located, for example, in Valletta, Malta, and affiliated with both the United Nations (to promote its promote its programme of action to establish zones of peace) and with the CSCE (to promote its process beyond Europe) would become a pertinent first step towards an institutionalization of a zone-of-peace practice. Moreover the Center would provide for the updating of neutrality and non alignment in the post-Cold War eara and for sustaining the idea of a one of peace Movement.